COME, FOLLOW ME!
VOLUME I

ELAINE CLANTON HARPINE

ABINGDON PRESS / Nashville

COME, FOLLOW ME! A WORSHIP PROGRAM FOR TEACHING
THE GOSPEL TO CHILDREN, VOLUME 1

This book is printed on recycled, acid-free, elemental-chlorine–free paper.

Library of Congress Cataloging-in-Publication Data

ISBN 0-687-09207-8

01 02 03 04 05 06 07 08 09 10 — 10 9 8 7 6 5 4 3 2 1

MANUFACTURED IN THE UNITED STATES OF AMERICA

To

David,

Virginia,

and

Christina

CONTENTS

Acknowledgments

A special thank you to my loving husband, Bill. Thanks for taking the pictures for the book, for your carpentry expertise, and for believing in me.

Special thanks to my three wonderful children, David, Virginia, and Christina. I created this program for you. You've now grown up and become my best helpers. Thanks; I couldn't do it without you.

A heartfelt thank you to all the children I've had the privilege and honor of working with over the years at the First United Methodist Church in Cuyahoga Falls, Ohio. I love each of you dearly.

Thanks to Kathy Walker for her never-ending love and encouragement, and to Dr. Steven Bailey for believing in the program. Special thanks to Dean Wagner and Tate Newland for taking time out of their busy schedules to lend their musical talents, and to Wendy Gillespie for her weekly devotion and music ministry.

Thank you to the parents. Your support helped make our children's worship program a fabulous success. Thanks also to our many friends. Thank you for believing in children's worship.

INTRODUCTION

It was a flower-bedecked, sun-drenched, steamy spring morning. The McBride children were hesitant about attending the big church on the corner. It was new, unfamiliar.

Having moved to town only three days before, the children were nervous. Mary squirmed and couldn't sit still. Jacob sat bored, resentful, and sullen. Mark made paper airplanes from the offering envelopes in the pew.

The children were called to the front for the children's sermon. Fifty-two children sat listening as the minister read a five-minute story based on a parable from the Bible.

After the story, the children left the sanctuary and entered a room with cloths draped like awnings, a biblical playhouse, a tent, a wooden boat under full sail, and a table with a sign that read "Marketplace." An adult helper pointed out seven learning centers scattered around the room. The children were to travel from station to station reading the instructions on the signs posted. All ages worked together side by side. Youth and adult helpers were posted at each station to lend a hand where needed.

The McBride children were cautious as they arrived at their first workstation. A smiling teenager helped everyone dress in biblical costumes so that they could work at the pottery shop. The papier-mâché was cool to touch and lots of fun.

Time breezed by so quickly that the children hardly realized twenty minutes had passed. A shy first grader stepped forward to ring the church bell for worship.

A teenager accompanied the group on the guitar as the children sang songs from the hymnal and tapped in rhythm on cardboard drums they had made at the call to worship workstation. A third grader proudly stood with Bible in hand and read the lesson for the day.

The sermon was a story from the Bible. Several of the children acted out the parable as it was being read. Puppets popped into view at the puppet stage and began to explain how the lesson applies to us today. Three children in sunglasses and baseball caps stepped forward to act out a modern-day version.

This modern version was written by a sixth grader from the sermon workstation. As the sixth grader read, the children in costume pantomimed. The service ended with everyone saying the Lord's Prayer in sign language and joining hands in a prayer circle to sing the benediction.

Children gathered their crafts to take home as parents arrived at the door. The McBride children talked all the way home about what they wanted to do next week when they would once again return to the biblical village at their new church.

You, too, can set up a children's worship program that will encourage families to return week after week. It's easy. No prior teaching experience is necessary. The cost is minimal. Everything you need is contained in one single program.

Open the door for the children at your church. Answer the call from Jesus to "come, follow me" (Matthew 4:19 NIV).

PART ONE

GETTING STARTED

1

Why Does Our Church Need a Children's Worship Program?

Children do not learn in the same way that adults do. If children are to truly learn about worship, we must teach them in a way they comprehend. Children learn by doing.

Come, Follow Me!: A Worship Program for Teaching the Gospel to Children is a two-volume set with 53 thirty-five minute sessions, more than 300 Bible-related craft projects, 102 pages of full-scale patterns, and 371 different Bible verses. Each session comes complete with seven learning centers, a five-minute children's story, and a ten-minute worship service.

There are ready-to-use puppet plays, building projects, pantomimes, skits, a biblical village, a children's musical, challenging crafts for older children, banner making, sewing, a carpenter shop, and an endless supply of easy-to-do paper crafts for the younger set. There are wonderfully messy crafts and crafts that produce no mess at all.

Come, Follow Me! has age-appropriate material for ages four through twelve. Everything is included in one program and easily adapted to the needs of a small church with only five children or a downtown church with two hundred.

This hands-on discovery approach actually teaches children how to worship God. Children write and lead their own worship services, read and study Bible verses every week at the workstations, and learn what it means to be a follower or disciple of Jesus.

Cost is minimal. You don't have to purchase expensive supplies or buy separate programs for different age-groups. Crafts are made from easy to obtain household recyclable items.

Come, Follow Me! is for Sunday school teachers seeking a craft book to supplement their weekly curriculum, ministers needing Bible-based children's meditations for the Sunday worship service, after-school program directors who want biblical work-at-your-own-pace learning center activities, parents wanting hands-on Bible-based family activities, and especially churches wishing to establish a children's worship service.

The sessions have been arranged by topics rather than dates on a calendar so that you may use *Come, Follow Me!* year after year. Some chapters contain activities that take several weeks, such as building the puppet stage. In contrast, chapter 7 has five distinct programs that may be pulled out and used independently at any time of the year. This is particularly helpful for the Sundays that fall between seasonal holidays.

In volume I, there's something special for Thanksgiving, Advent, and Christmas. Volume II includes Easter, Pentecost, and a summer packet that may even be used for vacation Bible school.

So what are you waiting for? Turn your ordinary Sunday mornings into a wonderland of biblical adventure. Add to your existing children's worship program, or create a whole new worship time for the children at your church.

Setting Up a Children's Worship Program Is Easy

Custom-design a children's worship program for your church. Select a committee or individual to lead the way.

Step 1: Decide How You Want to Use the Material in This Book

How much time will you have each week?
How many children should you plan for?
What ages will you include?
Will you use the five-minute story in the sanctuary?
Who will be in charge of organizing the program?

These are questions that must be answered at the beginning of your planning process. Make a chart or poster. Outline how the children's worship time will fit into the worship hour.

Step 2: What Room or Rooms Will You Use?

Deciding which room(s) to use is probably one of the most difficult decisions to make. It would be ideal if each church had a large, unused room where the learning centers could be set up and left each week, but it is often hard to find an unused classroom in a church. Therefore, you will most likely be sharing a room. You may use one room or several rooms. My own program is spread out among five classrooms.

Select a room where the children will be allowed to make a mess. Ask some important questions:

Can projects be left to dry in the room till next week?

What can we do to make this a more exciting classroom?

Does each teacher have equal use of the room? If the room you have chosen is used by preschool, the youth, or adults, ask how the children's worship program will fit in and what materials they will be allowed to keep in the room.

Select rooms that invite compromise and shared space. Desks, cabinets with doors that close, and rooms with closets are ideal. If the room is a children's Sunday school classroom, check to see if learning centers are to be shared.

The benediction workstation at my church is set up in a room with six large tables, which provides ample workspace, but the room is occupied every single day of the week by a different group. It's bulging at the seams Sunday morning with an overstuffed Sunday school class that dismisses two minutes before my children arrive. It's impossible to leave anything set up in the room. Consequently, I have the supplies hidden from sight so that all I have to do is walk in, open the supply cabinet, place the instruction signs and patterns on the tables, and begin.

Each of the seven learning centers, or workstations, represents one of the seven parts of the worship service. All of the workstations stress teaching children how to share and work together in a spirit of Christian love.

There is no need to separate younger children. All ages may work together in one room side by side.

The workstations are graded for educational and fine-motor-skill appropriateness.

Workstation 1 (Call to Worship) is geared for first and second graders.

Workstation 2 (Affirmation of Faith) is specifically designed for third and fourth graders.

Workstations 3 (Offering or Carpenter Shop) and 4 (Sermon or Bible Study) are appropriate for all ages.

Workstation 5 (Witness to Faith) is designed to offer fifth and sixth graders a challenge.

Workstation 6 (Prayer and Sewing Center) is for all ages because both simple and challenging projects are available each week.

Workstation 7 (Benediction) is set up with very simple no-mess projects for four- and five-year-olds, but often older children enjoy the projects as well. This list does not mean that only third and fourth graders can work at Workstation 2, or that only four- and five-year-olds are allowed at Workstation 7. The age-level groupings simply ensure that you do in fact have an appropriate activity for each age level.

Step 3: How Many Teachers Do You Need?

The number of teachers needed depends on the number of children in your program and the number of rooms. You need one person to direct the program, the same or another person to be in charge of supplies, and volunteers to help at the stations.

You must have an adult or older teen working in the carpenter shop at all times. Children should never use tools without direct adult supervision.

The children's worship program works best when you have an adult or youth helper at each workstation. These volunteers may be parents or youth who rotate or volunteer to work only one Sunday a month. That's fine.

Step 4: How Much Work Must You Do Each Week?

If you organize supplies as described in chapter 3, the weekly chore is not difficult at all. You will need to photocopy the workstation "Instruction Sign" and patterns for each of the seven workstations. The youth or adult directing each workstation will need the directions and patterns to lead the activity at the learning center. The ready-to-use patterns make it easy to simply walk in the door and teach.

If you are the director of the children's worship program at your church, I do encourage you to read over the session each week. Sometimes it is suggested that the teacher might want to make the project ahead of time as an example, but it's not required. You really can walk in with the students, lay out the workstation Instruction Signs and patterns, and simply begin.

The craft patterns for each session are located at the back of the book.

3

Organizing Supplies

asy access to supplies is key to the success of your children's worship program. If available, closets and cabinets with doors are excellent. Children go to the cabinet, take out supplies as needed, and then the cabinet doors are closed at the end of the session to hide materials from others who use the room.

An old desk in one room can hold construction paper, glue, scissors, pencils, markers, a Bible, and crayons. The room may then be used throughout the week by other groups. Some churches use mobile carts. The carts are filled with the needed supplies and rolled into the hallway between classrooms. Children secure their own supplies from the cart. The cart is then rolled back into storage afterward.

Workstations sharing Sunday school classrooms may find Sunday school teachers eager to set up combined supply baskets. Each session has a complete "Supplies Needed" list. The supplies are listed, one through seven, by workstation.

Common Supplies Used by All

Construction paper is an essential item for Workstation 7, but all stations use construction paper from time to time. Keep construction paper in one central location on a low shelf near a scrap paper basket. Children can be free to use paper as needed with the understanding that they never waste paper. Conserving trees and protecting God's world are universal lessons.

Craft Supply Baskets

For glue and scissor-type supplies, make up four craft supply baskets. Use baskets or boxes, or store supplies in a desk. When these materials are needed, the Supply List will specify "craft supply basket."

1. a Bible
2. glue and tape
3. scissors
4. ruler
5. paintbrushes of various sizes
6. pencils, markers, crayons, and colored pencils
7. Popsicle sticks
8. stapler with extra staples
9. watercolors
10. buttons and beads for decorating
11. stickers
12. pipe cleaners of various colors

Storage Cabinet for Recyclable Materials

Many of the craft projects use household recyclable items. A cabinet with a door is best. Arrange materials at the proper height for children. Label shelves. Children will obtain supplies as needed. If a project calls for pop bottles, each child working at that station goes and gets a pop bottle.

Place a "Can You Donate?" list in your church's newsletter. You'll be surprised how willing church members are to donate.

1. 2-liter and smaller plastic pop bottles
2. empty cereal and cracker boxes (all sizes)
3. laundry soap boxes
4. frozen juice cans (cardboard) and lids (they do not have sharp edges)
5. empty tissue rolls and paper tubes of all sizes
6. tan, brown, or skin-tone stockings, socks, and other footwear
7. brown paper grocery bags and small lunch bags
8. yarn, floss, and thread (all colors)
9. rubber bands
10. ribbons, string, and cloth cord
11. leftover wrapping paper in foil and shiny colors
12. tissue paper in white and various colors
13. foam, paper, or plastic plates, trays, and cups
14. round cardboard or plastic containers with lids
15. cotton balls or polyester stuffing
16. beads of all shapes and sizes
17. cloth scraps (all kinds)
18. old Sunday school handout sheets, particularly pictures of people in biblical costumes
19. aluminum foil
20. unbleached basket-style coffee filters for drip machines

Always check supply lists several weeks in advance, request donations, and restock shelves before items are needed. This list includes materials that are used throughout the entire year, so keep the cabinet stocked.

Special Requirements of Individual Workstations

Workstations 1, 2, and 5:
Call to Worship; Affirmation; and Witness to Faith

These three workstations use a variety of supplies because the projects change from week to week. These three stations include the messy projects. Make sure the storage cabinet for recyclables, craft supply baskets, and construction paper are easily accessible to these three workstations.

Workstation 3:
Offering or Carpenter Shop

The carpenter shop uses the same tools each week. The wood will vary from project to project, but the tools remain basically the same. The carpenter shop uses only hand tools, and only one hammer and one saw. The lesson from the carpenter shop is not how to build, but how to take turns and work with your neighbor.

Store tools out of the reach of children when not in use. Never allow children to work with tools without adult supervision.

The carpenter shop should be stocked with the following items:

1. 1 hand saw and 1 hammer
2. sandpaper (fine and coarse)
3. wood glue and C-clamps
4. nails (all sizes)
5. scrap wood (see guide sheets for each session)
6. ruler, framing square, measuring string, and pencils
7. Bible and small, sturdy table to use for workbench

Seek donations. You will be surprised how many people have leftover wood. A new house being built is an excellent source of scrap wood. Do not use treated (outdoor) lumber.

Workstation 4: Sermon or Bible Study

The sermon always uses puppets or drama. You need a cloth for a puppet stage, two or three hand puppets, and a Bible.

Workstation 6:
Prayer and Sewing Center

The prayer station is the "Dorcas Upper Room Sewing Center." This workstation always has a sewing or weaving project in process, so stock the room with basic sewing supplies.

1. fabric scraps of all sizes
2. darning needles, hemming needles, and embroidery needles
3. sewing pins and pin cushion
4. scissors for cutting cloth
5. ruler, yardstick, and tape measure
6. pencils, paper, and a Bible
7. felt scraps (large and small)
8. fabric glue

Workstation 7: Benediction

The benediction supplies stay the same for all fifty-three sessions. This is a total paper-glue, no-mess station.
1. various colors of construction paper
2. glue and tape
3. scissors
4. markers, colored pencils, or crayons
5. hole punch, stapler, and extra staples
6. stickers
7. a ruler, Bible, and pencils

The "Supplies Needed" list at the beginning of each weekly session assumes that each workstation has (1) scissors, (2) pencils, (3) markers or crayons, (4) glue, (5) a Bible, (6) a stapler and staples, and (7) a designated place to put scrap paper. Children should save scrap construction paper instead of throwing it into the trash can. Teach your children to recycle and conserve.

A Teacher Training Workshop

I am sure that your church is much like ours and blessed with many dedicated teachers who do a fabulous job. But each year it is harder to find new teachers or to talk those dedicated teachers of many years into teaching for one more year. Why? There are many reasons, but one possibility is that we have lost our childlike enthusiasm for learning.

Christian education should be as important, if not more so, than reading, writing, and arithmetic. Yet, Christian education is often left in the hands of loving, well-meaning volunteers who feel lost and confused. They have no special training, no help, and not even a clue of where to turn for assistance.

Come, Follow Me! introduces a new way of teaching through learning centers, drama, action, and service projects. There are no lectures, no worksheets.

With *Come, Follow Me!,* stories and puppets replace lectures. Learning centers and crafts take the place of worksheets.

If your teaching staff is unfamiliar with learning centers, try a teacher training workshop. Once your congregation experiences a hands-on teaching approach, your church may want to totally redesign the children's education department to incorporate the learn-by-doing concept.

Teacher Training

Consider at least a one-hour workshop. You may instead plan an all-day session that includes setting up the rooms and making workstation signs.

Step 1: Explain the Learn-by-Doing Concept

Tell all volunteers that the goal of the program is to teach children how to worship. There are seven different workstations or approaches to teach the selected Bible verse every week.

Children are free to move from workstation to workstation or to work at one specific station. The workstation instruction sign teaches the Bible lesson. The craft project encourages the children to read the Bible. If one child finishes before others, simply encourage the child to move to another station and work there. The adult or youth helper's function is to read the workstation sign and lend a hand to anyone needing assistance.

This is a fast-paced, action-packed program that can be completed in thirty-five minutes or expanded to a full hour. The program is designed to have children work twenty minutes at a workstation, complete a project, and then close with worship.

The workstations change each week. Some projects are long term, some simple, but children never run out of interesting things to do. Each station teaches directly from the Bible and has been tested to ensure age appropriateness.

Step 2: Emphasize the Importance of Reading

There are two essential elements to *Come, Follow Me!*: (1) easy access to supplies, and (2) teaching everyone to *read the entire work-*

station sign. The workstation sign teaches the Bible lesson. The craft project is merely an incentive to encourage children to read and learn. You must insist that everyone read the sign.

Often children and adults will skip over the Bible verse and go directly to the step-by-step directions for the project. *Come, Follow Me!* is more than a mere craft session. Each station has a lesson to teach from the Bible, so it is important that children read or have someone else read the workstation sign.

Another mistake frequently made by older children and adults is looking at the pictures or examples without reading the written directions. If you can get your group into the habit of reading the workstation sign first, you have mastered the concept of teaching with learning centers.

Have the adult or teen working at each station read the workstation sign out loud. The information on the station sign ties the entire session together. The story or meditation, the workstation signs, Bible verse(s), and the puppet play sermon are all written and coordinated around a particular Bible lesson.

My children love "Rusty the Old Green Church Bus" from Session 2, so I remind them that Rusty says to "read the sign first." Before long the children are reminding one another, and older children are volunteering to read for younger ones. Use friendly reminders.

Step 3: Develop Creative Classrooms

Decide if your room will have tables or chairs. I rarely use chairs, but tables are essential. Children gather around tables to work. Chairs take up space. For worship, we sit on the floor.

Step 4: Work with Patterns

Most patterns in the book must be placed *on the fold.* This helps small children cut two equal sides more easily. Remind children and workstation helpers to place patterns on the fold.

Step 5: Make Workstation Signs

If you are conducting an all-day workshop, you may want to have the teachers make samples of some of the crafts.

The following projects work well for workstation signs:

Project #1: Make a peace pole. See directions from Session 14, Workstation 3.

Project #2: Make an offering box. See directions from Session 3, Workstation 1.

Project #3: Make a pop-bottle person. See directions from Sessions 19 and 20, Workstation 5.

Project #4: Make a church. See directions from Sessions 3, 4, and 5, Workstation 5.

Project #5: Prepare prayer banner and sew a letter. See directions from Session 1, Workstation 6.

Project #6: Make a rainbow stick puppet. See directions from Session 1, Workstations 1, 2, 5, 6, and 7.

We must rekindle a burning desire to learn in the lives of our children, God's children. *Come, Follow Me!* is your gateway to a new approach to teaching children about Jesus.

PART TWO

BECOMING A DISCIPLE OF JESUS CHRIST

5

· ·

Creating a Worship Center

Session 1
The Meaning of the Rainbow

The Bible Lesson

The children's meditation is from the story of the prodigal son (Luke 15:11-32). The rainbow reminds us that God loves us.

What the Children Will Learn Today

The children will make rainbow puppets. The rainbows explain the meaning of worship.

Time Needed

5 minutes for story or children's meditation
20 minutes for workstations
10 minutes for worship

Supplies Needed (by Workstation)

Story: White paper, pattern, scissors, and markers

1. Small heart pattern for "L," markers, and scrap paper
2. Scrap paper, markers, and pattern for "O"
3. Wood scraps, sandpaper, and woodworking basket
4. Craft supply basket, scrap paper, and pattern for "V"
5. Construction paper supply basket and face and hat patterns
6. 37" x 28" piece Aida cloth, embroidery thread or baby-weight yarn, needles for prayer banner, craft supply basket, and pattern for "E"
7. Construction paper supply basket

Children's Meditation

GETTING READY

Prepare rainbow heart before story.

STORY

The Path to the Rainbow

The view from Hannah's bedroom window was magnificent. A faraway field was dotted with wildflowers, sprawling farms, and a small village nestled into the side of the mountain. Most days were sunny and perfect for playing, but Hannah didn't play. Hannah couldn't walk.

Hannah had been injured in a car accident. Hannah's mother and father both died in the accident, and her twin sister, Shannon, was also injured but soon recovered. Shannon now lived with their uncle and his family in New York. The apartment building and city were too much for Hannah to manage in a wheelchair so she had been sent to the mountains to live with her grandparents.

Shannon was coming to visit this summer. Hannah and Shannon hadn't really talked to each other much since the accident. Hannah resented that Shannon could still run and play as before, while she could only sit and watch.

When the day of Shannon's visit finally arrived, Hannah was surprised to see her grandmother fixing up the cottage with balloons and streamers. The decorations made Hannah a little jealous.

As Shannon walked through the door, Hannah thought how different her sister looked.

Shannon had grown taller and cut her hair. As the two girls stared at each other, their grandmother swung open the kitchen door [fold paper in half to represent door] and swooshed into the room carrying a heart-shaped cake [cut heart] with two lit candles on top.

"Whose birthday?" Hannah asked.

"It's not a birthday, but it is a celebration," Grandmother said. As Hannah looked more closely at the cake, she saw a rainbow spread atop the cake in beautiful icing colors [open heart and show rainbow in the middle of white heart].

"Shannon has come home to be with us this summer," their grandmother said, "and Hannah has sold her first painting."

"I have?" Hannah blurted out.

"I took two of your rainbow paintings to the gallery last week, and both of them sold," said Grandmother. "The buyer says you have talent. He wants to set up an art show to display your work.

"Every day is a new beginning," Grandmother added. "We simply have to look for new opportunities. It's sort of like the rainbow.

"Sometimes everything seems dark and gloomy, and no matter what we do, everything seems to go wrong. Yet God always stands ready to give us another chance. The rainbow is sort of God's sign of hope that reminds us not to give up but to try again. If we believe in God and are willing to try to improve or do better, then every day can be the pathway to a new day."

We, too, are embarking on a new beginning this morning. Today is the first day of our new children's worship program. Each Sunday we will have seven workstations that represent the seven parts of the worship service. Today, you will travel around to all seven stations putting together a puzzle. The puzzle starts with a heart and a rainbow. Fold your paper as I did in the story and cut out a heart.

Patterns are available if you need help. Draw the shape of a rainbow in the center of your heart and write your name underneath the rainbow.

Make a new piece for your puzzle at each station. You should have seven puzzle pieces. You may start at any station, but go to Station 7 last.

Workstations

Workstation 1: Call to Worship

GETTING READY

Have craft supply basket and patterns ready. Make an example of the rainbow puppet to show younger children.

<table>
<tr><td>

INSTRUCTION SIGN

Today, we are traveling around the room to learn about worship. Workstation 1 is the "Call to Worship."

STEP 1: Read Psalm 66:4.
STEP 2: Add a color to your rainbow.
STEP 3: Cut out a small heart. Write the letter "L" on your heart.
STEP 4: Carry each piece you make with you to the next workstation. Can you guess what we're making?

</td></tr>
</table>

Workstation 2: Affirmation of Faith

> ### INSTRUCTION SIGN
>
> "Peace be with you!" was a traditional greeting used in biblical times. You would answer: "Peace with you" or "Also with you." Try this biblical greeting as you travel from station to station today. This is Workstation 2, our "Affirmation of Faith," or a statement of what you believe.
>
> STEP 1: Add another color to your rainbow. Decode this message:
>
> ### OGD SI EOLV
>
> Write the unscrambled message above your rainbow.
>
> STEP 2: The unscrambled words will help you finish the sentence "I believe . . ." Write the answer on your white rainbow heart.
> STEP 3: Read Luke 4:8. Use the pattern; make a small heart.
> STEP 4: Write the letter "O" on the small heart. Carry pieces to next station.

Workstation 3: Offering or Carpenter Shop

GETTING READY

Need long thin wood scraps, 1" x 2" or 2" x 2", to prepare for next week's session.

> ### INSTRUCTION SIGN
>
> The "Offering" workstation is our carpenter shop each week. You may come and offer your time to work. We are sanding today. No one likes to sand wood. It's hard work and it's boring.
>
> STEP 1: Add a third color to your rainbow and write down something that's hard for you to do.
> STEP 2: Read Psalm 95:6. Help sand wood before going on.

Workstation 4: Sermon or Bible Study

> ### INSTRUCTION SIGN
>
> Each week we use seven workstations. The "Sermon" workstation tells how the Bible is important today.
>
> STEP 1: Add a fourth color to your rainbow and finish this sentence: "Worship is . . ." Read Psalm 100:1-5 for help.
> STEP 2: Make another small heart, using the pattern. Write the letter "V" on the heart.

Workstation 5: Witness to Faith

GETTING READY

Have an example of a face with a hat glued in place.

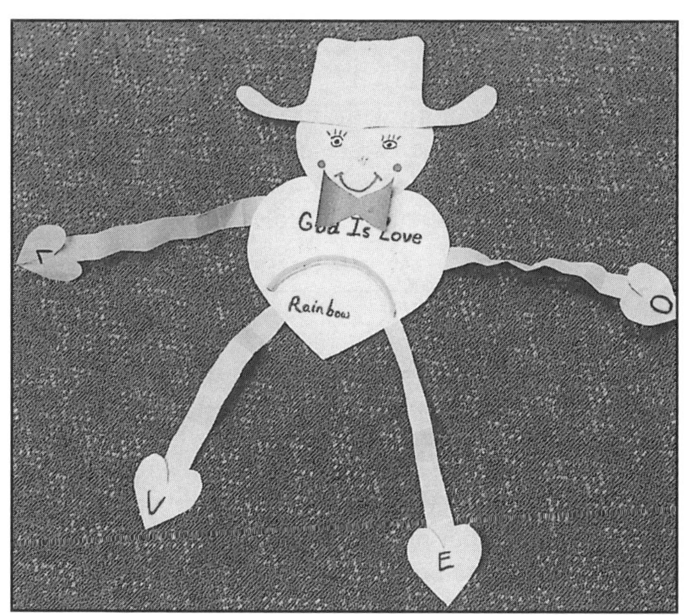

INSTRUCTION SIGN

When we "witness," we tell others about our faith.

STEP 1: Use patterns for heart and hat. Draw a face on the heart. If you have trouble drawing a nose, wad up a tiny scrap of paper for a nose. When something is hard to do, don't give up—try a different way to do the same job. Glue hat onto face.
STEP 2: Have someone read Luke 15:11-32 while you work.
STEP 3: Add another color to your rainbow and write down a rule that you find difficult to follow.

Workstation 6: Prayer and Sewing Center

GETTING READY

Cut Aida cloth to 37" x 28" size. Write Luke 10:25-28 on cloth with ink, not marker. Have a helper today who can teach how to thread a needle and sew a simple outline stitch. You may also want to have some needles already threaded to save time.

INSTRUCTION SIGN

Sewing is a peaceful activity that gives you time to think. Workstation 6, our "Prayer" station, is also used as a sewing center each week. We are starting a new commandment prayer banner today. It will probably take us a year to finish.

With the help of the seamstress, sew a few stitches. Read Luke 10:25-28 to learn what our banner will say when complete. While you are waiting for a turn, add another color to your rainbow and write down how you can be more patient at school, home, or with your friends. Use the pattern to cut a heart. Write the letter "E" on the small heart.

Workstation 7: Benediction

GETTING READY

Make an example to show.

INSTRUCTION SIGN

"Go now in peace!" The "Benediction," or closing to the service, sends everyone out to share the teachings of Jesus.

STEP 1: Read Genesis 9:16.
STEP 2: Cut 4 strips of paper 11" long and 1" wide.
STEP 3: Fold each strip as if you were making a fan.
STEP 4: Glue the L, O, V, and E hearts from Workstations 1, 2, 4, and 6 to the ends of these 4 folded strips of paper.
STEP 5: Glue other end of folded strips to the back of white rainbow heart. L-O-V-E should be spelled out on the hands and feet.
STEP 6: Glue face and hat to top of the rainbow heart. See example.

The Worship Celebration

GETTING READY

Have someone volunteer to be Rainbow. Tape puppet to ruler. Ask a youth to speak for Rainbow. Use a blanket for the puppet stage.

PUPPET PLAY FOR SERMON

Rainbow

[Puppet slowly peeks out over blanket.]

RAINBOW: Hi! I'm supposed to lead today's worship service, but I'm a little scared. Will you help me? [pause] Let's see, a worship service starts off with a *call to worship*. Maybe we could ring a bell. [Ring bell.]

RAINBOW: No, that's not enough. We need to explain why we're here. That's important, I'm sure. Another important part of worship is to tell others that we are Christians and that we follow Jesus. When you tell or show others what you believe, you're making a statement or *affirmation* about your faith.

Finish the sentence "I believe . . ." [Pause, have several children read their "I believe" statements.]

RAINBOW: Sometimes it's hard for me to talk in front of people. I get sort of shy.

When I heard I had to give the *sermon* today, I was really scared. I'm not sure I know what worship is. What did you write on your rainbows to say worship means to you? [Encourage everyone to read his or her "Worship is" statement.]

RAINBOW: That sure sounds like a good sermon to me. Oh dear, we forgot to pray. I get embarrassed when people ask me to lead the *prayer*. I forget what to say.

I've been told that doing something hard is a good way to show you're growing up. It's hard to follow rules. Do you ever have trouble following a rule? [Have someone tell a rule that it is hard to follow.]

RAINBOW: While we've been sharing all of these ideas together, we've been *witnessing* to God and to each other.

God wants us to come together each week to share our feelings and problems. God also wants us to help one another. Worship is a time to share together. Worship is a time to celebrate and tell God "thank you" for all that God has given us. Worship is also a time to learn.

I have to learn to be patient. It's hard to be patient. Can you think of ways to be more patient? [Have several children give examples of patience.]

RAINBOW: I've sure learned a lot from listening to you today. It's time to say good-bye for now, but I'll come again. [Close with Lord's Prayer.]

ITEMS TO GO HOME TODAY: RAINBOW PUPPETS

The Bible Lesson

Worship is a time to share God's love (Romans 12:10-18).

What the Children Will Learn Today

Being humble and grateful is a good way to begin worship.

Time Needed

5 minutes for story
20 minutes for workstations
10 minutes for closing service

Supplies Needed (by Workstation)

Story: Bells, hand puppets if desired (cow, cat, and dog) and a hand drum or empty cardboard box

1. Craft supply basket, pattern, tissue holders, and jingle bells
2. Old bedsheet, tempera paint, paper plates for handprints, newspapers, paint brushes, cleanup supplies, and cover-ups
3 and 5. Scraps of wood from last week, paper plates, construction paper, brown paper sacks, and craft supply basket
4. Puppet play scripts and two puppets
6. Embroidery basket and sewing supplies
7. Construction paper supply basket and bus pattern

Children's Meditation

STORY

Rusty
The Old Green Church Bus

For today's story, I need some helpers. I need someone who can ring a bell each time I say the word *bell* in the story. [Hand one of the children the bell.] I need someone who can "Moo" like a cow. [Give someone a cow puppet.] I want you to say "Moo!" every time I say "Daisy the Cow."

Who can meow like a cat? [Give someone a cat puppet.] You need to meow loudly one time when you hear Fluffy the Cat's name.

I also need someone who can bark like a dog. [Give a dog puppet to someone who rarely gets selected to do special jobs.] When you hear me say "Huey," you are to bark three times.

We need someone to be the bumpy road and tap this [hold up a box] every time I say "bumpy road."

The rest of us will do the "puff, puff, puff . . ." sound for Rusty's engine each time we hear the name "Rusty."

Okay, let's go!

RUSTY was an old green church bus with a bouncy luggage door. A big puff of blue-black smoke came out of the tailpipe as RUSTY chugged along the old BUMPY road to and from church.

RUSTY was very proud and thought he was just about the finest church bus that had ever been made, even though he was getting quite old and a little worn out. The old green church bus didn't always follow directions or listen to advice. RUSTY thought he knew everything he needed to know.

Every Sunday, RUSTY drove around the neighborhood ringing his BELL and bringing the children to Sunday school and worship. Well, on this particular Sunday morning the old bus pulled out of the church parking lot right on time and very proudly started on his rounds to pick up the children. The old green church bus puffed along very happily and rang his BELL. At his first stop, he picked up three children. As he drove by, the old bus also rang his BELL to say "Good Morning" to DAISY THE COW. DAISY called out, "You'd better read the sign." The old green church bus drove on by and stopped at the end of the street to pick up even more children.

"I don't need to read the sign," said RUSTY somewhat indignantly. "I know which houses to stop at."

All of a sudden, the bus clattered to a screeching halt right in front of where a bridge *used* to be and a sign saying: "Bridge Out! Detour 5 Miles." Oh dear, why hadn't someone told him there was a detour? RUSTY had six more children to pick up on the other side of the bridge. All of the children would be late for Sunday school if he had to go around to Humble Road. As the old church bus backed up and turned on to the even BUMPIER Humble Road, he remembered DAISY THE COW warning him to read the sign.

The old bus puffed up the hill blowing blue-black smoke everywhere and furiously rang his BELL at FLUFFY THE CAT who was sauntering across the road. FLUFFY called back over her shoulder, "You'd better read the sign."

"I read the sign. I know about the detour," said RUSTY.

FLUFFY called out again, "Don't forget to read everything on the sign."

As the old church bus drove around the S curve, he screeched to a stop again. This time he stopped in front of a sign across the road that read: "Road Closed! Go Back."

This is awful! Why hadn't someone told him that the shortcut was closed? RUSTY had to turn around again. He remembered that DAISY and FLUFFY both had warned him to read the signs, and he had seen the "Road Closed" sign. What else could they have meant?

Finally, the old bus had boarded his last passenger. If he hurried, RUSTY still might get the children to Sunday school on time. Chugging along faster than before, the old green bus rattled off toward church. HUEY chased alongside and said, "You better go back. You didn't read the sign."

"I don't have time to go back and read the signs," said the old church bus. "I have to hurry or I'll be late."

Without warning, RUSTY screeched to a halt a third time. There across the road was another ROAD CLOSED! sign. The sign read: "Road Closed for 3 Weeks, New Water Lines Being Laid, Take Alternate Route." And there, lying just beyond the big ditch that had been dug for the water line, was the little country church.

As HUEY ran along the shoulder of the road and scooted under the "Road Closed" sign, he shouted back over his shoulder, "You have to read the signs, RUSTY."

RUSTY the old green church bus was so close, but unfortunately, he would have to go all the way back around. He would never make it in time. The roads were too BUMPY. DAISY, FLUFFY, and HUEY were right. He should have stopped and read everything on the sign.

In our children's worship program, you have to stop and read the signs. There are signs at each workstation. Each sign tells you exactly what you are to do or make to help us get ready for our worship service. If you can't read the sign, ask for help.

Workstations

Workstation 1: Call to Worship

INSTRUCTION SIGN

Many churches use a bell to call people to worship. Make a simple handbell to ring at the beginning of our worship service today. Read Romans 12:2.

STEP 1: Use pattern and cut bell out of scrap paper.

STEP 2: Make a rainbow. Begin with BLUE. Write something that makes you feel sad.

STEP 3: For RED, write something that makes you angry.

STEP 4: Add PINK and tell something you can give to others.

STEP 5: Add PURPLE above the pink and write something you can do that makes you feel very proud.

STEP 6: For YELLOW, tell something that makes you happy.

STEP 7: Above your rainbow, write: "God loves everyone." Then, write today's Bible verse (Romans 12:2) and one thing you can do to be a better follower of Jesus.

STEP 8: Glue the rainbow around a tissue roll. Punch holes, attach handle. Add a jingle bell. Use only one bell. If we use only what we need in life instead of everything we want, there will always be enough for others. Decorate bell with streamers.

Workstation 2: Affirmation of Faith

GETTING READY

Make a portable, easy-to-use puppet stage from an old bedsheet. Fold cloth in half for thickness. Spread newspapers across a large table or space on the floor. Lay cloth on top of papers. Put tempera paint on paper plates. Have children work from only one side of banner so handprints will show right side up. Be ready with cover-ups and cleanup supplies.

INSTRUCTION SIGN

STEP 1: Put on a cover-up. Place hand, palm and fingers outstretched, on plate with favorite color of paint.

STEP 2: Place your handprint on "Helping Hands" banner to say you're a follower, a disciple of Jesus. Work with your neighbor to arrange all the hands in a RAINBOW ARCH.

STEP 3: Press hand with paint on clean piece of paper; make your handprint to take home as a reminder of your commitment. Wash hands.

STEP 4: With a paintbrush, decorate your handprint.

STEP 5: Read Romans 12:1. On your handprint paper, write: "I'm a Follower of Jesus" and the Bible verse. Sign up to read Romans 12:10-18 in the service today.

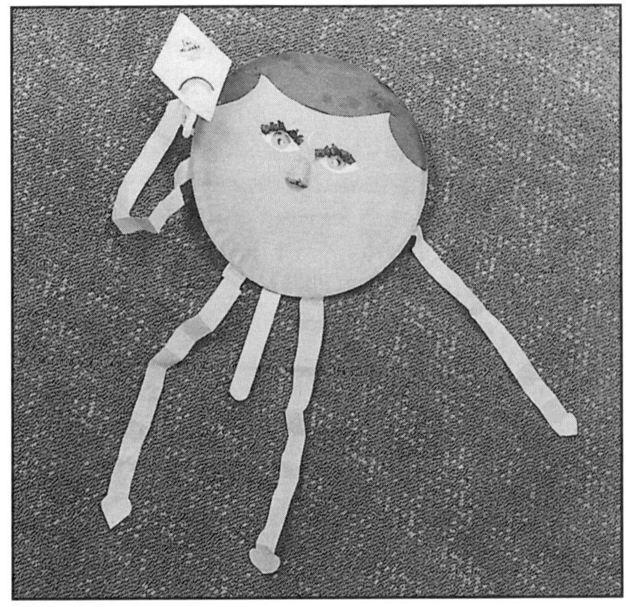

Workstations 3 (Offering or Carpenter Shop) and 5 (Witness to Faith) Combined

GETTING READY

Use puppet patterns from Session 1. Use wood sanded from last week. Save two puppets from today for Session 4.

INSTRUCTION SIGN
STEP 1: Cover back of paper plate with brown paper sack or skin-tone paper.
STEP 2: Draw or use paper to make hair, eyes, and a mouth.
STEP 3: Wad a dampened piece of paper to match face for nose.
STEP 4: Trace arm, leg, and foot patterns. Fold strips as if making a paper fan. Tape arms and legs to back of plate. Read Bible verse and write verse on back of plate to remind yourself to volunteer to read for the service today (Romans 12:20-21).
STEP 5: Tape long chenille stem to back of plate at right arm for kite string. Trace kite pattern. Add bows to kite tail. Glue right hand to chenille stem as if holding string of kite.
STEP 6: Select a wood scrap for a handle. Sand smooth or cover with paper. Glue puppet onto sanded wood for handle.

Workstation 4: Sermon or Bible Study

INSTRUCTION SIGN
You don't have to carry your Bible with you to tell others you're a Christian. They should know you're a follower of Jesus by how you act and talk. Read Romans 12:14-18. Your job is to act out the sermon. Today, finish writing the puppet play. Write in lines where indicated. You need 2 puppeteers and 2 readers. Read slowly and loudly.

PUPPET PLAY FOR SERMON

What Is a Church?

[Have one of the puppets poke its head out and look all around. Give each puppet a name.]

1ST PUPPET:	It's clear. Come on up.
2ND PUPPET:	Are you sure? There sure have been a lot of children running around here lately. Why do the children come here so much anyway?
1ST PUPPET:	This is a church, and the children come here to learn how to worship God.
2ND PUPPET:	What's a church?
1ST PUPPET:	A church is a special place where Christians gather to worship God every Sunday.
2ND PUPPET:	They come every Sunday?
1ST PUPPET:	Every Sunday is a day of celebration! Christians get together on Sunday to learn more about God and to praise God.
2ND PUPPET:	Christians! Are the children Christians too?
1ST PUPPET:	Yes, a Christian is anyone who follows the teachings of Jesus and . . . [Read Matthew 22:36-40 and Proverbs 15:31-33 for help. Write an answer for puppet.]

1ST PUPPET: The children show others they are Christians by . . . [Read Luke 10:30-37 for help. Finish skit in your own words. Remember, our puppets never use bad words or fight.]

Workstation 6: Prayer and Sewing Center

GETTING READY

Children will work on same prayer banner as last week.

INSTRUCTION SIGN

"Amen!" We often close prayers by saying Amen. "Amen" is a Hebrew word used to say "that's right." Amen is said at the end of a prayer to tell others you agree with what was said. Follow the directions of the seamstress and continue sewing today. Read Psalm 106:48 while waiting for a turn.

You are in charge of closing our worship service today by leading us in saying the Lord's Prayer.

Workstation 7: Benediction

INSTRUCTION SIGN

Trace pattern and make Rusty the old green church bus. Draw windows and doors for Rusty or cut scrap paper for doors and windows that open. Write today's Bible verse (Romans 12:10-13) and a slogan to follow inside: "Share a Smile with Someone Today" or "Stop and Read the Bible Every Day." Your bus will stand up when finished. Sign up to read your slogan for worship today.

The Worship Celebration

GETTING READY

Use bell to call everyone to worship.

SIGN-UP SHEET FOR TODAY'S WORSHIP CELEBRATION

Call to Worship: Have children ring their rainbow bells.

Affirmation (read Romans 12:10-18):

Offering/Witness (read Romans 12:19-21):

Sermon (2 puppeteers and 2 readers for "What Is a Church?"):

Prayer (lead the Lord's Prayer):

Benediction (read church bus slogans):

ITEMS TO GO HOME TODAY: RAINBOW HANDBELLS; PAPER-PLATE PUPPETS; HANDPRINTS; AND BUSES

6

Building the Sunshine Share-a-Lot Puppet Theater

The Bible Lesson

To be a follower of Jesus, we must live a life based on love for God and all God's creation (1 John 4:7-8, 19-21).

What the Children Will Learn Today

Working on long-term projects helps build group togetherness.

Time Needed

5 minutes for story
20 minutes for workstations
10 minutes for closing service

Supplies Needed (by Workstation)

Story: Folding church from Workstation 5, small scrap of wood that you can easily break, old tin can with coins, and simple church from Workstation 1.

1. Cereal boxes to use as collection containers, Mission Project poster, green paper or leftover gift wrap to cover boxes, copied small church pattern, and craft supply basket

2. Cloud and sun patterns, cotton balls, cardboard, and blue construction paper

3. Tools and lumber for carpenter shop

4. Puppet play, Helping Hands cloth, and four puppets

5. Patterns, stiff white paper, and self-sticking plastic

6. Embroidery banner and sewing supplies, yarn, tape, newspapers, and cereal boxes for weaving travel bags

7. Construction paper supply basket, plus a stapler or tape

Children's Meditation

GETTING READY

Make church examples. See Workstations 1 and 5.

STORY

The Little White Church

A small white church once sat at the edge of town. It didn't have a fancy parking lot. It was just a plain little church where people came to worship God [show small church].

One Sunday morning, a terrible thunderstorm was brewing. Everyone was sort of hoping the preacher wouldn't talk as long as usual so they could get home before the rain started, but much to their surprise, the preacher went up and down the aisles passing out buckets and tin cans. You see, if it rained while you were at church, you would most likely get wet, because the roof on the little white church *leaked*.

As the rain began to drip through the ceiling, the preacher unfolded a large drawing he had made and began to talk about building a new church. The preacher went on for what seemed like hours with the constant drip, drip, drip of

35

raindrops in metal containers echoing from every corner of the church. Then the preacher asked everyone to follow him outside.

"It's a great idea, Preacher," said Mr. Hamilton as he stood looking up at the drawing from the front lawn, "but we'll never be able to raise the money. It's impossible!"

"Sure you can," said the preacher as he reached and pulled off a rotten plank [break the piece of wood in half]. "All you have to do is pull a plank and name your price. If everyone helps we'll have this church built in no time."

The preacher wrote his name and $5 on the board he pulled off. All at once everyone seemed to be yanking off boards and tacking up $10, $100, and even a $500 donation pledge.

Mr. Gordon, a local dairy farmer, went to his truck and brought back a shiny silver milk can and set it right underneath the drawing. Mr. Gordon then emptied out his pockets and put everything he had in the milk can [drop coins into can]. One year later, they started the new church. The walls went up one by one [unfold large paper church]. Everyone helped with the roof [place roof on top]. The steeple bell rang loud and clear [put steeple on roof].

Each week the families gathered to build new pews, paint, lay carpeting, and finish the interior until, finally, the new church was complete [open floor to show pews].

You can build a church, too, a paper church. Building a church can remind you that you, too, can accomplish seemingly impossible tasks, if you try. Don't give up when something looks hard, and never say, "I can't." Instead say, "I'll try."

Workstations

Workstation 1: Call to Worship

GETTING READY

Have children save money for a local food bank or international organization. Make a poster describing project. Boxes will be collected in Session 10. Send a letter home with the children about the project.

Photocopy paper church pattern. Cut holes in boxes for money slots.

Use green construction paper for grass or left-over gift wrap to emphasize that the collection is a gift.

INSTRUCTION SIGN

Read poster about Mission Project. Then make a paper church collection box to remind you to collect money for our service project. Sign up to read Matthew 7:1-2 for our service today.

STEP 1: Church—cut on solid lines; fold on dotted lines.

STEP 2: Decorate church with stickers or draw windows.

STEP 3: Cover box with green paper. Write Bible verse on box. Push paper through hole for money. Glue church in place.

Place collection containers on worship table for service. Sign up to lead hymn. Take box home and start saving for collection in Session 10.

Workstation 2: Affirmation of Faith

GETTING READY

We will be making affirmation booklets. Use cotton or white construction paper for clouds. Children will add to booklet for several weeks. They may take booklets home and add pages at home or display on bulletin board.

INSTRUCTION SIGN

At age eighteen, Jewish boys who wanted to continue their education lived and traveled with a teacher. These students were called "disciples," which means "follower or someone who obeys the teachings of" another person. We are followers of Jesus. Make an affirmation booklet telling what it means to follow Jesus.

STEP 1: Glue cotton onto blue paper for clouds.

STEP 2: At bottom of blue page, complete the following statement:
God is . . .
  You may answer: "God is Love" or "God is the Creator." Read: John 4:24; 1 John 4:7-8, 19-21; and Romans 11:36.

STEP 3: Glue blue page to a stiff piece of cardboard.

Sign up to read today's Bible verses from 1 John for our service.

Workstation 3: Offering or Carpenter Shop

GETTING READY

Copy "Guide Sheet for Building the Sunshine Share-a-Lot Puppet Theater." Have an adult supervise use of saw and hammer.

INSTRUCTION SIGN

Welcome to Joseph's Carpenter Shop! As a young boy Jesus learned to work with wood. You will too.

One of the lessons Jesus taught his disciples was that the amount of your offering wasn't as important as your willingness to give. Read Mark 12:41-44. Follow instructions of master carpenter to build "Sunshine Share-a-Lot's Helping Hands Puppet Theater." Display first piece of wood cut at service.

Guide Sheet for Building the Sunshine Share-a-Lot Puppet Theater

Three general rules to follow: (1) Always measure a board twice to make sure you measured correctly, (2) ask an adult to check your work before you saw, and (3) lightly pencil on each board you cut a description of where it belongs (for example, "bottom right—46" long").

Lumber Needed

1. Lumber, 1" x 2" nominal thickness (measures actually 3/4" thick). These are sold as furring strips, and often go on sale. You need 12 pieces that are 6 feet in length.

2. Lumber, 2" x 2" nominal thickness. These are used to add stability to the bottom. The plans call for 3 pieces that are 6 feet in length.

3. 3" hinges. You need 6.

4. A box of 1 1/4" nails. These are short so the points won't stick out of the boards.

5. Four 48" long 3/4" dowel rods.

6. Eight 1" eye hooks

Sawing

Step 1: Measure and cut three 2" x 2" boards 46" long to go across the bottom. Measure carefully. Cut straight.

Step 2: Measure and cut six 1" x 2" boards 46" long for top and middle. See drawing.

Step 3: Measure and cut six 1" x 2" boards 72" long for sides. Sometimes you are lucky enough to be able to purchase the exact length you need and won't even have to cut the 72" boards.

Step 4: Measure and cut braces for corners from leftover 1" x 2" scrap wood. See diagram. You may also purchase metal corner braces.

Step 5: Cut dowel rods for curtain rods. You will need someone to drill the holes for the curtain eye hooks.

Save all wood scraps. You will use them for projects throughout the year. You have now finished cutting all of the boards needed to build your puppet stage. Congratulations!

Sanding

Sand all boards until they are smooth. Do not nail any boards together until they have been sanded.

Hammering

Step 6: Build the puppet stage one panel at a time. Start with a side panel. Lay out the panel. Lay the top, middle, and bottom boards on top of the 72" side boards. Use your framing square to make sure all corners are the same. Measure twice before you hammer. Add a little glue to the corners to make the joints secure. Then nail on the middle side board for support. Hammer braces into place at the corner as marked on drawing.

Step 7: Repeat the same process for other side panel.

Step 8: Repeat process for center panel. Add curtain rods. Sand smooth. Your puppet stage is together. Good work!

Step 9: Attaching the hinges will depend somewhat on the type of hinges you have. Before you attach hinges, stand the puppet stage up with adult help and test out the placement of your hinges. Make sure the puppet stage will fold up.

Step 10: Attach one hinge according to the package directions and then stand the puppet stage up again and test for accuracy before attaching the remaining hinges. If you happen to make a mistake, don't worry. Take the hinge off. Attach correctly. Fill any holes with wood putty before you paint. You have completed the Sunshine Share-a-Lot Puppet Theater.

Workstation 4: Sermon or Bible Study

INSTRUCTION SIGN

During his three-year ministry, Jesus traveled from town to town preaching on hillsides, beside the Sea of Galilee, and in the temple courtyards, but never in a church. There were no churches and no Christians. The first church wasn't built until almost 200 years after Jesus died. Read 1 John 4:7-8, 19-21.

STEP 1: The first step to being a puppeteer is to speak loudly and slowly so that everyone can hear what you're saying.

STEP 2: Cooperation always makes for a better sermon. Have one person be the puppeteer and make the puppet move. Have a second person be the voice for the puppet and read the script. You need 4 puppeteers and 4 readers today.

PUPPET PLAY FOR SERMON
A Good Excuse

JAKE: I don't need to read that silly workstation sign. I can tell how to build this church without reading that old sign.

JUDY: Then why are you gluing the sides of your church together instead of using tape? The directions say that if you tape the walls together the church will fold flat for storage. There's no way your church will fold.

JAKE: I'll never finish if I stop to read the sign.

MIKE: The point of the workstation is not simply to build a church. The Bible verses teach the lesson for the day. If you skip the Bible, you've missed the reason for doing the project.

BARBARA: Jesus gave us specific directions to follow in life, but we won't know what they are if we don't read the Bible.

JUDY: Life hasn't changed all that much. We still have cheating, lying, stealing, teasing, and people constantly trying to prove that they are better than someone else. The primary goal for most people is still money, and there are many people living in poverty while others live in lavish luxury.

JAKE: I did it! While you've been talking, I've been working. I have all four of my windows finished.

BARBARA: You did something wrong.

JAKE: It takes too long to cut those little tiny pieces.

MIKE: In life, it's important to take the time to do things right. If we rush and do sloppy work, we won't be giving our best. In the end, we only cheat ourselves.

JAKE: My church is a mess. I'm throwing it away.

JUDY: Don't give up and quit. You can fix it. God always forgives us for our mistakes and lets us try again.

BARBARA: It'll take a long time, but if we work slowly and do our best, we can build a church that we'll be proud of.

JAKE: I can't. It's too hard.

MIKE: No task is too hard if you really try, and if you need help, I'll be glad to help you.

BARBARA: Maybe we can work together.

JUDY: After all, that's what a church is all about: people working together to help each other.

JAKE: We'd better get started, then, 'cause my church needs lots of help.

Workstation 5: Witness to Faith

GETTING READY

Use stiff poster paper for the church. Have a paper sack for each worker to store unfinished pieces in each week.

INSTRUCTION SIGN

We are building a church. It takes commitment to finish the job. First, read the answer Jesus gave in Mark 10:17-21.

STEP 1: Use pattern and make walls for church.

STEP 2: Cut 8 small windows from clear self-sticking plastic. Cut tiny pieces of tissue paper. Place on sticky side of plastic. Cover tissue with second piece of plastic.

STEP 3: Glue windows in place. Cut black frames and glue over each window on inside and outside.

STEP 4: Place a finished window or wall on the worship table today to show that construction has begun on the church.

Workstation 6: Prayer and Sewing Center

GETTING READY

Make an example. Keep a travel bag for the Christmas play.

INSTRUCTION SIGN

Welcome to the Dorcas Upper Room Sewing Center! Dorcas was a follower of the teachings of Jesus and helped to build the early church. When Dorcas and her family traveled, they would have carried a small woven travel bag instead of suitcases.

Weave a cloth travel bag. Reread Luke 10:27 while you wait to sew or weave. Sign up to lead the Lord's Prayer today.

STEP 1: Stuff cereal box with newspapers. Wrap 7 STRANDS of yarn tightly around cereal box.

STEP 2: Wrap a contrasting color of yarn around a small scrap of cardboard to make a shuttle. Start to weave over and then under the strands of yarn tied around your cereal box. Continue all the way around the box. Keep yarn tight.

STEP 3: When weaving is complete, cut yarn evenly across the top. Do NOT cut too close to the edge of weaving or you will not be able to tie the ends together.

STEP 4: Tie sides together.

STEP 5: Do NOT tie top together; tie along edge.

STEP 6: Braid yarn handle. Tie in place.

Workstation 7: Benediction

GETTING READY

For young children, cut the paper to be woven beforehand or make plain unwoven paper bags. Use old Sunday school leaflets for pictures of biblical clothing to go in travel bags.

INSTRUCTION SIGN

Travelers carried clothes or a pair of sandals in a handwoven cloth travel bag as they walked from town to town.

Make a paper travel bag. Write 1 John 4:7-8, 19-21 on your bag to remind you what it means to be a follower of Jesus. Sign up to tell one way to show God's love during the service.

STEP 1: Fold paper in half. Cut slashes, 2" apart, from fold to about 2" from edge. Do not cut through edge.

STEP 2: Cut different colors into 2" strips for weaving.

STEP 3: Begin to weave over and under.

STEP 4: Staple edges and strips on top for handles.

STEP 5: Cut out paper biblical clothes or draw your own. Travel bag opens for you to put clothes inside.

The Worship Celebration

SIGN-UP SHEET FOR TODAY'S WORSHIP CELEBRATION

Call to Worship (read Matthew 7:1-2):

Affirmation (read 1 John 4:7-8, 19-21):

Offering (show first piece of wood cut for puppet theater):

Sermon (4 puppeteers and 4 readers for "A Good Excuse"):

Prayer (lead the Lord's Prayer):

Benediction (tell one way to show God's love):

ITEMS TO GO HOME TODAY: COLLECTION BOXES; TRAVEL BAGS

Session 4
What Do I Have to Give?

The Bible Lesson

The Bible lesson comes from Luke 6:27-36 and answers the question "What do I have to give?"

What the Children Will Learn Today

The children will learn that there are many ways to share love with others. Making cards for people in a nursing home is one way.

Time Needed

5 minutes for story
20 minutes for workstations
10 minutes for closing service

Supplies Needed (by Workstation)

Story: An empty jar and $3.23 in pennies for story

1. Boxes, paper, and church patterns from last week [Session 3, Workstation 1]

2. Pink, yellow, and purple construction paper, sunrise patterns, and gold glitter

3. Guide Sheet, tools, and lumber for puppet stage

4. Two paper-plate puppets from Session 2, Helping Hands puppet cloth, a puppet to use all year for Sunshine, and script

5. Paper for building churches, tissue paper for stained-glass windows, clear self-sticking plastic to cover windows, tape and glue, construction paper, and patterns for windows and walls

6. Construction paper, embroidery banner, yarn for travel bags, scraps of yarn and thread for cards, and craft supply basket

7. Construction paper supply basket and Lovegram patterns

Children's Meditation

GETTING READY

Use jar and pennies to tell story.

STORY

Twenty-Three Cents

"One, two, three, four, five, six, seven, eight, nine, ten. This'll take forever," Joey moaned. "Why don't we watch TV?"

"No TV. We have to keep counting," Maggie insisted.

Maggie and Joey had been saving every penny they found for about three years now. They were saving for a bicycle. Sometimes Joey wished they'd never started. It all seemed so hopeless.

"By the time we save enough, we'll have outgrown the bike and won't even be able to ride it," Joey said.

"We have $3.22," Maggie announced.

"Pennies are worthless," said Joey.

"A single penny by itself may not be worth much, but if we put them all together, then they can amount to something. Cheer up! You'll see; we'll make it. Let's walk by the bike shop after school," said Maggie. [Put pennies in jar.]

Every day after school, the children stopped at the bike shop and ran their fingers longingly across the handlebars of the old red bike. The old bike had actually seen its better days. There were patches of rust eating away at the metal, the tires were bald, and the seat was bent and torn, but to Maggie and Joey the old junker looked brand-new.

On Sunday morning in church, Mr. McFrancis from the bike shop stepped up to the lectern to tell about flood victims in the valley and how they needed blankets. Two teenagers from the youth group held up a hideously ugly blanket for everyone to see.

"That blanket is so ugly that no one will even want one," whispered Joey.

Mr. McFrancis explained that the church

hoped to send one hundred blankets by Tuesday. The blankets cost $3.00. Mr. McFrancis went on to explain how the flood victims had nothing left and were using the blankets for tents, coats, and beds.

"We could buy a blanket," Maggie suggested as they left church.

"No way. That's our bike money," said Joey.

Mr. McFrancis had ended his speech on Sunday by saying "it was better to give than to receive," but it still didn't seem fair to Joey on Monday after school as he stood beside Maggie and watched her give Mr. McFrancis the penny jar.

"We want to buy a blanket for the flood victims," Maggie said with sort of a shaky voice. "We have exactly $3.22."

"Twenty-three cents," Joey interrupted as he dropped a penny into the jar that he had found outside the door of the bike shop.

"That's kind of you, and the children in the valley will be grateful. The blankets cost $3.00. You have 23¢ left. I don't know if you're interested," Mr. McFrancis continued as Joey brushed away a tear from the corner of his eye, "but it so happens that we're having a sale on used bikes today. There's a certain old red bike that's been marked down to exactly 23¢." Then Mr. McFrancis walked over and wrote 23¢ in big print on the price tag.

"We'll take it!" Joey blurted out.

"Good," said Mr. McFrancis with a smile. "Let me write up your sales receipt."

Joey wasn't listening. He had the kickstand up and was riding the old junker around the store.

A minute ago all was lost, gone. They had given away all that they had and yet received more in return than Joey ever believed possible.

Workstations

Workstation 1: Call to Worship

GETTING READY

Have pennies from story for collection boxes. Use pattern from last week.

<table>
<tr><td>

INSTRUCTION SIGN

Last week, you made a church to take home to remind you to collect money for our mission project. This week, use the same pattern and work together to make a collection box for us to keep on our worship table. If you weren't here last week or didn't get a chance to make a church, take time to make one today. The word "church" comes from a Greek word meaning "Lord's house." Read 1 Timothy 1:12. Make a collection box. Take a penny from the jar for your box. Write today's Bible verse on your box. Place your box on the worship table to remind everyone of our mission project.

Sign up to help sing a song to begin the puppet play.

</td></tr>
</table>

Workstation 2: Affirmation of Faith

GETTING READY

Keep affirmation booklet instructions up for each week. Label Week 1, Week 2, Week 3, etc.

INSTRUCTION SIGN

We started with the last page of our affirmation booklet. This week, we'll add the sunrise to remind us of the resurrection. Each week we will add a new page and statement of our faith.

STEP 1: Trace sun. Cover with gold glitter. Let dry.

STEP 2: Trace pink and purple sunrise patterns. At bottom of pink page write: "Thank you, God, for . . ."

Complete the sentence by writing something special that you are thankful for in your life. Read Colossians 3:12-13, 17 for help. Sign up to read your statement during today's service.

STEP 3: Glue sun in place on pink page as marked on pattern. Punch holes. Tie sunrise pages on top of sky page.

Workstation 3: Offering or Carpenter Shop

INSTRUCTION SIGN

Are you a follower of the Way? The early Christians were said to be followers of the Way because they followed the teachings or the way of Jesus Christ. Read John 14:6 and follow the instructions of the master carpenter.

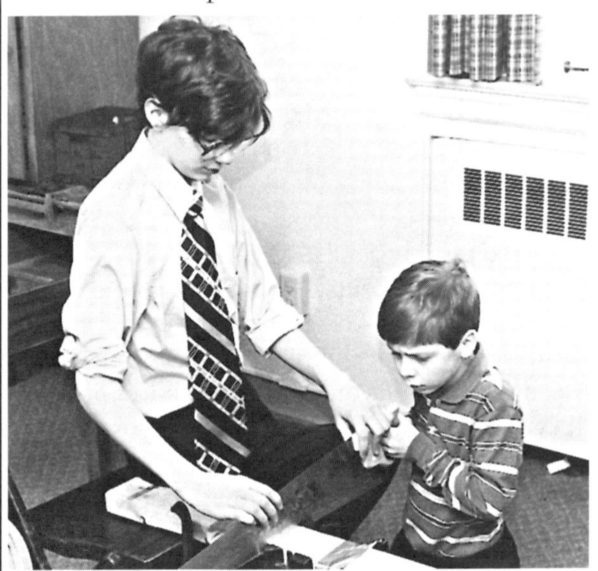

Count the offering received for the Mission Project each week. Write the total received on the Mission Poster and report at service.

Workstation 4: Sermon or Bible Study

GETTING READY

Use a favorite puppet for Sunshine. He returns often.

INSTRUCTION SIGN

You are in charge of introducing Sunshine-Share-a-Lot today. Sunshine is a puppet that we will use often. Sunshine likes to tell stories about how important it is to share God's love. Read Romans 13:8-10. Check skit and write responses for puppets. Have one person read and another person be puppeteer while doing this.

STEP 1: Have Sunshine enter as if climbing up a set of stairs instead of just popping up. A gradual movement upward gives the audience a chance to get ready for the puppet's arrival. Use the same descending pattern to exit at the end.

STEP 2: Practice having puppets turn to other puppets when talking, but never turn their backs to the audience.

STEP 3: Keep your puppet active throughout play but not in a distractive way. Remember, puppet should keep the audience's attention so that they will listen to the sermon. Practice and be ready. You need 3 puppeteers and 3 readers.

PUPPET PLAY FOR SERMON

How Sunshine Share-a-Lot Got His Name

SUNSHINE: Hi! I'm Sunshine Share-a-Lot. Welcome to the Helping Hands Puppet Theater. I'm glad you could come today. I feel a story coming on. That's how I got my name, you know. I tell stories about how you can share God's love. Would you like to hear a story? [Have 2 puppets pop out and say yes.]

SUNSHINE: One day, there was a little boy who thought no one liked him. He always sat alone in Sunday school. No one ever said, "Do you want to sit with us or be in our group?" Rimmey just sat by himself. [puppets say, "Ahhh!" very sadly]
  The teacher talked in class that day about how all Christians are "brothers and sisters in Christ."
  Rimmey raised his hand and said, "I don't have a brother." [puppets say, "Ahhh!" again]

SUNSHINE: The teacher smiled and said, "Well, now you do, Rimmey. As brothers and sisters, we learn to help each other and not be jealous or mean. That means you can't do something just to make the other person mad or to try to get him or her in trouble.
  Can you think of something you do that makes others unhappy? [Write an answer for puppets.]

SUNSHINE: Are you ever selfish? [Have puppets shake their heads *no* and then, reluctantly, nod *yes*.]

SUNSHINE: Do you ever feel jealous and want all of the attention? [Have puppets vigorously nod their heads *yes*.]

SUNSHINE: You have to remember that giving someone else a turn to feel special doesn't take anything away from you. You are still special in your own way, and you prove how special you really are when you think about the feelings of others.

PUPPET 2: I like this brother and sister stuff.

PUPPET 1: Me too!

SUNSHINE: Come on, let's all give it a try. You never know, you might like being nice to each other.

Workstation 5: Witness to Faith

GETTING READY

Children will work at different paces so leave instructions for folding church from previous weeks posted. Label as Week 1, Week 2, etc.

INSTRUCTION SIGN

"Lord" means "master" or "one who is in control." You may hear it said in church that Jesus is the "Lord of our life." This means that we follow the teachings of Jesus and let his teachings determine how we should live our lives. It's kind of like a building plan or blueprint, except instead of building a house, we are building a Christian way of life.

STEP 1:   If you did not finish the side walls or stained-glass windows last week, finish those first.

STEP 2:   Cut large stained-glass window and wall for end.

STEP 3:   Make large stained-glass window as before. Be ready to put the walls together next week. Volunteer to read Luke 6:32-36 for our service today. Sign up at worship table.

Workstation 6: Prayer and Sewing Center

GETTING READY

Continue working on the embroidery banner and travel bags. Have yarn scraps, paper, and glue for cards.

INSTRUCTION SIGN

In keeping with Dorcas's tradition of giving to those in need, we are making cards to send to nursing homes and hospitals.

Continue working on the embroidery banner and travel bags. Read 1 Corinthians 13:4-7 before starting to work today.

STEP 1:   Fold a piece of construction paper in half. On the inside write: "Have a Nice Day."

STEP 2:   On the outside, create a yarn picture for the cover. Make a flower garden, sunrise, rainbow, or house. Use your imagination. Simply put a dot of glue on the paper, then twist or coil yarn into different shapes to form pictures. Place cards on worship table for service.

Sign up to lead the Lord's Prayer in the service today.

Workstation 7: Benediction

INSTRUCTION SIGN

You have probably heard of a telegram; it's how you send a short message to someone. Well, today, you are going to send a Lovegram. All Lovegrams contain one simple short message: "God is Love." Read 1 John 4:16. Then make a Lovegram.

STEP 1: Fold paper in fourths. Open and cut on FOLDED lines. Start at FOLD and cut almost but not all the way to edge. Look at example. When finished, you have a Greek cross "+" cut in the middle. Curl each cut edge around a pencil. Set aside.

STEP 2: Use pattern and cut 10 hearts of different colors. Use scrap paper. Stack together and staple right in the middle.

STEP 3: Glue curled Greek cross page to plain paper.

STEP 4: Place heart in the middle of curled opening. Glue in place. Fold and crease heart to make a stand-up open heart.

STEP 5: Write on your Lovegram: "God is Love. (1 John 4:16)."

You may send your Lovegram to anyone you wish today. Sign up to read 1 John 4:16 for the benediction. Go in peace and share God's love.

The Worship Celebration

SIGN-UP SHEET FOR TODAY'S WORSHIP CELEBRATION

Call to Worship (help sing a song to begin the puppet play):

Affirmation (read thank-you statement from affirmation booklet):

Offering (report total received for Mission Project):

Sermon (3 puppeteers and 3 readers for "How Sunshine Share-a-Lot Got His Name")

Witness (read Luke 6:32-36):

Prayer (lead the Lord's Prayer):

Benediction (read 1 John 4:16):

ITEMS TO GO HOME TODAY: LOVEGRAM; COLLECTION BOX CHURCHES

Session 5
The Young Worshiper's Toolbox

The Bible Lesson

The parable of the two house builders tells the story of what it means to be a Christian (Matthew 7:24-27).

What the Children Will Learn Today

The house is our faith; its foundation is the teachings of Jesus

Time Needed

5 minutes for story
20 minutes for workstations
10 minutes for closing worship service

Supplies Needed (by Workstation)

1. Craft supply basket, paper plates, pop bottles, scraps of cloth and fake fur, rice or pebbles to put inside pop bottles
2. White and green paper for church and hill patterns
3. Guide sheet, tools, and lumber for puppet stage
4. Scrap wood, building blocks, Helping Hands banner, rattles and tin pans, 3 copies of script, small table, umbrella
5. Paper for churches, tissue paper, clear self-sticking plastic, tape, glue, construction paper, and patterns
6. Brown paper or paper sacks for covering blocks, detergent boxes, prayer banner, thread, yarn, and cereal boxes for bags
7. Construction paper supply basket and toolbox patterns

Children's Meditation

STORY

The Carpenter's Toolbox

Once there was a young boy who spent his days working in his father's carpenter shop. The boy spent his time building with leftover scraps. His father asked him one day what he was building. The boy said, "Oh, just a toolbox."

One by one the boy placed the tools his father had given him into the toolbox. He carefully lifted his saw. Sometimes he had to cut the pieces of wood apart so he could make something special with them. Second, he put in a hammer so that he could put things together and make them work. A pile of wood couldn't be called a table. To be useful, the different-sized pieces of wood had to work together. Third, he put his plane inside. He would definitely need to smooth things over and make them fit.

After he finished packing all of his tools, the boy set off to find work. For his first job the boy was asked to build a small boat. It was as fine a boat as any you've ever seen. The boy told its new owner, "This boat will only float as long as you take care of it every day." His first customer promised to take very good care of his new boat.

The boy's second job was to make a building that sparkled in the golden sunlight. The boy was not sure he liked this building because it seemed a little too fancy to be useful. The boy told the new owner that the building would only sparkle as long as everyone who wanted to go inside was granted entrance. The owner promised.

The boy's third project was to make a stand for a beautiful hand-painted water jar. The jar was broken and it seemed a little strange to be making a stand for it now.

One day, as the boy walked through the village, he paused to look over his work. The boat sat muddy and dejected. The beautiful building had turned an ugly brown because the new owner was charging admission. The water jar stand sat tall and proud in the corner and on top of it was a beautiful water jar that faintly showed the lines where it had painstakingly been pieced and glued back together.

The boy emptied his tools onto the ground. He took his toolbox and went throughout the village gathering everything that was broken and wouldn't work. Then he returned to where his tools lay waiting for him. Slowly, he began to mend and repair.

From that day on, the boy carried an empty toolbox. The boy filled it with the broken pieces of life that he found scattered throughout the village. He never once built another fancy building or boat from new wood. Instead, the boy merely took the broken things of life, repaired them, and returned them to be useful and appreciated once again.

Workstations

Workstation 1: Call to Worship

GETTING READY

Use patterns from Session 2 for puppet face. Have a craft basket with supplies: glitter, buttons, sequins, yarn, paper, macaroni, rice, coffee filters, scraps of cloth, or construction paper.

INSTRUCTION SIGN

Use paper plates and craft supplies to create a puppet. We need 9 people for today's play (see Workstation 4 sign). Sign up to help. Read Matthew 7:24-27 for a description.

STEP 1: Add ½ cup dry rice, pebbles, or salt to an empty 2-liter pop bottle. Glue paper or cloth around pop bottle. The neck of the bottle will form the handle for the puppet. Cloth should hang down over hand, so leave cloth long.

STEP 2: Trace patterns or draw a face on a paper plate. Decorate face of puppet. Use bright colors so the face will show up clearly. Use paper or yarn for hair.

STEP 3: Glue and tape paper-plate puppet face to end of pop bottle. Go to Workstation 4 and practice for the sermon.

Workstation 2: Affirmation of Faith

INSTRUCTION SIGN

In the church, we often talk about Jesus as being the rock or foundation of our faith. Add the church to your affirmation booklet today.

STEP 1: Trace hill, church, and backing strip patterns.

STEP 2: On the backing strip write: "As a follower of Jesus, I must try each day to . . ." Read Matthew 25:35-40.

STEP 3: Decorate church or just draw windows and door.

STEP 4: Fold backing strip as you would to make a paper fan. Glue to back of church. Attach to grassy hill as indicated on pattern. Church can be pulled forward to read message. Tie grassy hill page on top of sunrise. Sunrise will show over hill. Place your booklet on the worship table for the service today.

Workstation 3: Offering or Carpenter Shop

INSTRUCTION SIGN

Jesus used the example of two house builders in a parable. One was in a hurry and threw his house together. The second worked hard. What happened? Read Luke 6:46-49. What kind of builder are you?

Workstation 4: Sermon or Bible Study

GETTING READY

Have building blocks and scraps of wood available to build houses in skit. Use Helping Hands cloth for puppet stage.

INSTRUCTION SIGN

Palestine for the most part had a very hot, dry climate. The rains came twice a year. A level spot in summer became the middle of a raging stream in autumn. Houses were typically built from baked mud, bricks, stones, and wood. A mud house is easily washed away if not built on solid rock. Read Matthew 7:24-27.

The puppet technique you are learning today is to develop a character voice for each puppet. Give Fred a scratchy, sarcastic-sounding voice. Give Morgan a very slow, thoughtful voice. Make sure Sunshine speaks slowly and loudly enough to be understood.

Have 3 puppeteers, 3 readers, 2 builders, and 1 sound-effects person (use rattles and pans). Skit is entire service.

PUPPET PLAY FOR SERMON

How to Build Your House of Life

[Before Sunshine starts to speak, have some background noise: hammering on a wood block, sandpaper rubbing together, or rhythm sticks. Have a small table that wobbles when you shake it. Have wooden building blocks or scrap wood on the table. Have two volunteers silently build house as puppet talks. House Builder #1, for Fred, lays blocks on their shakiest edge. This house is built to fall down at the *end* of the story. House Builder #2, for Morgan, carefully lays foundation blocks flat; house shouldn't fall down when table is shaken.]

SUNSHINE: Welcome! Welcome! Welcome! It is wonderful to see each and every one of you here today. I have a great story today, and I have brought along two friends to help me.

First, I'd like you to meet Fred. Fred is a local builder. Fred guarantees that he can build you a house faster than anyone else in town. If you find someone who can build your house faster, Fred will build the house for you absolutely free. Now, you can't beat that, can you? [Fred puppet bows excessively.]

The second person I would like to introduce today is Morgan, who is also a builder. Morgan says that she is not the fastest, but she does guarantee that your house will last forever.

[Crash cymbols, shake pop bottles, or bang pans for thunder.]

SUNSHINE: From the looks of the sky, we may want to find a house to get inside of soon. Looks like rain.

FRED: I can have your house built for you before the rainstorm gets here. You'll be snug and dry inside your very own new home before the first raindrops begin to fall.

SUNSHINE: I don't know, Fred. [more thunder noises]

FRED: No problem. All I have to do is nail these two boards together [start to build House #1 with blocks shakily balanced], add a roof, and I'm ready for my paycheck.

SUNSHINE: Are you sure it will keep me dry?

FRED: Don't you believe me?

SUNSHINE: I'm not sure, Fred. Will your house be finished before the rain starts, Morgan?

MORGAN: I can't guarantee that I'll be done before it rains, Sunshine, but I can tell you that once I'm finished this house will keep you dry for many rainstorms to come.

FRED: Sure! Sure! Sure!

MORGAN: First, I pick a nice *peaceful* location for my house and *try to do the best I can* every day.

FRED: Are you saying my houses aren't peaceful?

SUNSHINE: Of course not, Fred. Shhhhh! Let Morgan explain.

MORGAN: Second, I dig down to a rock-hard foundation. It takes more time and *patience*, but if you put a lot of *hard work and love* into building the foundation, your house will stand up against the strongest rainstorms of criticism and teasing.

FRED: That sensational foundation is not going to do you much good when it starts to rain in a few minutes.

SUNSHINE: [sternly] Fred, will you stop interrupting?

MORGAN: Third, I *gently* build the sides. Everyone needs gentle words and kind thoughts. If I am *careful about what I say and do,* I can make someone feel better just by how I act or talk.

FRED: I feel better, too, when people pay me money.

SUNSHINE: Please ignore Fred; he's a little jealous.

MORGAN: Fourth, it takes *self-control. I stop and think before I talk or act.*

Fifth, I find you have to have *faith. Never quit, never give up.* When you start to become discouraged and think you'll never finish, think of something that makes you happy.

FRED: Getting paid makes me happy.

SUNSHINE: Morgan wasn't talking about money.

MORGAN: Sixth, I spread on a thick layer of *kindness*. You need to *treat each and every person with respect and forgiveness*.

SUNSHINE: Yes, a good rule to remember is not to say anything to anyone else that you wouldn't want said back to you.

FRED: Hmmmmm!

MORGAN: Seventh, use *good* building materials. Think about how your actions will make others feel. If you *work hard to make others happy*, you'll find your house filled with happiness too.

FRED: Enough! I'm going inside my house. [Fred exits.]

MORGAN: The eighth and final step is to cover your house with *love*. Try a little harder each day and be *forgiving*.

    If you put all of these special building blocks into your life, you'll find that your "house of life" is true *joy*.

[Make thunder sounds and shake the table till the quickly built house falls down. Sturdy house should stay up. You may have Sunshine put on a raincoat or use a small umbrella.]

SUNSHINE: I don't know about you, but I'm going to follow Morgan's advice. If you forget, remember the story that Jesus told. One man was in a hurry. The other man took his time. When the rain came, the first man who had been in such a hurry found out that his house was in the middle of a dry riverbed. The rain washed his house away. The man who built his house on solid rock stayed warm and dry. Bye for now from your friend Sunshine Share-a-Lot standing here in the rain.

Workstation 5: Witness to Faith

<table>
<tr><td colspan="2" align="center">INSTRUCTION SIGN</td></tr>
<tr><td colspan="2">Many Christian communities save and work for years to build a church. Ask someone how long it took to build the church you are now attending. Read Matthew 16:18. Continue building.</td></tr>
<tr><td>STEP 1:</td><td>Finish any windows and side walls from last week.</td></tr>
<tr><td>STEP 2:</td><td>Trace and cut doors and front wall. Glue doors in place. Glue ONLY edges of doors so that doors will open.</td></tr>
<tr><td>STEP 3:</td><td>TAPE walls of church together. Church should stand up. If built correctly, your church also folds flat.</td></tr>
<tr><td>STEP 4:</td><td>Make outside covering for church or leave plain. For bricks, cut red rectangles or color with a marker. For siding, glue strips of paper so they overlap. Another nice effect is a mosaic made with torn bits of different colors of paper.</td></tr>
</table>

Workstation 6: Prayer and Sewing Center

GETTING READY

Continue sewing and weaving. Cover boxes for house. Make example. Empty detergent boxes make excellent bricks.

INSTRUCTION SIGN

Dorcas used the upper room of her house as a sewing room. This was a room built up on the roof with its own door and possibly a window. She entered the upper room from the roof.

Our upper room is built of boxes stacked to make stones. Read Galatians 5:22 and add to upper room by wrapping a box with plain brown paper. Wrap boxes tightly. Use glue to seal the paper, NOT tape. Do not glue blocks together.

Workstation 7: Benediction

GETTING READY

Have four-year-olds simply color tools and church.

INSTRUCTION SIGN

Love is the foundation that Jesus tells us to build our lives upon. If we follow his teachings, we will know how to talk and act kindly toward others and how to be helpful to those in need. Make a paper toolbox and fill it with the teachings of Jesus.

STEP 1: Fold paper as shown by the dotted lines on toolbox pattern. Write: "Young Worshiper's Toolbox" on side. Use pattern for end pieces. Glue toolbox together. Make 1" wide handle by folding construction paper.

STEP 2: Fold paper width of church pattern as if making a paper fan. Trace pattern. Cut on solid lines.

STEP 3: On the inside of the church, write: "Rejoice and be happy, be humble, don't brag, do what is right, be kind and forgiving, think kind thoughts, and always work for peace." Then read Matthew 5:1-12. Decorate church and place in toolbox. Trace tool patterns. Set toolboxes on worship table

---

The Worship Celebration

SIGN-UP SHEET FOR TODAY'S WORSHIP CELEBRATION

Sermon (3 puppeteers, 3 readers, 2 builders, 1 sound-effects person for "How to Build Your House of Life"):

ITEMS TO GO HOME TODAY: PAPER-PLATE PUPPETS; TOOLBOXES

Session 6
Everyone Is Welcome
in God's Church

The Bible Lesson

The Bible lesson talks about judging others (Luke 6:37-38). Children know and understand the cruelty of teasing, but they often do not think themselves cruel when they tease. The Bible lesson stresses that it is worse to tease than to be teased.

What the Children Will Learn Today

The story and sermon today emphasize that God loves everyone and does not consider one person to be better or more likable than another. Children will practice giving compliments.

Time Needed

5 minutes for story
20 minutes for workstations
10 minutes for closing worship service

Supplies Needed (by Workstation)

Story: Freddy the Frog traced and ready to cut out

1. Newsprint or scrap paper, empty pop bottles, papier-mâché recipe, cover-ups to protect clothes, and plastic table and floor covers for messy crafts

2. Green and blue construction paper, sequins, markers or pink, yellow, purple, and blue tissue paper, and patterns

3. Guide sheet, tools, and lumber for puppet stage

4. 3 puppets (including Sunshine), Helping Hands cloth, and script

5. Church supplies, tape and glue, ruler, black construction paper for roof and scraps for banners, cardboard for roof, stiff white paper for balcony, and banner patterns

6. Embroidery banner, travel bags, craft sup-
ply basket, and brown paper bags or mailing paper for covering laundry detergent boxes

7. Construction paper supply basket and patterns for Freddy

Children's Meditation

GETTING READY

Have children make quiet frog noises every time you say "Freddy." Trace, decorate, and cut Freddy out as you tell story.

STORY

Freddy the Frog

Have you ever thought how lonely it must be to sit all by yourself beside a pond all day croaking like a frog? Well, this was exactly Freddy's problem. You see, Freddy was a frog, and people didn't come to the pond very often just to see Freddy.

Oh, the pond was nice enough all right. As a matter of fact, the pond was surrounded by beautiful flowers of every shape, color, and size. Imported Chinese goldfish lived in the pond. Many visitors and guests came to the pond to see such beautiful and rare goldfish, but no one came to see Freddy [cut out Freddy]. Freddy wasn't special. Freddy was an ordinary slimy-looking green frog who had a very long red tongue for catching flies. Freddy had two big round eyes that sat on top of his head. I suppose he was sort of funny-looking [open paper and show Freddy], but it hurt Freddy's feelings every time anyone teased or laughed at him.

The goldfish with their radiant beauty would swim over and say to Freddy, "Go away; don't sit here. No one will want to come to the pond today if you sit there making that awful noise. Go away, Freddy; we don't want you."

Freddy slowly hopped away feeling very dejected and unwanted. Freddy hopped over to the rose garden. The gardener had been out watering this morning, and the ground beneath the roses was still damp and cool.

"Oh, don't bring that horrible noise of

yours over here, Freddy," said the roses. "A rose garden is a place for quiet, peaceful meditation. You don't fit in. Besides, everything in this garden is beautiful, not fat and ugly like you. Go away, Freddy! Go away," said all of the roses.

Surely there was some place where even a frog was allowed. As Freddy hopped on through the garden he came upon a group of toads. *These guys will surely let me hop along with them,* thought Freddy. So he hopped over to say hi.

The toads took one look at Freddy and said, "Get lost! You're the wrong color. We don't allow your kind hanging around here. Go on, scram!"

Freddy hopped away. No one wanted Freddy or his song.

Freddy wasn't watching where he was going, but he stopped short when he heard a group of small boys running by say, "Hey, let's catch that frog. We can have a jumping contest and see who can make him jump the longest. I bet I can make him jump farther than you can."

Finally, Freddy had found someone who wanted him, but Freddy knew about little boys, and they weren't exactly the kind of friends he was looking for today. Freddy hopped faster than he could ever remember hopping before.

Freddy wasn't even watching where he was hopping as he dodged the maze of scurrying hands and feet that were chasing him. All of a sudden, Freddy hopped into a gigantic building. The stone floor was cool, and it felt nice to sit and rest where it was dark and shadowy. The boys would never find him here.

Freddy sat with his eyes closed, resting on the cool, dark stones, when a big, kind hand reached down and gently picked Freddy up. "You can't sit in the doorway like that," said the parson who worked at the garden chapel. "Someone will come along and step on you. Let's see if we can't find a safe place to rest."

The kind old parson took Freddy outside to a little garden. There was a fountain, a tiny pond, and lots of beautiful flowers. The parson sat down on a bench in the shade of an old oak tree.

"You're exactly what we need. When people come to sit and rest in the rose garden, you can sing them your little song," the parson said as he ever so gently put Freddy down beside the pond.

"You can remind people who come to the chapel that God loves everyone and has a special job for each and every one of us. Your job," continued the parson, "will be to call everyone for worship each day; so sing out loud and strong, little fellow."

Sing out, Freddy did. For finally Freddy had found a home, a friend, and someone who really wanted him just the way he was.

We have a friend, too, and God always wants us. God doesn't pick and choose. God loves everyone.

Workstations

Workstation 1: Call to Worship

GETTING READY

Mix papier-mâché. Save two water jars for Christmas.

INSTRUCTION SIGN

In biblical times, water had to be carried from the well every day in clay jars. Even though you didn't have to go to the well before church, help us get started today by signing up to lead a song or read a Bible verse. Read John 4:6-9, 11, 14. Then make a simple water jar as a reminder to help someone in need this week. Say a kind word to your neighbor as you work.

STEP 1:   Put on a cover-up to protect your clothing. Then set an empty pop bottle on a sheet of newsprint.
        Cover pop bottle with glue. Use a sponge or brush to spread glue evenly.

STEP 2:   Pull newspaper up and wrap newsprint around pop bottle. Make flared opening at top of pop bottle. See picture.

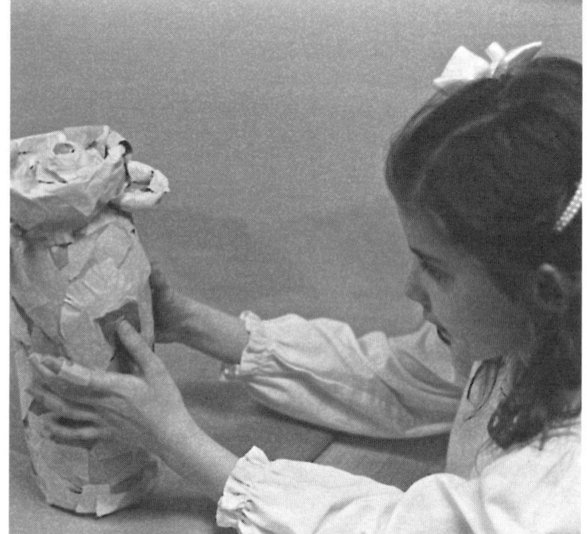

STEP 3:   Put your name on your bottle and set aside to dry. You will paint your water jar next week.

Workstation 2: Affirmation of Faith

INSTRUCTION SIGN

The Holy Spirit is said to be God's Spirit living within us. God's Spirit helps us to be kind to others.

STEP 1:   Trace patterns for river and hill.

STEP 2:   On the left-hand side of the river page (see pattern), write: "God's Spirit guides me to . . ." Tell one thing you can do to help others. Read Romans 8:5, 16 and 12:1-2.

STEP 3:   Use sequins or roll tiny bits of scrap tissue paper into a tight ball to form tiny flowers to dot the hillsides. When dry, punch holes for page and TIE onto your affirmation booklet. Compliment your neighbor's book. Place booklet on worship table.

Sign up to read John 8:7-11 in today's service.

Workstation 3: Offering or Carpenter Shop

INSTRUCTION SIGN

As followers of Jesus, we should not merely sit and listen to Bible verses, the stories in Sunday school, and sermons each week. We must also act. Jesus calls us to take action. Read Matthew 28:19-20 and James 1:22-25 and 2:15-17. Say a kind word to a fellow worker today. Compliment his or her sawing or hammering. Sign up to report the service project offering.

Workstation 4: Sermon or Bible Study

INSTRUCTION SIGN

Many teachers of Jesus' day wouldn't bother teaching the common, poor people. Jesus used simple examples from everyday life to teach everyone. Read Luke 6:37-38 and John 8:7-11.

Today's sermon has 3 puppets. The puppet technique we're working on today is showing feelings. How do you show sadness with a puppet? With your voice? How do you show joy? Remember: SLOWLY and LOUDLY. Use 3 puppeteers (including Sunshine) and 3 readers.

PUPPET PLAY FOR SERMON

Sunshine Share-a-Lot's Search for a Friend

SUNSHINE:	Hi! This is your friend Sunshine Share-a-Lot. I'm here on a special mission today. I'm looking for a friend. I'm not exactly sure I know what a friend is, though. Maybe we should find someone to help us. [Chester wanders onto the stage.] Look, there's someone now. Let's see if he knows. Hi! My name's Sunshine Share-a-Lot. What's yours? [Sunshine turns toward Chester to speak.]
CHESTER THE WHALE:	My name's Chester.
SUNSHINE:	Do you know how to find a friend?
CHESTER:	No, I've never had a friend. The kids at school laugh and tease me 'cause I'm kinda fat, so I play by myself.
SUNSHINE:	That's not fair. You should remind the children that friends come in all shapes and sizes. Some friends are tall and skinny, and some friends are short and a little heavier. A friend needs to be kind. Friends should think about the words they say. If you go around teasing someone about being fat, that's not being kind, and it's certainly not being a friend. Would you like to come along with me to look for a friend?
CHESTER:	Wow! You think I could find a friend too?
SUNSHINE:	Sure, we've already figured out one thing a friend needs to do. A friend needs to speak nicely about others and use kind words that will not hurt someone's feelings. I can remember to do that. How about you?
CHESTER:	It's not always easy to make sure that all of the words that come out of your mouth are nice words, especially if someone else is teasing you, but I'll try.
SUNSHINE:	Good! Then off we go. [Puppets move to the right, whistling as they go. A third puppet arrives.]
SUNSHINE:	Look, here comes someone else. Let's go see if she knows how to find a friend.
BETSY BUNNY:	[sniffling and crying] Boo hoo! Boo hoo hoo!
SUNSHINE:	What's the matter? Why are you crying?
BETSY:	I invited some friends over to my house yesterday to play, but they didn't want to play with me. They just wanted to play with my toys. They took my favorite stuffed kitty and threw it across the room playing catch. Now my kitty has a hole in it.
CHESTER:	If that's what having a friend is all about, maybe I don't need one.
SUNSHINE:	No! No! No! A friend is *not* someone who just comes over to play with your toys. A friend comes over to play with *you*. And when friends visits someone's home, they absolutely never play rough. You have to remember that as a friend you have a responsibility to be nice to the

person who invited you and to make sure that they are happy and having a good time too.

BETSY: Being a friend is a big *responsibility*.

CHESTER: Are you sure we can actually find a friend?

SUNSHINE: Of course. And see, we've been searching for a friend, and by working together we've become friends.

Friendship is not something you can buy or find. You have to work at being friends. You have to stop and think if what you're saying will make others feel happy or sad.

CHESTER: I want to make others feel happy.

SUNSHINE: You also have to think about how you act.

BETSY: When you go to someone's house, ask if it is all right to play with special toys.

SUNSHINE: Be on your best behavior.

CHESTER: I'll remember.

SUNSHINE: How about you? Will you work at being friends too? [Puppets leave stage whistling.]

Workstation 5: Witness to Faith

INSTRUCTION SIGN

The sanctuary is typically where worship services are held. Some sanctuaries are fancy. Others are plain and simple. Sign up to read today's Bible verses: Luke 6:37-38.

STEP 1: Finish any work on walls or windows not complete.

STEP 2: Use black paper and cardboard for roof.

STEP 3: Add banners to hang along the inside walls of the church, balcony, lights, or any other finishing touches desired. When complete, your church should fold flat for storage. Compliment your neighbors on something they added to their churches.

STEP 4: Trace patterns and make balcony. Cut on solid lines and fold on dotted lines. Glue ONLY TABS of balcony as marked on pattern. When folded, floor of balcony pushes down and balcony folds flat. Do NOT glue front floor of balcony to railing or balcony will not fold flat.

Workstation 6: Prayer and Sewing Center

INSTRUCTION SIGN

As a disciple of Jesus, see if someone needs help today. Perhaps you can help someone thread the needle or show someone new how to sew or weave. Find at least one person you can help by giving them a compliment. Read Luke 6:38. Sign up to lead the Lord's Prayer.

Workstation 7: Benediction

INSTRUCTION SIGN

Make Freddy the Frog from today's story to remind you that "God loves everyone" and welcomes everyone to God's church.

STEP 1: Fold a sheet of green paper lengthwise. Trace pattern. Remember to place pattern on fold of paper.
STEP 2: Decorate Freddy's face. Give Freddy a bow tie.
STEP 3: To make Freddy's long tongue, trace pattern onto red or pink paper. Cut tongue out. Read Luke 6:37, then write the Bible verse and something that others tease you about on Freddy's tongue. Curl tongue on a pencil. Glue just the tip of the tongue to Freddy's mouth so tongue will curl and uncurl. Sign up to read the words from Freddy's tongue during the service.

The Worship Celebration

SIGN-UP SHEET FOR TODAY'S WORSHIP CELEBRATION

Call to Worship (lead a song or read John 4:6-9, 11, 14):
Affirmation (read John 8:7-11):
Offering (report service project offering):
Sermon (3 puppeteers and 3 readers for "Sunshine Share-a-Lot's Search for a Friend"):
Witness (read Luke 6:37-38):
Prayer (lead the Lord's Prayer):
Benediction (read words written on Freddy the Frog's tongue):

ITEMS TO GO HOME TODAY: FREDDY THE FROG

Session 7
Learning to Serve the Needs of Others

The Bible Lesson

Today's lesson is about final judgment (Matthew 25:31-46).

What the Children Will Learn Today

The children will be given several opportunities to help one another in today's session at the workstations.

Time Needed

5 minutes for story
20 minutes for workstations
10 minutes for closing worship service

Supplies Needed (by Workstation)

1. Papier-mâché water jars from last week, brown tempera paint, sand, paintbrushes, cover-ups for messy crafts
2. Green construction paper, tissue paper (green and other colors), unused brown coffee filters, and tree patterns
3. Puppet stage wood, tools, and supplies
4. Script and 4 puppets (including Sunshine)
5. Church building supplies and construction paper scraps
6. Banner, travel bags, boxes, and curtains for puppet stage
7. Supply basket, heart and fish patterns, hole punch

Children's Meditation

STORY

By Your Hands You'll Be Fed

A long time ago, in a faraway mountain village, lived a king. His castle was gigantic and made of massive carved stones.

Inside was a great dining hall with a long table covered with a white linen cloth. Along each side of the table, tall, beautiful stained-glass windows seemed to reach straight up to the sky. As the sunlight filtered in through the stained glass, patterns of color danced to and fro across the white tablecloth.

Each night at dinnertime the king opened the heavy oak doors to the dining hall and stood at the top of the stairs to welcome anyone who might be waiting. For it was known throughout the land that every night at dinnertime if you were hungry and didn't have food to eat, you were welcome at the king's table. The king made only one request. You had to show the king your hands, palms up, when you came to the door.

One night when the king opened the huge oak doors, there stood before him a long line of people; some were even children. As people stepped forward to show the king their hands, the king directed them to a seat at the table.

One poor man was stooped and barely able to walk. He had no shoes. His clothes were tattered and worn out. His hands showed hard calluses and blisters. The king motioned the old man to the head of the table. The old man hobbled to his seat.

A woman stepped forward with four small children huddled near her for warmth. The woman's hands were cold, dry, and scratchy. The king motioned the woman and her children to sit right next to the fireplace with its roaring fire.

Person after person stepped forward to show the king their hands. The king directed each to a place at the table. Finally, a very elegantly dressed man stepped forward, bowed low before the king, and said, "Your Royal Highness, it is with great pleasure that we accept your invitation to dine with you this evening. It is most gracious of you to invite us into your home on such a cold night." And the man bowed again in a showy sort of way. The king examined the man's bleached white palms. They were soft, silky, and wrapped in wool to keep them warm.

The king quietly motioned the man to sit at the far end.

"Why, Your Majesty," the man protested, "it will be cold that far from the fire and the food will be nothing more than scraps by the time it travels past so many hungry mouths. Some of these people haven't eaten in days; they'll eat everything in sight. There'll be nothing left for me!"

The king looked at the man and gave a gentle smile. "The test of service is written on your hands. If you have given much to others, then much will be given to you. If you have cared and labored only for yourself, then you have earned only what is left. Your place," the king continued, "is at the end.

"When we think ourselves better than others or more deserving of a place of honor, we in fact reduce our importance. Your place is at the end of the table with me."

Workstations

Workstation 1: Call to Worship

GETTING READY

Mix brown tempera paint and sand together to make textured paint for water jars from last week. Have sponges, brushes, and songs to choose from.

INSTRUCTION SIGN

Worship is a time to celebrate and be happy as we think of the nice things that God has given to each of us: life, health, family, the beauty of the earth, special talents, and skills.

Sign up to lead a song and read the Bible verse for our call to worship today. Read Luke 6:31. Choose a new song or an old favorite. Then, put on a cover-up and paint your water jar from last week. The sand will give your jar a claylike surface.

Workstation 2: Affirmation of Faith

GETTING READY

Tree must dry till next week before being added to booklet. Have a drying space provided. Children will finish the affirmation booklets next week.

INSTRUCTION SIGN

The early Christians, apostles, and followers of Jesus were given the task of developing statements of belief as they formed communities of believers and new churches. Many were asking, as we are, "What do you believe?" Make a tree of knowledge to answer this question. Sign up to tell us what you wrote.

STEP 1: Trace tree pattern and make 2 trees on stiff paper. Use green paper for leaves and brown for trunk. Fold first tree in half and cut window as marked on pattern. In the center of the second tree, complete the statement "I believe . . ." Read James 2:14-18 for help.

Make sure your answer shows through tree window. Tree with cut window goes on top. Do NOT glue the two trees together.

STEP 2: Set tree with writing aside till next week. Glue unbleached coffee filter or brown paper onto tree trunk with cut window.

STEP 3: Roll green tissue paper and glue to top of tree or leave plain. Make sure window still opens. Let dry till next week. Set trees with "I believe" statements on worship table.

Workstation 3: Offering or Carpenter Shop

INSTRUCTION SIGN

A church is composed of people. You are part of the church because of what you give to others. In the church, you are called to make a commitment with your time, money, and faith. Read Matthew 5:6. Sign up to report money collected during service today.

Workstation 4 : Sermon or Bible Study

INSTRUCTION SIGN

Jesus often told a story to answer a question or teach an important rule about how to live life. We can learn from these same stories or parables today by reading them in the Bible or having a puppet tell us a modern-day version. Read Matthew 25:35-40. Then practice today's puppet play for the service. You need 4 puppeteers, including Sunshine, and 4 readers.

PUPPET PLAY FOR SERMON

Can You Have More Than One Best Friend?

LIZZY THE COW:	It's not fair; you always play with her.
RUGGLES THE PUPPY:	Well, you always insist that we play the game your way.
DANA THE DOLPHIN:	[spoken very sarcastically] I know; we'll do what I want. That will solve the whole problem.
SUNSHINE:	What's all the yelling about?
LIZZY:	It's not fair. Ruggles always gets to sit next to Dana, and that makes me feel that Dana likes Ruggles more than me. When Ruggles is not around, Dana and I get along fine. We never fight. And Dana is *my* best friend. Besides, Ruggles and I were best friends before Dana came along.
	It's too hard to get along when there are three of us together. All we do is compete to see who can be the best, the most important, the boss.
	Sometimes, I just feel like I want to sit down and cry.
SUNSHINE:	I know exactly how you feel. I had a best friend once. I introduced her to another friend of mine. They became best friends, and went off and abandoned me. Now, they play together all the time, but they don't like it when I play with them anymore. That made me angry, and I felt left out. I said lots of hateful things to them. One day, I stopped and thought about how I was acting and talking. I decided that I didn't want to act like that anymore, so now I'm spending all my time going out trying to help others. Would you like to be my friend?
LIZZY:	May I invite my *two* best friends to come along?
SUNSHINE:	Sure! God invites everyone; no one's ever left out.

Workstation 5: Witness to Faith

GETTING READY

Have example of floor of folding church. Show how it opens and folds.

INSTRUCTION SIGN

A church or congregation is often known by what it does to make life easier for others; this is called "outreach ministry." If you were creating an outreach ministry program, what would you include? Read Matthew 25:37-40 for ideas. Sign up to tell your outreach ministry ideas during the worship service today.

Finish the roof, walls, windows, or any other work not completed. Then, if desired, make the floor and pews.

Churches did not always have pews. Early churches were large rooms with space for people to stand during service. Pews or benches were placed along the wall for those too sick to stand.

STEP 1: Measure brown paper and cardboard for floor.

STEP 2: Use pattern and carefully cut out pews. The angle and fold lines shown on pattern are very important. Cut exactly as shown. Fold precisely on dotted line. Glue pews in place on church floor. Keep pews open till dry. Pews should fold flat.

Workstation 6: Prayer and Sewing Center

GETTING READY

Measure and pin cloth for curtains for puppet stage.

INSTRUCTION SIGN

Worship is a time to celebrate God's love, to be humble, and to think of the needs of others rather than ourselves. Worship is also a time to be forgiving. Read Mark 9:41.

Continue working on banner, travel bags, and blocks. Start hemming curtains for puppet stage. Sign up to lead the Lord's Prayer.

Workstation 7: Benediction

INSTRUCTION SIGN

We are encouraged to go and tell others about Jesus. Every word we speak, the way we act, and the way we treat others tell how committed we are as followers of Jesus. Make an "I'm a Follower of Jesus" card.

STEP 1: Fold paper in half. Trace fish pattern on front. Decorate with torn pieces of scrap paper or punch circles.

STEP 2: Open card. Trace heart pattern inside. Decorate with torn paper scraps or punched circles. Write a message inside the heart. Tell someone you love them, how important they are to you, or just say thank you. Give your card to someone special. Read Matthew 25:42-45 and write Bible verses on card. Sign up to read today's Bible verses for the Benediction.

The Worship Celebration

SIGN-UP SHEET FOR TODAY'S WORSHIP CELEBRATION

Call to Worship (lead a song and read Luke 6:31):

Affirmation (read statements from trees of knowledge):

Offering (report on service project collection):

Sermon (4 puppeteers and 4 readers for "Can You Have More Than One Best Friend?"):

Witness (tell outreach ministry ideas):

Prayer (lead the Lord's Prayer):

Benediction (read Matthew 25:42-45):

ITEMS TO GO HOME TODAY: I'M A FOLLOWER OF JESUS CARDS; WATER JARS

Session 8
What Does It Mean to Be a Witness for Christ?

The Bible Lesson

In the parable of the yeast (Matthew 13:33), God's love grows and changes us as persons, just as yeast changes dough.

What the Children Will Learn Today

The children will think about ways to change their lives and accept responsibilities at home, with friends, and at school.

Time Needed

5 minutes for story
20 minutes for workstations
10 minutes for closing worship service

Supplies Needed (by Workstation)

1 and 2. Affirmation booklets, trees from last week, paper
3. Puppet stage supplies
4. Skit and puppets
5. Church building supplies
6. Long scraps of cloth or ribbon, yarn, or cord, dowels
7. Construction paper supply basket and circle or plate

Children's Meditation

STORY:

A New Day for Cindy

One day, there was a little girl who didn't think anyone liked her. Cindy thought the whole entire world hated her.

Mom and Dad were always telling Cindy to clean her room. Cindy *hated* cleaning her room.

"No TV!

"No, you can't read 'The Mystery of the Runaway Train' instead of doing your home-work! It's a school night. No playtime till that math grade comes up."

All Cindy heard morning, noon, and night was *no*. Cindy was certain that Mrs. Pritchard at school despised her. Her parents griped at her constantly, and her friends barely talked to her anymore. Cindy sat down on the floor next to her bed amid dirty laundry, an up-ended bucket of wooden blocks, and a pile of other assorted toys.

Something had to change. Cindy was tired of being unhappy. Cindy decided, *Things are going to be different.* And change they did.

Cindy put a smile on her face. Smiling made Cindy feel better. Cindy also found that instead of always dreading cleaning her room, she could actually get it cleaned up without the lectures and arguments if she spent a mere fifteen minutes a day cleaning. You know, *really* cleaning, not the kind of cleaning where you sit down and build a tower out of the blocks or shove everything into the closet and slam the door. Instead, Cindy ran around pretending she was the VCR on fast-forward.

But the change that really made Cindy happy was when she started *looking out for others.* Cindy made it a point each and every day to think of some way to make those around her happier.

When she saw that her mom was tired, she went and helped. When friends were arguing, Cindy tried to help them work out a compromise.

Cindy liked her new way of behaving because Cindy had learned to *share-a-lot* of God's *love.* The more Cindy shared, the happier she became. Maybe you'd like to *share-a-lot* of *love* with someone at your house this week.

Think of someone in your family who argues and fights. Maybe it's over what TV show to watch or perhaps you argue over cleaning chores. Think of a way that *you* could solve the problem and eliminate the argument. No, you can't solve every problem, but if you think hard, even you could solve at least one problem in your house or family. But remember, the change must come from *you*, not from others. What should you change about yourself? [If time permits, ask children some of the actions they plan to try.]

Workstations

Workstations 1 (Call to Worship) and 2 (Affirmation of Faith) Combined

> INSTRUCTION SIGN
>
> You have worked hard for the past five weeks on your affirmation booklet. The final question to answer is: "What does your faith enable you to do that you couldn't do if you didn't believe in God and follow the teachings of Jesus?"
>
> STEP 1: Cut tree backing strip and write your answer saying: "Through faith, I can . . ." Read Romans 12:10-18, 21.
> STEP 2: Glue 2 trees together. Make sure window opens.
> STEP 3: Fold tree backing strip as if folding a fan. Glue to tree and glue tree in place on front hill. Your booklet, if put together correctly, should read from "I believe" to "God is." Sign up to read your affirmation for our worship service today.

Workstation 3: Offering or Carpenter Shop

> INSTRUCTION SIGN
>
> Jesus spent his life helping others. Before he became a traveling teacher, he probably helped young boys learn to saw and work with tools in Joseph's carpenter shop in Nazareth. Whenever you take the time to help someone, you are helping God. Read Romans 12:17-18. Then find someone you can help in the carpenter shop. Help someone saw or hammer. Help sand without complaining. Sign up to report offering from service project.

Workstation 4: Sermon or Bible Study

GETTING READY

Children may need help writing their portion of the sermon.

> INSTRUCTION SIGN
>
> A parable is a story that teaches a moral lesson. When Jesus used parables, the people could see more clearly why and how they were supposed to live.
>
> Today's puppet play gives you a chance to teach the lesson. You need 4 puppeteers and 4 readers today.

PUPPET PLAY FOR SERMON

How Many Times a Day Do
You Witness for God?

REPORTER: Excuse me! I'm _____________________ [make up a name for the reporter] with KTBT News. We're doing a survey. We would like to know how many times a day you witness for God.

PUPPET #1
______ [name]
answers: I don't know.

REPORTER: Have you ever been the last person chosen on a team at school? How did you respond?

PUPPET #1: [Write your own answer. Remember we never use rude words or actions.]

REPORTER: Do you think it's fair to choose teams? If you were in charge of choosing teams, how would you make it fair?

PUPPET #1: [Write your own answer. Write nice answers.]

REPORTER: Those are wonderful answers. Thanks for your time. [Puppet #1 leaves. Another puppet arrives.]

Good morning! I'm from KTBT News and we're conducting a survey. Could you answer a few questions?

PUPPET #2
______ [name]
answers: Sure!

REPORTER: Have you ever felt like the whole world was against you? Do you ever have days where everything seems to go wrong? If so, what do you do?

PUPPET #2: [Write your own answer. No silly answers.]

REPORTER: Some people say, if we look for positive ways to respond to bad days, it helps. Do you agree?

PUPPET #2: [Write your own answer. Be truthful.]

REPORTER: Very interesting. Thank you and have a nice day. [Puppet #2 leaves. Puppet #3 enters.]

Hello! I'm _____________ [name] from KTBT News. Do you have time to answer a few questions for a survey?

PUPPET #3
______ [name]
answers: Well, I suppose, as long as it doesn't take too long.

REPORTER: Thanks. Do people ever tease you or act rudely toward you?

PUPPET #3: [Write your own answer. Remember, no rude words.]

REPORTER: Have you ever felt like you didn't have any friends or that people didn't want you to be a part of their group? What did you do?

PUPPET #3: [Write your own answer. Be serious.]

REPORTER: What does it mean to share God's love?

PUPPET #3: [Write your own answer. Give a respectful answer.]

REPORTER: Is it easier to share at home with your family and friends or with total strangers?

PUPPET #3: [Write your own answer. Give a nice example.]

REPORTER: That's a good point to remember. Thanks. [Puppet #3 leaves and Reporter turns toward audience.]

I've learned a lot this morning. I learned that I can witness for God each and every day just by how I treat other people. I can try to make unfair situations better, and I can make sure that everyone feels included.

Sharing means including everyone and everyone's ideas. Sharing also means doing your fair share when there's a job to be done. Helping to create peace and harmony at home is a good beginning. Till we meet again, see if you can find a way in your life to witness for God.

Workstation 5: Witness to Faith

GETTING READY

Young children will not finish today, but instructions are easier to follow if presented at one time.

INSTRUCTION SIGN

Most sanctuaries are one large room. The chancel is the front of the sanctuary where the altar is and where the choir and ministers sit. The nave is where the pews are located.

The minister preaches from the pulpit. The lectern is where the Bible is read during the service.

Pulpits were not always found inside the church. They were outside in the church yard. When moved inside, pulpits were placed on a raised platform to allow everyone to see. Since there were no public address systems, they sometimes made pulpits on wheels and rolled them up and down the aisle so that everyone could hear. Later, sounding boards were hung over pulpits to reflect the preacher's voice. Sign up to read Romans 12:10-12 in the service today.

STEP 1: Trace pulpit, raised platform, and lectern patterns. Glue together as directed on pattern. Place in front of pews.

STEP 2: Trace pattern. Make altar or communion table. Write "In Remembrance of Me" or use a Christian symbol on front of altar or communion table. Fold altar on dotted lines. Glue tab. Make altar cloth. Place in center of raised platform.

STEP 3: There are 3 steps leading up to the altar for the Trinity: God the Father, Jesus the Son, and the Holy Spirit. The color blue near the altar represents "truth." Use patterns and cut stairs. Fold. Glue ONLY front edge of stairs in place. Leave carpet loose for church to fold.

STEP 4: Use pattern and cut communion rail. Glue in place.

STEP 5: Place finished floor of church on cardboard base. Decorate outside with green construction-paper grass.

Workstation 6: Prayer and Sewing Center

GETTING READY

A hanging loom is made with two dowel rods and yarn or cord. Stretch yarn between dowel rods. Pull loom tight.

INSTRUCTION SIGN

Dorcas spent her time sewing for the poor. She lived in Joppa, a seaport town on the coast of the Mediterranean Sea. The upper room of her house was filled with clothing she made to give to those in need. Read Acts 9:36. Continue working on the embroidery banner, the woven travel bags, the blocks for the house, and today add a woven sleeping mat to the list of jobs.

STEP 1: Cut strips of cloth or ribbon 3 feet long. Braid strips together TIGHTLY.

STEP 2: Weave braided cloth strips over and under on loom.

Sign up to lead the Lord's Prayer today.

Workstation 7: Benediction

GETTING READY

You may also use paper plates for this project if you wish.

INSTRUCTION SIGN

Most dishes in biblical times were simple clay pottery. The people painted or drew symbols on their dishes. The early Christians used a fish to tell others they were Christians.

Today, we often select fancy dishes to use at dinner. Think of the plates in your home. Then design a set of fancy china. Read 1 Peter 5:6-7 for ideas, and sign up to read these verses in the service.

Cut a circle. Draw a design or picture on it to show God's love. Write "God Loves You" on plate. Place on worship table.

The Worship Celebration

GETTING READY

Children from Workstation 2 will read their affirmation booklets today for the Call to Worship.

SIGN-UP SHEET FOR TODAY'S WORSHIP CELEBRATION

Call to Worship/Affirmation (read from affirmation booklets):
Offering (report service project offering):
Sermon (4 puppeteers and 4 readers for "How Many Times a Day Do You Witness for God?"):
Witness (read Romans 12:10-12):
Prayer (lead the Lord's Prayer):
Benediction (read 1 Peter 5:6-7):

ITEMS TO GO HOME TODAY:
AFFIRMATION BOOKLETS; FANCY CHINA

Session 9
I Don't Know How to Pray

The Bible Lesson

The Bible lesson comes from the Lord's Prayer today (Matthew 6:5-14) and the meaning of prayer.

What the Children Will Learn Today

The children will learn how to write prayers today.

Time Needed

5 minutes for story
20 minutes for workstations
10 minutes for closing worship service

Supplies Needed

1. Paper and pencils
2. Nice paper to write prayer on, self-drying or oven-baked modeling clay, cover-ups, table knives
3. Paint, paintbrushes, paint cover-ups for puppet stage
4. Puppets, cloth puppet stage, paper, pencil, and script
5. Church building supplies—to be finished next week
6. Banner, travel bag, blocks, woven mat, and curtains
7. Construction paper supply basket

Children's Meditation

STORY

Praying a Prayer That Works

A little girl named Jessica thought she was doing all the right things, or at least she tried. She brushed her teeth and combed her hair every day, always said please and thank you, dressed in her fanciest dress each week for church, and never forgot to say her daily prayers. Jessica knelt down to pray one day underneath a tree as she walked through the park.

"Dear God," she began, "please make me prettier than Sally Ann and make sure I win first place in the spelling bee this week. I've been very good, and I'm still waiting for the new bicycle that I asked for last week. Thank you, God, for all the special things you have done for me today. Amen.

"I don't know why I bother," Jessica said out loud to herself as she finished her prayer.

"Bother with what?" said a squeaky little voice from somewhere up in the tree.

"Who are you?" Jessica shouted as she stared up at a little bird chirping on a low branch in the tree over her head.

"I'm Robin," said the little bird, bowing graciously. "May I be of service?"

"No, I was just praying, but I'm not sure why I bother because God never answers my prayers."

"God answers all prayers in the way they need to be answered," said Robin. "Besides, did you listen to what you were saying? You weren't really praying. You were simply making out a want list—make me prettier than Sally Ann, first place, a bicycle. That's not a prayer."

"I should know what a prayer is; after all, I pray every single day," said Jessica.

"Prayer is when you make a humble request to God. Like, 'God, help me to study harder so that I'll be ready for this week's spelling bee. And God, help me not to be jealous if I don't win.'

"God never promised he'd send us a toy store or make us better than someone else. It says in Luke 11:13 that God will send the Holy Spirit to help us whenever we ask, but it doesn't say God'll send us a bicycle if we ask."

"If I start praying differently, do you think God will start answering my prayers?" inquired Jessica.

"God listens to every word you say, even when you're not praying, and God always answers every prayer. He may not answer your prayer in the way you want; instead, God answers your prayer in the way you need it answered. What we want and what we need are often two different things."

"Robin, will you help me learn to pray?" asked Jessica.

"I'll get you started. Once you're rolling, you'll find it's easy to talk to God. You don't have to raise your hand and ask permission. You don't wait in line. You don't even have to get dressed up to talk to God. God is always ready and waiting to talk with you," said Robin.

"It helps to first get yourself ready to pray. I often like to find a nice quiet place by myself. God can hear me just fine in between the noise, but sometimes I have trouble hearing him. I always start with 'Dear God,' or 'Our Father,' just so God knows that I'm getting myself in the mood to listen to what he has to say. Then I tell God how grateful I am for this life that he has given me, for the beautiful forest, and for each day. I also remember to tell God that I'm sorry for things I did today that I know I shouldn't have done. He knows I make mistakes, and after I tell God I'm sorry, I go out and try to do better. I always share my feelings with God and tell him how I plan to help others. When I've finished, I close my prayer by telling God thank you for something special in my life, like giving me such pretty little songs to sing each day. Then, I say 'Amen' and sit quietly to listen and to think. It's when I think quietly that God's answers come to me. He doesn't send bicycles; he just sends his love."

"What do you do if you can't think of what to say to God?" said Jessica.

"When I can't think of what to say," said Robin, "I pray the prayer that Jesus taught the disciples. Come on, pray it with me. You'll see; it really helps."

[Close story with everyone praying the Lord's Prayer together.]

Workstations

Workstation 1: Call to Worship

INSTRUCTION SIGN

Write a prayer for service today. A prayer should:

1. Address God—"Dear God," "Our Heavenly Father," or whatever way you would like to begin your prayer.

2. Your prayer should list things you are grateful for—family, home, life, and so on.

3. Your prayer should include something you have done that you are sorry for.

4. Your prayer could tell a wish or hope you have for the future.

5. You should close your prayer with a thank-you to God.

6. The last word in many prayers is "Amen." Saying the word "Amen" means you agree with what was said in the prayer. In other words, if you read a friend's prayer and say "Amen" at the end of the prayer, it means you agree even though you didn't write it. You may write "Amen" at the end of your prayer.

Read Matthew 6:5-15 to learn what Jesus said about prayer and to help you get started. You may want to read verses 9-13 in both a King James translation and a new modern translation.

Sign up to read the opening prayer for today's service.

Workstation 2: Affirmation of Faith

GETTING READY

Have nice paper to write the Lord's Prayer on. Use self-hardening clay or clay that can be baked.

INSTRUCTION SIGN

STEP 1: Read Matthew 6:5-10 and write the Lord's Prayer on paper provided. Use your neatest handwriting.

STEP 2: Roll out clay but not too thin. Trace around hands separately. Cut out clay hands with a table knife.

STEP 3: Wad ball of foil to place between hands. Round, mold, and shape hands around foil to resemble hands in prayer, but make sure foil doesn't show.

STEP 4: Bake clay or let air-dry. Place hands on top of paper with Lord's Prayer. Place on worship table for service.

Sign up to read Matthew 6:5-10 in the service today.

Workstation 3: Offering or Carpenter Shop

GETTING READY

Have paint, brushes, and cleanup supplies ready before you start. Have cover-ups for painters and floor.

INSTRUCTION SIGN

We are continually reminded to share love and kindness with others. As you paint, remember to share with your neighbor.

Read Matthew 6:7-9. Open your work session today with prayer. If you need help, remember the prayer Jesus taught. Sign up to report collection for service project during worship today.

Workstation 4: Sermon or Bible Study

GETTING READY

Sermon can be presented as puppet play or with actors.

INSTRUCTION SIGN

Each and every Sunday is a time to celebrate and say thank you to God. Explain the Lord's Prayer for the sermon. Read Luke 11:1-13, Matthew 6:5-14, and the Lord's Prayer. You need 2 puppeteers and 2 readers.

From the Ritual of the Former Methodist Church

Our Father, who art in heaven,
    hallowed be thy name.
    Thy kingdom come,
    thy will be done on earth as it is in heaven.
Give us this day our daily bread.
And forgive us our trespasses,
    as we forgive those who trespass against us.
And lead us not into temptation,
    but deliver us from evil.
For thine is the kingdom, and the power, and the glory,
    forever. Amen.

PUPPET PLAY FOR SERMON

The Lord's Prayer

ADRIAN: Look at this workstation sign. She expects us to do all of this. That's impossible.

GARY: Let's just skip reading all that stuff.

ADRIAN: No, we'd better read everything on the sign.

GARY: [sound of pages turning] Matthew 6:5-15. That's the Lord's Prayer. My mom made me memorize it when I was little, but it's never made one bit of sense.

ADRIAN: "Our Father, who art in heaven, hallowed be thy name." That means we're talking to God.

GARY: I understand that part, but what does "hallll-low-ed" [mispronounce word] mean?

ADRIAN: It means to honor. We're supposed to honor God's name and show respect.

GARY: You mean like not using God's name as part of a curse word when we're mad.

ADRIAN: That's right.

GARY: Next, it says, "Thy kingdom come, thy will be done on earth as it is in heaven." Does heaven look like earth?

ADRIAN: No! It means we're to do what's right, like being kind, even to people we don't like, and helping those in need. It means God wants us to actually be loving toward our neighbor instead of merely talking about it.

GARY: "Give us this day our daily bread." You don't have to explain that part; I understand food. It means thank goodness we finally get to eat.

ADRIAN: Will you be serious?

GARY: I am being serious. I'm hungry.

ADRIAN: You're always hungry. Jesus wasn't talking merely about food. In biblical times, one piece of bread was all the poor might have to eat. So "give us our daily bread" means saying thank you for what you have. It also means to share what you have with those who are less fortunate.

GARY: I brought $1.00 for the service project offering.

ADRIAN: Bringing our offering is important, but we also have to remember to care about people. As it says, "And forgive us our trespasses, as we forgive those who trespass against us."

GARY: I never walk across the neighbor's yard.

ADRIAN: It means more than staying out of the neighbor's yard. It also means you're not supposed to "trespass" on someone else's feelings.

GARY: Even if you are only being mean to your sister to get back at her for being mean to you yesterday? Even if she deserves it?

ADRIAN: Even if she deserves it. You're supposed to be forgiving. Just as God forgives you when you do something wrong, you're supposed to forgive others, including your sister.

GARY: Wait! I know the next part. "And lead us not into temptation, but deliver us from evil." That means to put a tighter lid on the cookie jar so that I won't be tempted to take a handful of cookies right before dinner.

ADRIAN: Well, something like that. And the last part says, "For thine is the kingdom, and the power, and the glory, forever. Amen." Each day we should do a little better than we did the day before, help a little more, show that we care.

GARY: We should also remember that God loves us, even if he's not overly happy with something we did. God always forgives us when we ask for forgiveness and then show him we're truly sorry by changing how we act.

ADRIAN: Now, what were we supposed to do at this station? Oh, it says we have to write a prayer. How should we start?

[Puppeteers should write a prayer to close puppet play. If you need help, see Workstation 1, Call to Worship.]

Workstation 5: Witness to Faith

> INSTRUCTION SIGN
>
> You don't have to be in church to pray to God, but every church service does include a prayer. You are going to write a prayer today to place inside your folding church. You may make a prayer banner to hang on the wall for all to see, or you may write your prayer on a door mat so that all who enter your church enter in an attitude of prayer. You decide. Read Matthew 6:7-12.
>
> Sign up to read your prayer today. The church will be finished next week.

Workstation 6: Prayer and Sewing Center

> INSTRUCTION SIGN
>
> Prayer and sewing both take patience. If you learned how to sew or weave last week, find a friend or someone you do not know and teach them. Teaching someone else is like having a "prayer chain." You keep God's love flowing from person to person. Read Matthew 6:14-15. Place the in-process embroidery banner on worship table today.
>
> Sign up to read the Lord's Prayer.

Workstation 7: Benediction

INSTRUCTION SIGN

People often close a prayer by saying that they are followers of Jesus, such as by saying "in Jesus' name we pray," or in "Christ's name." As a follower of Jesus, you are going to write a prayer and make a praying hands prayer card.

STEP 1: Fold a piece of paper in half. Place your hand with the thumb flat against the FOLD of the paper. Draw around your hand. Keep your thumb tight against the fold of the paper.

STEP 2: Cut around your hand-tracing. Be careful not to cut the hands apart at the fold.

STEP 3: Decorate the fingernails on your handprint or pretend you have gloves on and decorate the hands.

STEP 4: Open and write inside "Thank you, God, for . . ." Tell something you are thankful for—family, peace, friends, the beautiful world we live in . . . Read Matthew 6:5-6 for help. Write the Bible verses beneath your prayer and take your prayer card home with you as a reminder. Sign up to read your prayer for the service. Take praying hands card with you to service.

The Worship Celebration

GETTING READY

Make sure that you have all volunteers signed up before service and that they have prayers written. Remind children that a prayer does not have to be long. A prayer can be one sentence.

SIGN-UP SHEET FOR TODAY'S WORSHIP CELEBRATION

Call to Worship (read opening prayer):
Affirmation (read Matthew 6:5-10):
Offering (report service project collection):
Sermon (2 puppeteers and 2 readers for "The Lord's Prayer" play and closing prayer in play):
Witness (read prayers from folding churches):
Prayer (lead the Lord's Prayer):
Benediction (read prayers from praying hands cards):

ITEMS TO GO HOME TODAY: PRAYING HANDS CARDS; PRAYING CLAY HANDS (IF DRY)

Session 10
Witnessing in Thought, Word, and Action

The Bible Lesson

Jesus stressed throughout his ministry how to bring people closer to the kingdom of God (Matthew 13:1-9, 18-23).

What the Children Will Learn Today

As followers of Jesus, we should follow his teachings on even the simplest of everyday issues.

Time Needed

5 minutes for story
20 minutes for workstations
10 minutes for closing worship service

Supplies Needed (by Workstation)

1. Paper plates, elastic, craft supply basket, Session 2 patterns
2. Construction paper supply basket and flower patterns
3. Puppet stage supplies, curtains, and coverings for sides
4. Green, yellow, brown, and pink paper, craft supply basket, green pipe cleaners, paper-towel rolls or paper tubes, patterns, and puppet stage
5. Church supplies and steeple patterns
6. Green and brown paper, weed pattern, prayer banner
7. Construction paper supply basket and bird pattern

Children's Meditation

STORY

I'm Too Busy

The triplets had a problem. Sandy never bothered picking up her toys. Tommy, on the other hand, always said that he would, but if TV, a snack, or a good book interfered, Tommy forgot. Philip was much too busy.

Philip was busy building a town. His towns were creative but consumed the house.

When the triplets grew and entered school, their mother noticed the same problems with homework. Sandy would go in her room and close the door as if she were going to get right to work, but actually she got right to playing.

Tommy would come home, spread his books all over the dining room table, and then go to the kitchen to fix a snack. Two hours later, Tommy was still eating a snack.

Philip, on the other hand, never opened his book bag. Philip was outside climbing trees and riding his bike.

As late spring passed into early summer, the parents decided to give each child a garden.

Sandy poured her seeds on the ground. "I'll come back and plant later," she said. While Sandy was off swinging her doll, the birds came and ate the seeds.

Tommy was in a hurry. He found a clear spot without weeds, planted, watered, and was done.

Philip was so excited about his garden that he drew sketches, made a list of jobs to do, and vigorously pulled every single weed in his entire garden. At first Philip faithfully watered and weeded his garden, but then he forgot as he got busy with baseball. The garden sat unnoticed and unweeded.

As summer progressed, the triplets noticed that their parents' garden was filled with beautiful towering flowers.

Sally ran to her garden and began to scream. "My flowers, my flowers," she wailed.

As her mother comforted Sally, she asked, "Did you follow all of the steps we showed you?" Sally didn't answer.

Tommy was yelling and bellowing over at his garden. "I was given bad seeds," he said. "Look, the flowers started to grow, then they died."

Tommy's dad pushed his finger down into the garden soil. "The seeds were fine. It's that rock hidden underneath the soil that stopped your flowers. If you had not been in such a hurry, you could have put in a nice garden over here."

Philip sat in shock. His garden was filled with weeds. A few of Philip's flowers struggled to poke their way through, but mostly Philip had weeds.

"You can't tend a garden once," said Philip's mother. "You have to tend a garden every day. You have to combine a little play with a little work."

"Maybe we should try again," their father said. "God gives us a chance to try again."

"Yes!" the triplets yelled as their father distributed three new packets of seeds.

Workstations

Workstation 1: Call to Worship

GETTING READY

Use paper-plate puppet patterns from Session 2 if desired.

Take up project collection boxes from Session 3.

INSTRUCTION SIGN

Sunday is a time to make changes in how we live our daily lives. Many of us dress up to come to church. We should also "dress up" our lives. Think of one way you can change and follow the advice in the parable. Make a paper-plate puppet. Tape your puppet to a ruler or put it on a piece of elastic so that it will bounce during the story. Go to Workstation 4 and practice.

Workstation 2: Affirmation of Faith

INSTRUCTION SIGN

The fourth kind of soil described in the parable of the sower and the seed was good soil. Read Luke 8:15. Make a flower. Be prepared to hold your flower up high during verses for "good soil."

STEP 1: Trace patterns for petals, center, and leaves.

STEP 2: Cut 4" x 8" piece of construction paper for stem.

STEP 3: Roll stem around a pencil and glue in place on paper. Crease leaves. Glue leaves to back of stem.

STEP 4: Write on petals before gluing in place. Write: "I am a Follower of Jesus" on flower center. Write the Bible verse on a petal. On other petals, write five ways you can follow the teachings of Jesus this week at school, at home, on the playground, with friends, or by helping someone in need around the world. Glue flower in place on paper.

Sign up to read what you wrote on your flower for the worship service.

Workstation 3: Offering or Carpenter Shop

INSTRUCTION SIGN

The sower and the seed parable mentions four different kinds of soil. The first soil was the hard path or road. The fields were divided into long, narrow strips in Palestine. No fences divided the property. There was only a hard-packed path or road made hard by the travel of many people beside the field. Seed that fell on the path had no chance to grow. Jesus compared such ground to people who think they know everything and do not listen. Someone who has all of the answers is like the path. Read Matthew 13:4, 18-19, then finish the puppet stage so it can be used for the sermon today.

Hang curtains in front. Staple coverings to sides. You will make fancy banners for the sides later. Congratulations!

Workstation 4: Sermon or Bible Study

GETTING READY

You must have one paper tube that fits easily inside another for the pop-up flower that grows. For example, use a thin gift-wrap paper tube inside a larger jumbo wrapping tube.

INSTRUCTION SIGN

As followers of Jesus, we are to go out every day to help others, share kindness, be understanding and loving, and treat others as we would like for them to treat us. Read Matthew 13:1-9, 18-23 and act out the parable for our sermon today. Everyone is helping. The call to worship station is making puppets, the affirmation station is making the flowers in the good soil, the prayer station is making the weeds, and the benediction station is making the birds to help tell today's sermon. Work on other props needed.

STEP 1: Trace patterns and make pop-up flowers, thorn bushes, and a big, friendly sun to tell today's story.

STEP 2: Punch paper circles for seeds. Do NOT use real seeds. Paper can be harmlessly tossed; seeds cannot.

STEP 3: Trace flower, roll in tight cluster. Tape flower to pipe cleaner to simulate wilting when needed in story.

STEP 4: Use two paper tubes. One should easily fit inside the other. Cover both with green paper. Make a second flower (patterns from Step 3). Roll and tape flower to inside tube. Place flower inside larger tube. To make grow, push up slowly.

STEP 5: Glue thorn bushes and weeds to paper towel or tissue rolls so that you will have a stiff handle and can make the thorn bushes and weeds grow faster than flowers.

STEP 6: Glue sun to a wrapping paper tube so that you can make it show high over puppet stage.

You will need someone who can read LOUDLY and SLOWLY so that everyone will understand parable. Use the new puppet stage.

Workstation 5: Witness to Faith

GETTING READY

If children started late and have not finished, have them finish in stages. For example, finish the walls, windows, roof, and steeple so that they can enjoy taking their folding church home.

INSTRUCTION SIGN

The second soil in the sower and the seed parable is the rocky soil. This means a thin layer of soil sitting over the top of rock. The seeds sprout but cannot grow because the rock blocks the roots from reaching moisture. Jesus compared this kind of soil to shallow faith. Read Mark 4:5-6, 16-17. Sign up to read Matthew 13:18-23 in service today.

It has been hard to work for eight weeks on building a single project, but you have almost finished. Use steeple pattern and cut steeple from paper to match outside of church. Fold on dotted lines and glue tabs.

STEP 1: Use pattern and cut bell. Make a foldout bell if desired by cutting 5 copies of bell. Fold and staple in middle.

STEP 2: Cut steeple roof and glue to steeple. Attach string to bell. Tape string to inside steeple. Set steeple on roof. Your church is finished. Place on worship table.

Workstation 6: Prayer and Sewing Center

GETTING READY

Keep the various sewing projects going until finished. The embroidery banner will take all year. You will use a travel bag, the sleeping mat, and the blocks for the Christmas Eve service.

INSTRUCTION SIGN

The third kind of soil mentioned in the sower and the seed parable was the soil covered by thorn bushes. If you have ever cleared a garden by pulling weeds, you know how frustrating it can be to stand and watch new weeds sprout faster than the seeds. Weeds always seem to grow faster. If the garden becomes too thick with weeds, the new seeds and plants will not get enough sunlight, moisture, or space to grow. Read Matthew 13:7, 22.

Jesus said our lives are the same. If our lives become too busy with details, we don't have time to think of the needs of our neighbor. Use green paper scraps and cut weeds using pattern. Take weeds to Workstation 4 and help practice sermon. Also continue working on sewing projects. Hang embroidery banner on puppet stage and sign up to write a prayer for service.

Workstation 7: Benediction

INSTRUCTION SIGN

It was the custom in biblical times for farmers to plant crops by throwing seed all over the ground or sowing. The farmer knew some of the seed would fall on bad soil and not grow, but he hoped that most would end up in good soil.

Read Mark 4:3-8. You are in charge of making the birds.

Trace bird pattern. Write Bible verses on bird. Decorate. Fold wings up. Roll a sheet of paper on a pencil, tape together. Glue bird to end of paper stick. Be prepared to make your bird fly when birds are mentioned in the parable.

The Worship Celebration

SIGN-UP SHEET FOR TODAY'S WORSHIP CELEBRATION

Call to Worship (puppets for parable of the soil; read Matthew 13:1-9):

Affirmation ("good" soil flowers for parable; read ways to follow Jesus from petals):

Offering (puppet theater finished today for parable):

Sermon (act out parable of the soil):

Witness (read Matthew 13:18-23):

Prayer (weeds for parable; write a prayer):

Benediction (birds for parable):

ITEMS TO GO HOME TODAY:
PAPER-PLATE PUPPETS; FLOWERS;
BIRDS; FOLDING CHURCHES

7

Symbols of the Church and What They Mean

(Sessions in this chapter may be used as independent pull-out programs as suggested in chapter 1.)

Session 11
The Purpose of Symbols
in the Sanctuary

The Bible Lesson

Luke 10:25-37 calls everyone to a life of action.

What the Children Will Learn Today

Children learn meanings of various symbols at workstations.

Time Needed

  5 minutes for story
20 minutes for workstations
10 minutes for closing worship service

Supplies Needed (by Workstation)

1. Pop bottles, brown, yellow, and orange construction paper, brown lunch bags, owl pattern, and craft supply basket
2. Paper plates, Popsicle sticks, pipe cleaners, glue, tape
3. Construction paper basket, scrap paper, and altar pattern
4. 3 puppets (including Sunshine), puppet stage, and skit
5. Foil, candles, and salt dough recipe from Appendix

6. Netting (fabric store), heavy string, darning needles, macramé wooden beads, and heavy cord
7. Construction paper, scrap paper, stapler, and pattern

Children's Meditation

STORY

You Can't Be in Our Children's Choir

Rutherford was a gangly, tall, thin boy who didn't say much. He just stood in the corner, slumped over, staring at the floor.

Rutherford was hard of hearing and wore a hearing aid in each ear. Rutherford was also dyslexic and had trouble reading.

Rutherford knew that he was different, that he'd never be able to play baseball or do the things others did. Rutherford desperately wanted to be part of the group, to go places with the children, to have a friend—even one friend would do.

Rutherford showed up one day for children's choir practice. Mrs. Smith, the choir director, flew into a rage. "We can't have that child in the choir," she said. "We're planning a special concert for Children's Day. We're doing serious music. We can't have Rutherford slumped over on the front row. You'll have to tell his parents to keep him home till after the concert. Children like Rutherford don't belong."

The Children's Day concert was to be a wonderful collection of music telling of God's love

80

for everyone. A dramatic conclusion would show how everyone was invited to come and worship God together.

Tears filled Rutherford's eyes. The word *everyone* didn't include Rutherford.

When he went to the mall, kids from school would pause and say, "Hi, Rutherford. How are you doing?" Then rush off to another store before Rutherford managed to say, "Fine." No one ever wanted Rutherford to tag along or sit next to them. And now they didn't even want him in the church choir.

On the day of the concert, the children started with a lively song about how everyone should come together and worship God in peace and love. Rutherford sat rejected and hurt. During the chorus, Jimmy Gordon marched into the audience, much to the shock and horror of Mrs. Smith, and brought Rutherford up to stand beside him. Mrs. Smith looked mortified. Rutherford didn't know what to do. Jimmy wrapped his arm around Rutherford's shoulder. "Just follow me," Jimmy whispered.

Rutherford swayed to the music and even joined in a little on the chorus of one song. Rutherford would always remember Jimmy's single act of kindness on the day the children's choir did more than sing the words to a song.

God never picks favorites or leaves anyone sitting out in the audience feeling rejected. God loves everyone equally and challenges us to do the same.

Workstations

Workstation 1: Call to Worship

INSTRUCTION SIGN

Make a wise old owl to remind you to read your Bible. Read Proverbs 18:8-9; 19:11; 20:11; and 22:2.

STEP 1: Place pop bottle inside paper lunch bag. Cover with second bag. Bottle is completely hidden.

STEP 2: Trace and cut 2 owls. Glue in place.

STEP 3: Cut eyes and beak using patterns. Fold beak.

STEP 4: Trace your hands on brown paper. Glue hands to bottom of owl. Write your favorite proverb on owl's feet. Place owls on worship table. Sign up to read your favorite proverb.

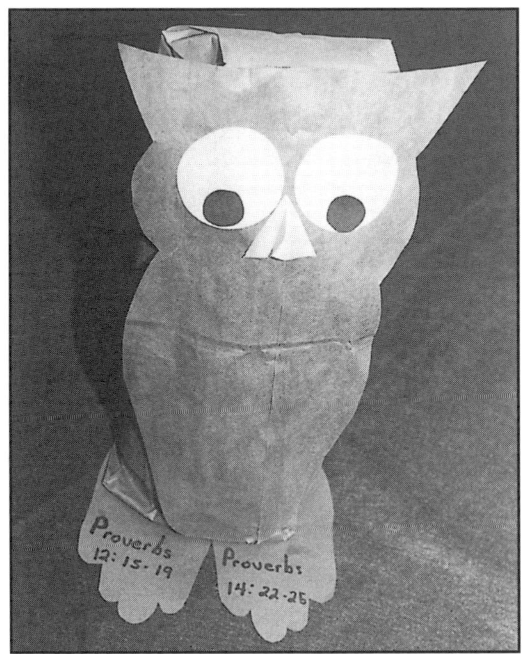

Workstation 2: Affirmation of Faith

INSTRUCTION SIGN

The butterfly is the Christian symbol for "new life." Often we think that we cannot change the way we act or how we treat other people, but we can. Read Luke 10:25-37.

STEP 1: Fold and cut a paper plate in half.

STEP 2: On first half, write words or draw pictures that describe the person you are: kind, moody, loves horses, plays piano, etc.

STEP 3: On second half, write or draw pictures telling how you're different. Remember, being different is what makes you special. You're the only one in all of God's creation like you.

STEP 4: Color and decorate butterfly. Make it the most beautiful butterfly ever. Color a Popsicle stick to match.

STEP 5: Tape round edges of plate together in the middle. Glue stick in place for body. Fold a pipe cleaner in half and curl the edges to make the antennae. Tape antennae to stick. Sign up to read what makes you special for today's affirmation.

Workstation 3: Offering or Carpenter Shop

INSTRUCTION SIGN

"Jesus" was a common Jewish name for boys in biblical times. Read Matthew 27:16-17 and Colossians 4:11. "Jesus" means "savior" or one who has come to save. The word "Christ" means "anointed or chosen one" in Greek. In Hebrew, "Christ" means "Messiah" or "Jesus is the chosen or appointed leader." We often see the Greek Chi "X" and Rho "P" for Christ on the altar (**symbol**).

STEP 1: Fold paper in half to fit pattern. Mark lines and make a card that opens to form altar or communion table.

STEP 2: To cut candles, fold upper portion of table and cut candles. Place the Greek symbol for Christ on the altar cloth.

Trace pattern and make a Bible. Trace around a quarter or round circle for an offering plate. Sign up to read Luke 10:25-37.

Workstation 4: Sermon or Bible Study

INSTRUCTION SIGN

People continuously asked Jesus, "What must I do to improve my life and live as God wants me to?" Read Luke 10:25-37. You need 3 puppeteers (including Sunshine) and 3 readers.

PUPPET PLAY FOR SERMON

Love Your Neighbor

SIMON:	"Love the Lord your God with all your heart, and with all your soul, and with all your strength, and with all your mind; and your neighbor as yourself" (Luke 10:27).
SUNSHINE:	That's great, but it doesn't mean anything unless you put the words into action.
SIMON:	Action?
SUNSHINE:	It's important to read the Bible, but it's even more important to act upon what you read.
SIMON:	[spoken proudly] I've memorized thirty-three Bible verses.
SUNSHINE:	Memorizing's not enough.
SIMON:	If I memorize one hundred verses by the end of the year, I get a gold-plated bookmark to put in my Bible.
CAREY:	You're not listening, Simon.
SUNSHINE:	Jesus says that if we love God, we will love our neighbor as we love ourselves.
SIMON:	I know what that means. That means to treat my neighbor the same way I want to be treated. If I don't want someone hitting me, then I shouldn't hit someone else.
SUNSHINE:	It also means that just as you want to feel important and have lots of friends, so does the shy person standing alone in the corner with no one to talk to. Everyone wants to feel important and have friends. It's our job to help.
SIMON:	Trying to follow what the Bible says is sure a lot harder than memorizing.
SUNSHINE:	Every day we should help others.
SIMON:	Even people we don't like?
SUNSHINE:	Even people we don't like. If we love God with all our heart, soul, strength, and mind, then we'll always be looking out for what's best for others.
CAREY:	Amanda thinks she's better than I am. [pause] I'm going to try to treat Amanda the way I wish she treated me.
SUNSHINE:	You won't see a change right away, but if you continue to be kind, polite, and look for the good in others, you'll eventually feel your love being returned to you.
SIMON:	I'll try.
SUNSHINE:	Let's all try!

Workstation 5: Witness to Faith

GETTING READY

Have salt dough mixed and ready (see appendix). Place cross on foil to bake later. Bake slowly at 250° for 3 hours or until hard and slightly brown. Save cross and use for Lent.

INSTRUCTION SIGN

The cross is a symbol of sacrifice. The cross can also be a reminder of our cruelty toward others: teasing, rude words, laughing at and rejecting others.

Read 1 Corinthians 13:4-7 and sign up to read these verses in today's service. Make a salt dough cross. Add six candle holes on the cross for six qualities we should show others: patience, kindness, humility, generosity, truthfulness, and eternal or never-ending love. Use a candle to shape hole. Leave cross on foil and place on worship table for service.

Workstation 6: Prayer and Sewing Center

GETTING READY

Cut netting ahead of time. Use yardstick and measure a three-foot circle. Save fishing net to use for Easter and musical.

INSTRUCTION SIGN

Cast-net fishing was done from the shore when a school of fish could be spotted in shallow water. An open, circular, weighted cast net was thrown out flat, allowed to sink, drawn closed, and pulled in, hopefully full of fish. Jesus said if we follow his teachings, we're like fishermen. Our actions help others believe in God. Read Matthew 4:18-20. The fishing net reminds us to bring others to Christ.

STEP 1:   Cut a 3-foot circle of netting. Thread 2 darning needles with doubled lengths of string. Lay the string on top of the circle to measure how much thread is needed.

STEP 2:   Tie a BIG knot in end of doubled string. Sew string in and out of netting so that you can draw the net up into a closed bag. Leave ends long. Tie wooden beads for weights along edge of net.

STEP 3:   You are now ready to go fishing. Gently throw your net out. Have a friend place some fish inside. Place net and fish on worship table for service today. Sign up to lead the Lord's Prayer.

Workstation 7: Benediction

INSTRUCTION SIGN

Being a follower of Jesus in the early church often meant risking your life or going to secret hiding places for worship. The secret sign of the fish was a welcome sign to the early Christians. The fish reminds us even today to love and accept one another. Read Luke 10:25-37 and sign up to read the parable of the good Samaritan in the service today.

STEP 1:   Trace fish pattern on paper and make 2 fish.

STEP 2:   Glue and staple fish together, except leave one side open for stuffing. Decorate fish.

STEP 3:   Stuff fish with scrap paper. Glue and staple shut.

Go fishing at Workstation 6. Place fish on net for service.

The Worship Celebration

SIGN-UP SHEET FOR TODAY'S WORSHIP CELEBRATION

Call to Worship (read favorite proverb):
Affirmation (read characteristics that make you special):
Offering (read Luke 10:25-37):
Sermon (3 puppeteers and 3 readers for "Love Your Neighbor"):
Witness (read 1 Corinthians 13:4-7):
Prayer (read the Lord's Prayer):
Benediction (read Luke 10:25-37):

ITEMS TO GO HOME TODAY: OWLS; BUTTERFLIES; FISH; ALTARS

Session 12
The Story of Stained-Glass Windows

The Bible Lesson

Verses from Proverbs reinforce teachings of Jesus.

What the Children Will Learn Today

To count your blessings instead of complaints.

Time Needed

5 minutes for story
20 minutes for workstations
10 minutes for closing worship service

Supplies Needed (by Workstation)

1, 2, and 4. Cardboard box, four pastel sheets of paper to cover sides of box, black tape, and craft supply basket
3. 1" x 2" boards for weaving loom, tools, pencil, and yardstick
5. Tissue paper, tape, hole punch, scallop craft scissors (if available), string or thread, and a circle to trace
6. Stiff white paper or poster board, black construction paper, craft supply basket, church pattern, and tape
7. Craft supply basket, white paper, and circle to trace

Children's Meditation

STORY

The Gift of Sight

Lucy had been blind since birth. She had never seen anything but darkness. Lucy's mother spent hours describing the stained-glass windows till Lucy could see them in her mind.

"Each window's different, like people. No two windows are exactly alike," her mother explained.

"Who made the first window?" Lucy asked one day.

"We're not sure," said her mother. "Books tell of stained-glass windows in early churches in Rome and the Near East as long ago as A.D. 500. The oldest window is a picture of the prophets in the Cathedral of Augsburg, Germany, and they were made in the 1100s. The windows of St. Denis in Paris were made about the same time and are probably the most famous."

"Is it hard to make a window?"

"Yes, it's also very expensive. First, the artist makes a color sketch. Then a full-scale color drawing is made. This drawing is then numbered and cut into pieces like a puzzle. The puzzle pieces are used as patterns to make the window. Each colored piece of glass is cut and hand-painted for details.

"The thickness and color of the glass determine how much light will shine through. It's God's light that actually makes the window beautiful. Light in medieval times was considered magical. The light coming through the beautiful stained-glass windows was believed to be able to change one's soul.

"In the early churches, many people couldn't read. The windows taught them the stories from the Bible.

"Twelve sections of glass are placed in a rose window to signify the joining together of heaven and earth. The circular rose window represents truth and God's never-ending love.

"Just as you don't crawl over the pews in church the way you crawl over the stadium bleachers at a football game, the beauty of stained glass was believed to help prepare the congregation for worship and to call them to repent and change," said Lucy's mother.

Lucy sighed. "It must be wonderful to see. I would never take it for granted if I could see. I'd cherish every moment."

Since most of us have always been able to see, we don't think about what it would be like to be blind. Take a moment this week to stop and look at the beauty of God's creation all around you and cherish the gift of sight.

Workstations

Workstations 1 (Call to Worship), 2 (Affirmation of Faith), and 4 (Sermon or Bible Study) Combined

GETTING READY

Select a cardboard box suitable for project. Have four large sheets of paper of size needed to cover each side of box. White side of wrapping paper can be used or light pastels. Photocopy and cut following list of Bible verses into strips.

1. Jesus was born in Bethlehem (Luke 2:1-7).
2. As a young boy, Jesus helped Joseph in his carpenter shop in Nazareth (Luke 2:39-40).
3. When he was twelve, Jesus walked with his family from Nazareth to Jerusalem to celebrate the Jewish festival of Passover (Luke 2:41-42).
4. Jesus joined those being baptized in the river Jordan by John the Baptist (Matthew 3:13).
5. Jesus called Peter, Andrew, James, and John to follow him and become fishers of men (Matthew 4:18-22).
6. Jesus selected twelve disciples. Matthew the tax collector was despised by the people (Luke 5:27-32).
7. Jesus told many stories about how the people were to live their daily lives (Matthew 7:1-2, 12).
8. Jesus taught about prayer (Matthew 6:5-15).
9. Jesus said to help your neighbor (Luke 10:25-37).
10. Jesus returned riding on a donkey (Mark 11:1-10).
11. The Last Supper, trial, crucifixion, and resurrection marked a new beginning (Luke 22:14-20; Mark 16:15).
12. The church began (Acts 2:44-47).

Glue each Bible verse onto the paper in sequence, three verses on each sheet of paper. Remember to leave space for drawings. Do not glue paper to box.

INSTRUCTION SIGN

You are said to be a witness for Christ if you go and tell others what you know or have learned about Jesus. We are going to be witnesses by drawing pictures on a "Story Cube." It will be your job to read the Bible verse and supply the pictures.

Draw a picture describing what's happening in your part of the story. Take your time. Most of all, remember to work together as a group. When we finish, we will have a story telling of the life and teachings of Jesus.

Workstation 3: Offering or Carpenter Shop

GETTING READY

Help children cut notches straight so yarn will line up.

INSTRUCTION SIGN

Every piece of cloth was woven by hand in biblical times. Build a weaving loom to help us appreciate how much easier life is today. Read Proverbs 27:1-4 and Matthew 5:5. Follow diagram.

Workstation 5: Witness to Faith

INSTRUCTION SIGN

Stained-glass windows were originally designed to teach stories from the Bible. Each window told a different story.

Rose windows were designed to be the focal point. Read Proverbs 25:9-14; 29:23; and Matthew 5:7. Make a rose window.

STEP 1: Cut 3 circles from different colors of tissue paper.

STEP 2: Fold each piece of tissue paper as you would to make a snowflake. First in half, then in fourths.

STEP 3: Cut notches in folded tissue as if you were making a paper snowflake. Work carefully; tissue tears easily. Make 3. The more intricate your cuts, the prettier your window.

STEP 4: Trace and cut a fourth circle. Cut a fancy edge. Do NOT fold or cut notches. Gently open tissue. Place on solid circle. Roll tiny piece of tape, put between tissue to hold together. Do NOT use glue. Take your rose window home and tape to a window as a reminder of the beauty of God's creation.

Workstation 6: Prayer and Sewing Center

GETTING READY

Use stiff white paper or poster board.

INSTRUCTION SIGN

Make a stand-up church to remind yourself to read the Bible.

STEP 1: Trace and cut out church, if possible, from one piece of stiff white paper.

STEP 2: Cut roof, steeple, and doors from black construction paper. Glue doors and steeple in place. Save roof.

STEP 3: Draw windows. To draw your own stained-glass windows, trace around window pattern. Let each window tell a story. Use small pieces of paper or markers to color windows. Read Proverbs 20:3, 11 and Matthew 5:11.

STEP 4: When all windows are finished, fold and tape edges of church together. Glue roof in place. Place on worship table.

Workstation 7: Benediction

INSTRUCTION SIGN

Create your own rose window today. Trace or cut a circle on white paper. Draw a picture in the center that tells about the life of Jesus. Color window with markers or crayons for stained-glass effect. Place on worship table for service.

The Worship Celebration

GETTING READY

Sermon is from story cube. Artists will read a Bible verse and show their pictures. Glue paper to box after worship. Use as storage box or craft supply box. Tape edges with black tape.

SIGN-UP SHEET FOR TODAY'S WORSHIP CELEBRATION

Participants who worked on story cube:

ITEMS TO GO HOME TODAY: CHURCHES; ROSE WINDOWS

Session 13
Who Is My Neighbor?

The Bible Lesson

The parable of the friend at midnight in Luke 11:5-13 reminds children to help those in need whether near or faraway.

What the Children Will Learn Today

Four of the workstations are working together today to make a world friendship banner. The idea is to teach cooperation.

Time Needed

5 minutes for story
25 minutes for workstations
5 minutes for closing worship service

Supplies Needed (by Workstation)

1. Skin-tone felt, various colors of yarn for hair, fake fur, sharp scissors, patterns, fabric glue, and felt scraps
2. Papier-mâché, foil, plastic bowls
3. Light blue felt for banner and dark blue felt for world
4. Actors, Bible, and any props desired for pantomime
5. Felt scraps for letters and sharp sewing scissors
6. Light tan felt for continents, make pattern
7. Skin-tone paper, patterns, and craft supply basket

Children's Meditation

STORY

To Buy a Calf

The children had been saving money for six months to buy a heifer calf. The children needed to raise $500 by June. Last year, the children only brought in $120.

They bought baby chicks. Baby chicks were nice and provided eggs for hungry children, but somehow, buying a calf seemed better.

The children counted the coins. There were several dollar bills, and someone had even placed a ten-dollar bill in the pickle jar. Excitement grew as the children and adults counted. Finally, the count was official. The children had collected $150. The sound of disappointment echoed throughout the room.

The teacher suggested they plan a special project. The children made a list. Everyone's favorite was to host a dinner.

The food would be donated by families. It would be like a big Thanksgiving feast. Families would sign up to bring a turkey, pie, pan of dressing, or whatever was needed. After worship, everyone who had bought a ticket would come and eat.

Finally, the day arrived. Everything was going as planned. Silence fell across the room when the teacher rose to announce the total contributions from the Thanksgiving feast. Everyone listened and waited.

"We'd like to thank you for your generosity, and we're pleased to announce that with your help the children have been able to raise $1,050." Applause filled the room.

"We'll be able to send not one but two heifer calves to families in Africa this year and also fifty baby chicks." As they bowed their heads for the closing prayer, the children would never forget how wonderful it felt to be helped by *your neighbor*.

Workstations

Workstation 1: Call to Worship

GETTING READY

Children are making felt banner to hang on puppet stage. Have pictures of faces from different countries. Have various colors of yarn and fake fur for hair. Have different colors of felt for skin. Use scraps for eyes.

INSTRUCTION SIGN

In biblical times, it was your duty to provide food and a place to sleep to anyone who came to your home seeking help. Hospitality was considered a sacred duty, so you would want to provide the best possible meal and lodging. Read the parable of the friend at midnight in Luke 11:5-8. Think how you would respond to such an unexpected guest who arrived at midnight.

Make a world friendship banner today. Be persistent. Make 20 faces from different countries. Make each face different just as we are all different. Make braided hair, hats, different colors of skin, and all shapes of mouths and eyes.

Workstation 2: Affirmation of Faith

GETTING READY

Mix papier-mâché. Have ready. Depending upon the humidity, the bowl, plate, and lamp may be dry enough to use for service. If not, use a brown or wooden bowl for service and place papier-mâché on worship table.

Have a variety of round plastic margarine tubs or larger bowls for papier-mâché. Save bowls for Easter service.

INSTRUCTION SIGN

When Jesus was a boy, it was the custom to provide an abundance of food, a feast, to any guest who came to your home. Yet, because there was no refrigeration or means of keeping food from spoiling, it was also the custom to bake only what the family was likely to eat. A guest who arrived at midnight would find the family asleep and the food bowls empty as was the case in the parable of the friend at midnight. Read Luke 11:5-8.

STEP 1: You are going to make papier-mâché bowls, plates, cups, and a hand lamp to use for our service today. Use brown scrap paper to give a brown clay color. Use foil to make a form for the bowls or cover the Styrofoam and plastic bowls provided.

STEP 2: Dip brown paper in papier-mâché. Cover objects.

STEP 3: The hand lamp that would have provided light in the house at night was a small round bowl with a spout. Use foil to make a spout. Place on worship table to dry.

Workstation 3: Offering or Carpenter Shop

GETTING READY

Have light blue felt for banner and dark blue for world.

INSTRUCTION SIGN

In Palestine, neighborhoods were public. The door was opened in the morning, left open all day, and only closed with the bar in place when everyone had gone to bed. Anyone passing by during the day was welcome to enter your home and visit. Once the door was closed, neighbors knew the family did not wish to be disturbed and would not knock. Read Luke 11:5-13.

We're working on a world friendship banner. Your job is to cut the circle for the world and make sure the banner edges are even. Make a paper pattern first. Then cut the felt.

STEP 1: Use a yardstick or string and pencil and make a circle on a large piece of paper.

STEP 2: Make sure pattern is right, then cut dark blue felt for the world using the pattern you made.

STEP 3: Check measurements for banner. This banner is the right size to hang on the side of the Sunshine Share-a-Lot Helping Hands Puppet Theater.

STEP 4: Glue blue world in center of banner. See photo for exact placement.

Measure twice before gluing.

Workstation 4: Sermon or Bible Study

GETTING READY

Have a round loaf of bread for play.

INSTRUCTION SIGN

You are going to be acting out the parable of the friend at midnight for today's service. First, read Luke 11:5-13. The sermon is the entire five-minute worship service today.

Set up two groups or households. One is the house of the neighbor who has closed his door and gone to sleep. Have his family spread out on the floor sleeping with one or two snoring.

The second household is the persistent friend who has an unexpected guest arrive. The persistent friend has no food in the house and goes next door to ask his neighbor for bread.

Knock on a table for knocking sounds. Use the bowls from Workstation 2 (if they are dry enough) to show there is no food. When the neighbor does finally get up to give his persistent friend some bread, have entire household wake up and be noisy.

Read Luke 11:5-9 as actors pantomime. Read verses 10-13 as benediction with all actors motionless. Close service with Lord's Prayer. You need a reader and at least 5 actors today.

Workstation 5: Witness to Faith

GETTING READY

Have stencils or patterns and scraps of felt to use for letters. The children will need sharp scissors to cut letters.

INSTRUCTION SIGN

In Palestine, where Jesus lived, most houses were one-room structures with one window and one door. The family's animals lived on the ground floor. The family slept on flat woven mats on a raised, hard earthen platform at the opposite end of the house from the door. Families were large. The raised platform would have been covered with sleeping family members. For the neighbor to get up after his family had gone to sleep would awaken his family and arouse the animals. Read Luke 11:5-8.

We want to be as persistent as the neighbor seeking bread. Cut letters for world friendship banner. Go slowly and do a nice job. Cut letters from scraps of felt to give a rainbow effect.

STEP 1: Decide on colors of felt to be used. Use stencils. Trace letters for: "FRIENDS AROUND THE WORLD." Cut felt.

STEP 2: Glue letters on banner. Check placement of letters with banner photo before gluing letters in place.

Workstation 6: Prayer and Sewing Center

GETTING READY

You will need to enlarge continent patterns before session or have children draw them freehand.

INSTRUCTION SIGN

We should make it a habit not to merely pray to God when we want something from him, but we should pray to say thank you without expecting anything in return. Read Luke 11:5-13.

Today, you are making the pattern and cutting the continents of the world for our world friendship banner. Work slowly and carefully. This is not an easy job.

Make pattern first. Then trace and cut felt. Finally, glue in place on banner. Check photo for placement.

Workstation 7: Benediction

GETTING READY

Young children may find the banner too difficult. They can make paper faces similar to what are being made at Workstation 1.

Have a variety of skin-tone colors of paper available.

INSTRUCTION SIGN

Make paper faces of children from around the world. Cut circles of different colors for skin, use patterns for hair, and draw different eyes and mouths on each face to remind us that even though we are different we are all children of God.

The Worship Celebration

GETTING READY

The entire service is the parable of the friend at midnight.

SIGN-UP SHEET FOR TODAY'S WORSHIP CELEBRATION

Sermon (reader and 5 actors for parable of friend at midnight):

ITEMS TO GO HOME TODAY: PAPER FACES FROM AROUND THE WORLD

Session 14
The Helping Hands Club

The Bible Lesson

Proverbs tell children how to be peacemakers.

What the Children Will Learn Today

The children are making a banner for the puppet stage.

Time Needed

5 minutes for story
25 minutes for workstations
5 minutes for closing worship service

Supplies Needed (by Workstation)

1. Pink and purple felt, patterns, and sharp scissors
2. Yellow and green felt, patterns, and sharp scissors
3. Paper juice cans, duct tape, wrapping paper, craft supply basket
4. Skit, two puppets, and Sunday school leaflet as prop
5. White felt, dove pattern, stencils for letters, sharp scissors, fabric glue, and blue felt to cover side of stage
6. Egg cartons, yarn, scissors to cut cartons, and patterns
7. Construction paper supply basket and banner patterns (Need: blue, green, pink, yellow, and white construction paper)

Children's Meditation

STORY

To Share a Bedroom

Jennifer and Roxanne are sisters and share a bedroom. It was fine when Roxanne was little, but Jennifer is five years older than Roxanne, and now she's tired of having a dollhouse, stroller, and kitchen set all over the room.

When the girls were little, they pretended to be twins, but not anymore. Their mother said it made her sad to hear the girls squabble and fight so much.

One day, a new girl moved to Jennifer's school. Jennifer invited Katy to sleep over one weekend. Katy barely even noticed Jennifer the whole evening. All Katy seemed to want to do was play with Roxanne. Roxanne, of course, loved the attention.

Finally, Jennifer couldn't take it any longer and she yelled, "Stop it! What are you doing? Why are you playing with her? You're supposed to be visiting me."

"I'm sorry," said Katy, "I didn't mean to be rude. [pause] My little sister, I miss her. She died three years ago.

"We did everything together. She'd climb in my bed. We'd hide under the covers and giggle and tell jokes.

"She hated thunderstorms and always climbed in bed with me when it rained. Then she got sick. I didn't understand. I got jealous, resentful of all the attention she was getting. We started fighting and arguing. I felt guilty after she died. I knew it wasn't my fault that she died, but I still regret that I wasted any of the days we had together by fighting.

"If I could do things over, I wouldn't waste even one second. I'd make sure she knew how much I loved her.

"I didn't mean to ignore you, Jennifer. Roxanne reminded me of all the wonderful times I no longer have. I suppose we don't appreciate what we have until we no longer have it."

"I'm sorry. I didn't realize," said Jennifer as she went over and hugged both Roxanne and Katy. "You're right, we don't appreciate the things we have in life, like a little sister.

"I know I can't help you miss your sister less, but I'll share mine with you, especially when she's driving me crazy. And maybe," Jennifer said very slowly, "we could all play together."

Workstations

Workstation 1: Call to Worship

> **INSTRUCTION SIGN**
>
> The color red in the church reminds us of the Holy Spirit. The morning sunrise, with shades of red, purple, and pink, reminds us that God forgives the wrongs we've done and surrounds us with his love. Read Proverbs 25:23, 28.
>
> Draw sunrise patterns for a banner to go on Sunshine Share-a-Lot Helping Hands Theater. Use patterns from Workstation 7 for an example. Take the sunrise to Workstation 5 to glue on banner.
>
> Sign up to read Proverbs 19:17 in service today.

Workstation 2: Affirmation of Faith

> **INSTRUCTION SIGN**
>
> Green reminds us to study and learn about God. Read Proverbs 22:1-4. Draw green hill pattern and sun for new banner. Take completed pieces to Workstation 5. Glue in place. Sign up to read for service.

Workstation 3: Offering or Carpenter Shop

GETTING READY

Use frozen-juice cans or other containers that stack.

> **INSTRUCTION SIGN**
>
> Peace poles are four-sided wooden posts. You find them at churches, libraries, and schools. The words "May Peace Prevail on Earth" are written in four different languages on the pole.
>
> Read Proverbs 18:2 (and sign up to read this verse in the service) and John 14:27-29. Make a peace pole.
>
> STEP 1: Select 3 containers. Tape cans vertically with duct tape. Help your neighbors tape their peace poles together.
>
> STEP 2: Cut paper to cover peace pole. Write "May Peace Prevail on Earth" vertically on peace pole. Also write the phrase in another language: "Reine solo la Paz en la Tierra." "Peace" is "paz" in Spanish; "friedan" in German; "paix" in French; "shalom" in Hebrew; and "salaam" in Arabic. Place on worship table.

Workstation 4: Sermon or Bible Study

> **INSTRUCTION SIGN**
>
> Avoiding gossip, trying to prevent fights, stopping an argument, not inventing stories or telling lies to get attention, and not trying to be better than someone else are a few of the different ways that we can help others at home and at school. Read Proverbs 26:20-28; 27:1-4; and Matthew 5:9. Practice skit. You need 2 puppeteers and 2 readers.

PUPPET PLAY FOR SERMON
The Mission

JACK: [spoken with shock and disbelief] Did you read this story? Look at these pictures? I can't believe this.

MARGIE: What are you talking about?

JACK: There's a story in our Sunday school leaflet this morning about a mission off the coast. It tells how the islands have become a big vacation resort. Developers are building fancy communities surrounded by brick walls and iron fences. The only way inside is through a guarded gate.

MARGIE: So?

JACK: The island's covered with migrant farmworkers and people who are too poor to buy food to eat.

Listen! [reads from leaflet] "Only one road leads into the resort community. It is lined with tar-paper shacks, lean-tos, and rotting unrepaired one-room houses. Many children only eat one meal a day, and often that is provided by the mission."

MARGIE: That's awful! Can you imagine living right next to so much wealth and money and not even having anything to eat? Why doesn't someone do something?

JACK: It would make me mad to live like that.

MARGIE: Getting angry never solves anything.

JACK: But it's not fair.

MARGIE: Does the story tell what's being done to help?

JACK: Yes, and it says we can help. They invite churches to plan work camp projects during the summer to help build, repair, or renovate houses for the island residents who can't afford to replace broken windows or repair leaky roofs. It says they also need health kits with basic medical supplies.

MARGIE: We could do that.

JACK: How?

MARGIE: Our children's worship class is always looking for new service projects. We could collect health kits.

JACK: We're only children.

MARGIE: We can still make a difference. Maybe we can even change the world. Maybe, someday, we can make sure there aren't poor people living outside the gates of rich resort communities. Health kits may not seem like much, but it's a start.

JACK: All right! All right! Don't start preaching. You're worse than the minister.

MARGIE: We could organize a special group and call it the "Helping Hands Club."

JACK: Each time we go to the grocery store, we could buy an extra bag of food and put it in the food pantry at church.

MARGIE: Let's make a list. Put down health kits to the mission, a bag of groceries to the food pantry . . .

JACK: There's also an organization the minister talked about one Sunday where every penny you raise buys food for hungry people at home and around the world. I remember because the minister said, "Even a penny could feed someone who's hungry."

MARGIE: That's great. Let's tell the class. Maybe the whole church would like to help!

Workstation 5: Witness to Faith

GETTING READY

Use a cloth or felt glue so that glue will not show through and ruin banner. Follow diagram when putting pieces together. Older children or helpers will need to cut dove and letters. Have blue felt banner measured and ready before session begins.

INSTRUCTION SIGN

The white dove is used as a symbol of peace all around the world. As children, we can't go around the world stopping wars, but we can help prevent squabbles that erupt and happen in our home or neighborhood. Read Proverbs 12:1 (and sign up to read this verse in the service), 14-20, 25.

As you trace and cut the dove and white letters for PEACE, think of an argument or problem at your house that you could make better. Work on bringing peace to your home this week. The banner will hang on the Sunshine Share-a-Lot puppet stage.

Workstation 6: Prayer and Sewing Center

GETTING READY

Most of the children have learned to weave from working on travel bags. Bookmarks are a little harder to weave because you do not have the cereal box to hold the weaving in shape. Teach children not to pull weaving too tightly today so that sides will stay even up and down the bookmark.

INSTRUCTION SIGN

Sewing is a very peaceful activity until you run into a problem or a new technique that is hard to learn. When we're frustrated, we often lash out in anger at others. Read Proverbs 18:9; 19:11, 17; and 20:11. Learn to weave an egg-carton bookmark. Use patience and compliment each other as you work.

STEP 1: Use pattern and cut out egg-carton weaving loom.

STEP 2: Wind yarn around loom. See example. Start at top and continue around each prong. Keep yarn only on one side.

STEP 3: Wrap contrasting yarn around a piece of scrap cardboard for shuttle. Tie loose end to weaving loom. Start to weave over and under. Remember that you can change colors or develop patterns when weaving. Be creative. Sign up to lead the Lord's Prayer for service. Take your bookmark and loom home.

Workstation 7: Benediction

INSTRUCTION SIGN

Do you often lose your temper? Do you yell at others over small problems that arise? If someone is rude to you, do you think you have to be rude back to them? Become a peacemaker. Read Proverbs 21:21, 23-24. Then make a paper copy of our cloth banner to take home today.

STEP 1: Use blue paper for sky. Trace patterns on colors indicated by patterns and glue grass and sunrise onto blue paper.

STEP 2: Trace dove pattern. Glue body of dove but not wings. Fold wings forward to make dove fly. Fold on dotted lines. Write "PEACE," Bible verses, and one way you can help bring peace to your home on the bottom of your paper banner and volunteer to read it during the service.

Place banners on worship table. Take your banner home as a reminder to be a peacemaker in your home.

The Worship Celebration

SIGN-UP SHEET FOR TODAY'S WORSHIP CELEBRATION

Call to Worship (read Proverbs 19:17):
Affirmation (read Proverbs 22:1-24)
Offering (read Proverbs 18:2):
Sermon (2 puppeteers and 2 readers for "The Mission"):
Witness (read Proverbs 12:1):
Prayer (lead the Lord's Prayer):
Benediction (read one way you can help bring peace to your home):

ITEMS TO GO HOME TODAY: WOVEN BOOKMARKS; PAPER BANNER

Session 15
Symbols of Love

The Bible Lesson

Love was the central message of Jesus' ministry; it is our central message too (1 Corinthians 13; 1 John 4:8-10).

What the Children Will Learn Today

The workstations stress learning to love one another.

Time Needed

5 minutes for story
20 minutes for workstations
10 minutes for closing worship service

Supplies Needed (by Workstation)

1. Laundry soap boxes, oatmeal containers, and other boxes, paper to cover boxes, patterns, stickers, and craft supply basket
2. Heart patterns, construction paper, and craft supply basket
3. Scrap wood, heart pattern, craft supply basket with decorating supplies (beans, sequins, or torn scrap paper), paint (if desired)
4. 3 puppets, skit, tiny boxes, and paper to cover boxes
5. Heart patterns, paper streamers (leftovers from birthday parties work fine for this project), and craft supply basket
6. Paper or cloth for quilt squares, patterns, and glue
7. Construction paper supply basket and patterns

Children's Meditation

STORY

If You Love Me

Julie Anne stormed and stomped off down the hallway to her room one more time. She was mad. Her mother had said *no* again.

"If you really loved me, you'd let me have the new pink and purple bike," yelled Julie Anne as she slammed the door to her room. "All you care about is yourself. I hate you."

Julie Anne didn't really hate her mother, but Julie Anne's feelings were hurt. "Katrina got a new bike. Why can't I? It's not fair," whined Julie Anne.

"Love is not expressed by buying presents," said her mother. "When you love someone, sometimes you have to say no."

"That's the most ridiculous thing I've ever heard," screamed Julie Anne.

"Does God give us everything we want? No, God gives us everything we need," said Julie Anne's mother. "God doesn't always give us what we want. God loves us and knows that it is often good for us to make do with less.

"As a parent," continued Julie Anne's mother, "God has given me the challenge of teaching you how to make wise decisions so that you can grow up to be a responsible adult and someday teach your own children. It doesn't make me happy to tell you NO, but you and I both know that it's the best decision for our family. We really don't have the money for a new bike, and your old bike's still fine."

"Getting a new bike will make me happy. Don't you want me to be happy?" Julie Anne thought that she would try a new angle on her mother. Perhaps the "poor me" approach would work better.

"A new bike won't really make you happy," said Julie Anne's mother. "Love will make you happy, and I love you very much. God loves you too. Now it's your turn."

"I'm sorry, Mommy, and I love you very, very, very much," said Julie Anne as she wrapped her arms tightly around her mother.

"I love you too," said her mother.

Workstations

Workstation 1: Call to Worship

<table>
<tr><td colspan="2" align="center">INSTRUCTION SIGN</td></tr>
<tr><td>STEP 1:</td><td>Make a drum for worship. Cover box with paper.</td></tr>
<tr><td>STEP 2:</td><td>Read 1 John 4:7-8, 12, 16, 19-21; and 1 Peter 4:8-10. Write these sentences and the Bible verses on your drum: "Love comes from God"; "God is love"; "Love one another."</td></tr>
<tr><td>STEP 3:</td><td>Decorate drum. Take drum to worship and sign up to help at the start of the service. Practice with puppeteers.</td></tr>
</table>

Workstation 2: Affirmation of Faith

GETTING READY

Have pictures from book or example of heart for children to see.

<table>
<tr><td colspan="2" align="center">INSTRUCTION SIGN</td></tr>
<tr><td colspan="2">Jesus said if you truly love someone, you would never say unkind words to them or try to hurt them, and if you did, you'd always say you're sorry.</td></tr>
<tr><td>STEP 1:</td><td>Trace and cut large heart. Trace and cut small heart in half. You need 2 halves. See example.</td></tr>
<tr><td>STEP 2:</td><td>Glue only the rounded EDGES of the small heart. Make sure that your small heart will open. Write "Jesus Loves" on the outside of the small heart halves. Open the small heart and write "ME" on the inside.</td></tr>
<tr><td>STEP 3:</td><td>Open large heart and write: "I show my love for Jesus when . . ." Then, write down a way you show love for Jesus, such as, "I share kindly with you."

Decorate your heart with sequins, glitter, or any supplies available in the craft supply basket. Read John 14:15, 23 and John 15:12. Write the Bible verses on your heart. Place on worship table and sign up to read them during the service. Take home to remind yourself to share kindly with others.</td></tr>
</table>

Workstation 3: Offering or Carpenter Shop

GETTING READY

If you have not finished the weaving loom from Session 12, finish today. Any size scraps of wood can be used for wooden plaques. Craft supply basket should have items to be used for decorating plaques. Paint can also be used.

INSTRUCTION SIGN

"Love" is an action word. To love your mother and father or brothers and sisters means to act kindly toward them. To love your neighbor means to act kindly to everyone. Read Romans 13:8-10 and sign up to read these verses in the service. Select a wooden board from the leftover scraps and turn it into a love plaque to give as a present.

STEP 1:   Select and sand board smooth.
STEP 2:   Trace heart pattern onto board.

Workstation 4 : Sermon or Bible Study

GETTING READY

Use tiny boxes for drums for puppets.

INSTRUCTION SIGN

Your job today is to explain what it means to love. Read 1 Corinthians 13. Practice skit. Need 3 puppeteers and 3 readers today. Cover small boxes to make drums for puppets. Practice with musicians from Workstation 1 before the service.

PUPPET PLAY FOR SERMON

Drums of Love

MUSICIANS: [Play cardboard box drums and sing a song of praise to the Lord for beginning of puppet play. Have musicians stand in front of puppet stage playing drums and singing. Puppets will be in puppet stage singing along and pretending to play their paper drums. As musicians are playing drums and singing, have one musician pretend to hit his drum really hard and try to tear it up. Remember, acting is only pretending.]

MARTY: Hey! What are you doing? [All music stops. Musicians sit down.]

JIM: What does it look like? I'm playing the drum.

CAROL: If you hit the drum that hard, you'll tear it up.

JIM: Who cares? It's only cardboard.

CAROL: You're supposed to care about everything, even the seemingly unimportant things.

JIM: I suppose you're going to tell me that God cares about cockroaches and skunks too.

MARTY: Probably; God created them.

JIM: So, I'm to be nice to cockroaches now.

CAROL: You're supposed to love everyone and everything in God's world, but I have to admit I don't like cockroaches. Yuck!

MARTY: Stop changing the subject.

JIM: I was just trying to get a clear picture of exactly how loving I'm to be.

MARTY: Sure you were.

CAROL: You shouldn't be mean or tear something up. Taking care of seemingly insignificant things is a good way to help us practice taking care of important things.

JIM: I was simply having fun tearing up a box.

CAROL: Violence is never fun, even if it seems harmless.

JIM: I never thought of it like that. Could we sing the song again?

[Musicians stand in front of puppet stage again.]

Workstation 5: Witness to Faith

INSTRUCTION SIGN

Fancy hearts with lacy edges have been used to say "I love you" for many years. God loves everyone and wants us to show our love for him in the way we treat other people. God wants us to be patient and kind, never jealous or conceited. God does not want us to act rudely to others, even if it's someone we don't like. God wants us to always tell the truth and to remember that love is the greatest gift we can ever give.

Read Luke 6:27-28, 32-36 and 1 Corinthians 13:4-7. Then make a lacy heart to remind yourself to go out into the world and share God's love with everyone you meet. Sign up to help with the service today.

STEP 1: Trace 2 identical hearts from pattern.

STEP 2: Cut a 36" strip of paper streamer.

STEP 3: Gather 3" of streamer at a time and glue to heart. You are making a paper ruffle.

Continue gathering streamer until you completely cover edge of heart. Add more streamer if needed or cut away any extra.

STEP 4: Glue other heart over top of streamer. Ruffled edge will stick out from hearts. Write "Love is patient and kind" on heart. Place on worship table today. Take heart home as a reminder to be patient and kind to everyone you meet.

Workstation 6: Prayer and Sewing Center

GETTING READY

My daughter created a quilt square from scraps of felt. She cut alternate contrasting squares and sewed them in place to make a nine-count square. Some of the older children might enjoy the challenge. The paper quilt square described below is easier.

INSTRUCTION SIGN

In pioneer and colonial days, girls would learn to sew a quilt. A quilt was considered to be a work of art and a special gift of love. Make your own quilt pattern using paper or felt.

STEP 1: Cut a 12" x 12" piece of paper or felt.

STEP 2: Cut four 4" squares of paper or felt. Glue squares in place according to diagram on pattern. This will give you a division of 9 equal squares on your quilt.

STEP 3: Read 1 John 4:7-8. Write "God is Love" on your quilt square. Decorate quilt squares.

Sign up to lead the Lord's Prayer today.

Workstation 7: Benediction

The Worship Celebration

INSTRUCTION SIGN

When you love someone, you show your love through your kind and helpful words and actions. Take God's love home with you and think of a way to share it with your family.

STEP 1: Make a paper house as a reminder to fill your home with God's love. Trace pattern. Decorate outside of house.

STEP 2: Use stickers, a drawing, or cut pictures from a magazine to tell one way you are going to share love this week.

STEP 3: Read John 13:34-35. Write Bible verses and a family slogan inside your house:

Put a Smile on your face,
a Kind word in your mouth,
and a Loving thought in your heart.

Place houses on the worship table and sign up to read your slogan for today's service.

SIGN-UP SHEET FOR TODAY'S WORSHIP CELEBRATION

Call to Worship (play drums and sing at beginning of puppet play):
Affirmation (read John 14:15, 23; 15:12):
Offering (read Romans 13:8-10):
Sermon (3 puppeteers and 3 readers for "Drums of Love"):
Witness (read Luke 6:27-28, 32-36):
Prayer (lead the Lord's Prayer):
Benediction (read slogans from houses):

ITEMS TO GO HOME TODAY: DRUMS; HEARTS; PLAQUES; QUILTS; HOUSES

PART THREE

WORSHIPING TOGETHER: PROGRAMS FOR THE HOLIDAYS

8

Missionaries: Go and Teach the Gospel

The Bible Lesson

This is a special program for World Communion Sunday, the first Sunday in October (1 Corinthians 10:17; John 6:35).

What the Children Will Learn Today

Children will learn the symbolic meaning of bread.

Time Needed

5 minutes for story
20 minutes for workstations
10 minutes for closing service

Supplies Needed (by Workstation)

Story: props: water jar, woven mat, and bread
1 and 2. Paper lunch bags, scrap paper, hole punch, stapler, glitter, patterns, tissue rolls, and craft supply basket
3 and 5. Bread dough, foil, and bread recipe from Session 18
4. Puppets, bread to serve to everyone, and skit
6. Embroidery banner and sewing supplies
7. Brown and yellow paper, pattern, and scrap paper

Children's Meditation

GETTING READY

Story is shorter than normal. Use the extra time to tell about Communion at your church.

STORY

One Piece for Everyone

Rachel hurried about the house sweeping the dirt floor one last time. She unrolled the sleeping mats [unroll mat]. The stew was cooking over the fire. All twelve round loaves of bread were baked and stacked near the oven to stay warm.

The followers of the Way were gathering at Rachel's house for worship this evening. It was the custom to eat dinner together before worship. There was talk of forming a church.

Rachel stood in the corner counting as everyone filtered in. Where had everyone come from? Rachel was happy to see so many, but would she have enough food? There was no way she had enough bread for so many people.

Rachel began to break the loaves of bread into small pieces and arrange them in a basket. She counted again. Still not enough! She must save one loaf for the Lord's Supper.

I'll break the bread again, she thought [break round loaf or paper example]. *If one person is to have bread, then everyone must have bread, even if it is only a small piece.*

Rachel smiled as everyone quieted down for the service. Sitting beside the empty bowl of stew was one small crust of bread. If we share what we have, there is truly enough for all.

Today, on World Communion Sunday, we join with Christians around the world to remember the life and teachings of Jesus and to remember that it is our responsibility to make sure all people, no matter where they live, have at least one piece of bread.

Workstations

Workstations 1 (Call to Worship) and 2 (Affirmation of Faith) Combined

INSTRUCTION SIGN

The early Christian sign of the fish and bread are Christian symbols for Holy Communion. Read 1 Corinthians 10:17. Make a fish with a bread basket.

STEP 1: Trace fish pattern onto a paper bag. Add eyes.

STEP 2: Glue or staple fish together, except for opening.

STEP 3: Tear scrap paper into tiny pieces and gently stuff inside fish. Glue and staple shut.

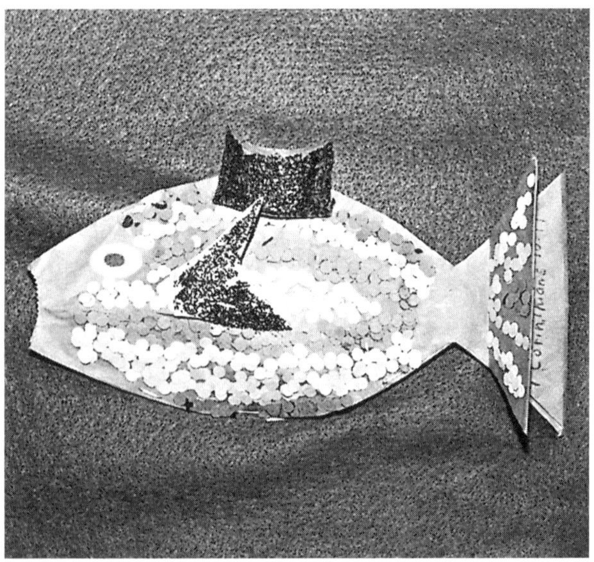

STEP 4: Decorate fish with paper, glitter, or sequins.

STEP 5: Use pattern. Cut fins. Write Bible verse on fin.

STEP 6: Trace bread basket pattern on tissue roll. Fold and cut slits as shown on pattern. Glue in place. Decorate. Place pictures of bread from magazines in basket or make round loaves of bread. Sign up to be the song leader for our service today.

Workstation 4: Sermon or Bible Study

GETTING READY

Bring bread. Make sure that there is a small piece of bread for each person in your group. Serve bread after sermon.

INSTRUCTION SIGN

Jesus did not grow up in a rich household. There might have been only one round loaf of bread to share at some meals.

Practice puppet play. Some spaces have been left blank for you to fill in. Read 1 Corinthians 10:17; 11:23-24 before you start. Remember to read the puppet parts LOUDLY so that everyone can hear the sermon. Need 4 puppeteers and 4 readers.

PUPPET PLAY FOR SERMON:

The Leftover Bread

[Have bread that you plan to serve after sermon sitting in the center of the worship table today.]

**PUPPET #1
_________:** Wow! Look how much bread there is.

**PUPPET #2
_________:** Scoot closer so we'll be first in line.

**PUPPET #3
_________:** I want the biggest piece.

PUPPET #2: Not if I get there first.

**PUPPET #4
_________:** Wait a minute! Didn't the teacher say something about how we're supposed to share? Isn't that the purpose of having bread each Sunday?

PUPPET #1: Nobody will know. And besides, there's always leftover bread.

PUPPET #4: But the idea is to share. Jesus shared his life and teachings with the disciples. The disciples went out and shared, and we're called to share.

PUPPET #3: What does that have to do with bread? We were talking about bread, remember.

PUPPET #2: I'm hungry. Let's eat.

PUPPET #1: Shhh! She'll hear you. Then we'll have to go to the end of the line.

PUPPET #4: You're missing the whole point. The idea is not to stuff our mouths full. The idea is to share.

PUPPET #3: If we each only take one small piece of bread, there'll always be enough bread for everyone to have a piece.

PUPPET #2: I get it. By sharing bread together each week we share kindness, love, and all the things Jesus taught.

PUPPET #1: If you're so smart, figure out these Bible verses: Luke 13:20-21. It says something about heaven being like the yeast making bread dough rise.

PUPPET #3: I think that means we'll have to let those two new boys that moved in down the street play baseball with us this afternoon after church.

PUPPET #1: I suppose we'll also have to let them use our ball and bat.

PUPPET #4: It might not be so bad.

PUPPET #1: I guess that means we aren't going to grab a handful of bread either?

PUPPET #2: Sounds like it!

PUPPET #3: Well, this sharing stuff may not be all bad.

PUPPET #4: We might decide we like it. Maybe that's why we come to church.

PUPPET #2: Will you stop? You sound like the teacher.

**ALL PUPPETS
TOGETHER:** Only _one_ piece.

*Workstations 3 (Offering or Carpenter Shop)
and 5 (Witness to Faith) Combined*

GETTING READY

Have enough bread dough for each child to make a small loaf of bread. See recipe in Session 18. Have bread dough mixed ahead of time so that children only knead and braid bread today. Work on a piece of foil and take bread home to rise and bake. Small loaves are best when baked at 300°F.

INSTRUCTION SIGN

Each year Christian churches around the world join together on the first Sunday in October and celebrate "World Communion Sunday." Communion is when people share in the Lord's Supper by eating bread as a part of the worship service. This service may take many forms and be called by many names: the Lord's Supper, Eucharist, or Holy Communion.

Read Matthew 26:26 and 1 Corinthians 10:17. Make bread to take home and share with your family. Shape bread into a round loaf or braid with three strands for the Trinity: Father, Son, and Holy Spirit. Let rise at home for an hour. Then, bake at 300° F. Sign up to be the Bible reader today for our service.

Workstation 6: Prayer and Sewing Center

INSTRUCTION SIGN

Continue working on commandment banner today. Read Luke 11:3. Sign up to lead the Lord's Prayer for our service today.

Workstation 7: Benediction

INSTRUCTION SIGN

In Jesus' time, bread was served at every meal and had to be made fresh every morning because it spoiled so easily. It was usually served in small, round loaves. Bread was not cut with a knife because bread was a symbol of life. Instead, bread was broken apart with the hands. Make a round loaf of bread.

STEP 1: Trace "bottom crust" patterns. Make one yellow and one brown crust.

STEP 2: The word "bread" is also used in the Bible to mean that Jesus is the "Bread of Life" or the necessary ingredient that makes our lives complete. Read John 6:35. On yellow crust, write: "Jesus is the bread of life" (John 6:35).

STEP 3: Tear scrap paper into small pieces. Place scrap paper between bread-crust circles. Glue edges closed. Do not wad paper; wadded paper doesn't work as well. Layers of scrap paper inside provide thickness for bread.

STEP 4: For top of bread, select either yellow or brown paper for top crust. Fold paper in half. Trace "top broken half" patterns. Remember to place pattern on FOLD of paper.

STEP 5: Again, place scrap paper inside each "top broken half." Glue edges closed. Staple to bottom crust. Make sure top halves still open to reveal Bible verse.

STEP 6: For a bumpy top crust, roll scrap pieces of brown paper into small balls and glue on top of round loaf. Sign up to read the Bible verse during the worship service today.

The Worship Celebration

SIGN-UP SHEET FOR TODAY'S WORSHIP
CELEBRATION

Call to Worship/Affirmation (lead a favorite
song):
Offering/Witness (read 1 Corinthians 10:17):
Sermon (4 puppeteers and 4 readers for "The
Leftover Bread"):
Prayer (lead the Lord's Prayer):
Benediction (read John 6:35):

ITEMS TO GO HOME TODAY: FISH; BREAD
TO BAKE; PAPER BREAD

Session 17
What Is a Missionary?

The Bible Lesson

To teach the gospel through our daily actions (Mark 16:15).

What the Children Will Learn Today

Each workstation tells about a missionary country.

Time Needed

5 minutes for story
20 minutes for workstations
10 minutes for closing worship service

Supplies Needed (by Workstation)

1. Balloons, juice cans, construction paper supply basket
2. White paper for paper chains, scrap paper and cloth, pictures of people from different countries, and craft supply basket
3. Frozen-juice lids, a nail, a hammer, felt, and string
4. Japanese lantern, puppets, and script for sermon
5. Cereal boxes, brown paper, patterns, tissue paper rolls, white paper, brown tissue paper, and craft supply basket
6. 2-liter plastic pop bottles, brown paper (grocery bags), patterns, stockings, yarn for hair, and craft supply basket
7. Construction paper, craft supply basket, and tepee pattern

Children's Meditation

STORY

The Eight-Year-Old Missionary

Terry sat quietly in church staring at the Sunday bulletin. On the front cover was a photograph of a banner that read "Come Follow Me." Under the picture were the words "Be a Missionary."

Today was Missionary Sunday. The anthem was an African prayer song with conga drums. Can you imagine having conga drums right in the middle of the service? Terry was impressed.

There were appeals to save soup labels for the mission project in the Appalachian Mountains. A man spoke about needing volunteers to sign up to go to South America this summer and establish an agricultural center.

Terry was beginning to daydream when he heard the minister say something about how all people could volunteer to be missionaries, no matter what their age or where they lived. This must be a trick. Terry knew for certain his mother would never let him sign up; after all, his mother said no to everything.

How's an eight-year-old boy supposed to help farmers in South America anyway? His mother certainly wasn't going to let him volunteer to go to South America, and besides, he didn't know a thing about farming.

The minister went on to say that missionaries are nothing more than representatives who go out on a specific mission to teach others about Jesus. The minister said children at school could be missionaries by being nice to someone who was unpopular; family members could treat one another kindly instead of fighting and arguing; even the youngest child could serve as a missionary by sharing smiles instead of frowns.

Me, a missionary for Christ! Terry mused.

When Terry's sister made an annoying humming noise on the way home, instead of kicking her, Terry ignored her. When she hummed louder, Terry still didn't respond. After about fifteen minutes, she quit. *It's working,* thought Terry.

Terry decided to see how many arguments and fights he could avoid. He laid a piece of paper on the desk in his room to keep a tally. Who knows, maybe the minister was right, perhaps an eight-year-old could become a missionary without ever leaving home.

Workstations

Workstation 1: Call to Worship

GETTING READY

Use 12-inch balloons. If you use a different size balloon, make your own pattern. Plan a simple song for the Call to Worship. Have children play drums as they sing together.

INSTRUCTION SIGN

A missionary might be sent to a small village in the African jungle or to the rice paddies of Korea. You can become a missionary, too, without ever leaving home. All you have to do is learn to tell others about Jesus by how you live your life. The first step is to say kind words. Read Proverbs 21:23-24.

Make an African drum to play along with the Call to Worship.

STEP 1:   Cut paper and cover sides of juice can.

STEP 2:   Decorate drum with kind words and a Bible verse.

STEP 3:   Cut and stretch balloon over open end of juice can. Keep balloon tight. Play drum with your fingers.

Workstation 2: Affirmation of Faith

GETTING READY

You need pictures of people from different cultures. An encyclopedia, "C" for clothing, works fine.

INSTRUCTION SIGN

Missionaries travel all around the world. Read Mark 16:15. Where would you send missionaries? Make a paper people chain.

STEP 1:   Fold paper to make a paper fan but wider. Fold width of pattern. Trace pattern. Remember to place the fold of the pattern on the fold of paper. Write Bible verse on chain.

STEP 2:   Make clothes for the people on your paper chain to represent people from around the world. Use the craft supplies available and dress person in their native costume. Cut clothes from scrap paper or simply draw costumes. Draw faces. Sign up to be the Bible reader for today's service (Mark 16:15).

Workstation 3: Offering or Carpenter Shop

GETTING READY

Use a board as a backing for the tin-punching because tin-punching leaves an imprint. Adult supervision required.

INSTRUCTION SIGN

Missionaries often wear a Christian symbol telling others they are followers of Jesus. Read Acts 1:8 and sign up to read this verse in the service today. Make a fish necklace. Nail punch around the pattern of the fish on a juice lid. Punch a large hole in the top of the lid and run a string through for necklace. Cut and glue circle of felt to cover the back of lid. Wear fish home as a reminder to be a missionary.

Workstation 4: Sermon or Bible Study

INSTRUCTION SIGN

We often think that missionaries only go to poor, underdeveloped countries, but many missionaries go to industrialized countries too. Missionaries teach farming, provide medical services, and even build universities. Make Japanese lanterns (fold paper, cut slashes, staple together, and make handle) for the puppets to use and to remind yourself that Jesus is the Light that Christians all around the world follow. Read John 8:12 and 3:21. Write answers for puppets as needed in play. You need 2 puppeteers, 2 readers, and 2 lanterns.

PUPPET PLAY FOR SERMON

The Missionaries

MARK:	[Hold lantern and speak loudly.] Go into all the world and tell everyone that Jesus is the Light of the World.
JUDY:	What is that supposed to mean? [no lantern yet]
MARK:	I'm not sure, but I think it means we should follow Jesus and encourage others to follow him too.
JUDY:	How can we encourage others to follow Jesus?
MARK:	[Write your own answer. Reread Matthew 5:43-48 for help.]
JUDY:	For as long as I can remember, my Sunday school teachers, Mom, and Dad have all said, "Follow Jesus!" but no one ever tells me how.
MARK:	You begin by reading the Bible.
JUDY:	Jesus talked about life a long time ago. I mean today—here and now.
MARK:	Many of the problems we face today are the same problems people faced in Jesus' time. Problems like greed, anger, cheating, being mean to someone, teasing, and people thinking they're better or more important than someone else.
JUDY:	You mean nothing has changed?
MARK:	The clothes we wear and the houses we live in have changed, but the problems stay the same.
JUDY:	We want to wear fancier clothes than our neighbor, be more important, and [write in your own end to the sentence].
MARK:	Maybe we can't change the world, but we could at least change ourselves and change how we act. It's a start.
JUDY:	What should we do first?
MARK:	We could [write your own answer. Read Luke 6:32-36].
JUDY:	That sounds great! Do you have another lantern?
MARK AND JUDY:	Go into all the world and tell everyone that Jesus is the Light of the World. [Use lanterns.]

Workstation 5: Witness to Faith

INSTRUCTION SIGN

Missionaries also help build hospitals in remote areas. A missionary sent to build a hospital with the Alaskan Indians might want to learn about the customs and traditions of the people.

Alaskan Indians of the Northwest make totem poles to tell about their family history and beliefs. Make an Alaskan Log Cabin Hospital with a Totem Pole that tells about God's love. Read Proverbs 18:1-4; 20-21.

Easy Version: Tape 2 empty cereal boxes together. Cover the boxes with brown paper. Draw windows and doors on the cabin. Use totem pole patterns. Draw pictures on your totem pole paper to tell the story of God's love. Glue to a paper towel tube. Add wings and beak for bird. Glue pole to side of hospital.

Harder Version:

STEP 1: Use pattern and cut a floor for the hospital. Make paper logs by rolling brown paper on a pencil. Glue logs onto floor. Alternate logs to make log cabin. If you want a door and windows, be sure to leave space for them as you work.

STEP 2: Use pattern and cut totem pole paper. Decorate and tell a story with your totem pole. Totem poles are elaborate and colorful. Sign up to tell others about God's love with your totem pole in the service. Write today's Bible verse at bottom of pole. Add wings and beak.

STEP 3: You may also add a stone chimney to the hospital by rolling brown tissue paper into tight balls and gluing onto chimney. Trace pattern for chimney. Place cotton in top for smoke. Place hospital on worship table to remind us to help.

Workstation 6: Prayer and Sewing Center

GETTING READY

Make examples of fringe or doll.

INSTRUCTION SIGN

Some of the first missionaries to the United States came to tell the Native Americans about Jesus. Make a Native American Indian Doll as a reminder that missionaries once came to our country just as we now send missionaries to other countries.

Read Mark 16:15 and Acts 1:8.

STEP 1: Trace patterns. Cut fringe for hem on dress. Glue dress to bottle. Put rubber band around neck of bottle.

STEP 2: Trace pattern for apron. Cut fringe for apron. Glue TOP EDGE ONLY of apron to neck of bottle.

STEP 3: Cut 2 sleeves. Fringe ends. Glue sleeve to neck. Stuff round ball of scrap stocking or cloth in end for hand.

STEP 4: Roll brown stocking into round ball, forming a hole in center. Glue to bottle cap. Use sequins or beads for face.

STEP 5: Wrap black yarn around book 15 times. Keep yarn flat. Tape center of yarn. Cut yarn in half. Glue tape side down from face to back of neck. Braid yarn for headband or add elastic headband. You can braid hair or leave straight.

STEP 6: Trace pattern for shirt. Fringe edges. Glue over arms. Place your finished Native American Indian doll on the worship table today to remind us to be missionaries this week. Sign up to lead the Lord's Prayer for today's service.

Workstation 7: Benediction

INSTRUCTION SIGN

We often think of missionaries overseas, but we have missionaries right here in our country. Many missionaries work as teachers. There are mission schools in the Appalachian Mountains, on Indian reservations, and in big cities for minorities and migrant farmworkers' children.

In the past, Native Americans of the plains lived in tepees and moved following the great buffalo herds. Today, many of the Native Americans live on reservations. Some of them do not have much money and often cannot build adequate schools for their children. Missionary Schools help children to get an education and also teach about God's love.

Use the pattern and make a tepee to remind us of the proud traditions of the Native Americans. The Plains Indians painted pictures on the outsides of their tepees to tell a story. Draw or paint pictures on your tepee to tell the story of the life and teachings of Jesus.

You are a missionary for Christ every time you are kind to someone. Read Proverbs 22:9 and Mark 16:15. Sign up to tell how to avoid an argument in today's service. Write today's Bible verse on your tepee. Then, glue edges of tepee together. Place tepee on the worship table.

The Worship Celebration

SIGN-UP SHEET FOR TODAY'S WORSHIP CELEBRATION

Call to Worship (song with drums):
Affirmation (read Mark 16:15):
Offering (read Acts 1:8):
Sermon (2 puppeteers and 2 readers for "The Missionaries"):
Witness (tell about God's love with totem pole):
Prayer (lead the Lord's Prayer):
Benediction (tell one way to avoid an argument):

ITEMS TO GO HOME TODAY: INDIAN DOLL; TEPEE; HOSPITAL; AFRICAN DRUM; PEOPLE CHAIN; FISH NECKLACE; JAPANESE LANTERNS

Session 18
The Thanksgiving Dinner

The Bible Lesson

Matthew 25:40 reminds us to give to others every day.

What the Children Will Learn Today

Children enjoy cooking. Thanksgiving dinner can become a tradition. Workstations provide historical facts and crafts.

Time Needed

5 minutes for story
30 minutes for workstations
closing circle with Lord's Prayer for benediction

Supplies Needed (by Workstation)

Story: table card (Benediction)
1. See recipe for bread.
2. See recipe for cake and icing.
3. See recipe for fruit salad. Cover box for donation.
4. See recipe for sweet potatoes.
5. Construction paper, Thanksgiving center-piece patterns, old stockings or unbleached coffee filters, and stapler
6. See recipe for pie.
7. Construction paper supply basket and patterns

(Some recipes need to be cooked after session. Adult supervision is required for using stove. Seek donations. Families or adult Sunday school classes are often happy to help.)

Children's Meditation

GETTING READY

Use example of the Thanksgiving table card.

STORY

The Thanksgiving Basket

Jessica selected thirty-five big, shiny red apples to take to church. The children's worship class at Jessica's church was cooking Thanksgiving dinner for a needy family. Jessica had volunteered to bring apples. Jessica only needed to bring three apples, but Jessica picked out thirty-five of the store's juiciest apples.

Jessica's class was cooking a complete Thanksgiving dinner. They were going to have turkey, a cake, pies, cookies, sweet potatoes, fruit salad, and homemade bread.

Jessica made a card to go with her apples. When the card was opened [show card] there was a table set for Thanksgiving.

The card read "Happy Thanksgiving! We've included all of our special favorites, even peanut butter and jelly. You'll also find 35 juicy apples in the box. You only need 3 for the salad. The extras represent the 32 children in our class. We hope you have the happiest Thanksgiving ever."

Workstations

Workstation 1: Call to Worship

GETTING READY

Divide into work teams. Have one group mix bread dough, another peel and cook apples, and another prepare icing. Younger children should not work with hot pans or stove. Baking done after session. Look through recipe and make a shopping list.

INSTRUCTION SIGN

The Hebrews celebrate the Feast of Tabernacles, as they did when Jesus was a boy. Usually in October, they build tabernacles or booths to mark the end of the farming and harvest season. Celebration lasts for seven days. Read Nehemiah 8:13-18.

CARAMEL APPLE STRUDEL BREAD
Ingredients for bread:

½ cup water
½ cup milk
½ cup margarine
2 eggs
5 cups flour
½ cup sugar
2 teaspoons salt
3 small packets quick-rise yeast

Oven temperature: 325°

Bread: Heat water, milk, and margarine in a pan till it starts to bubble. Do not let boil. Adult supervision for stove.

Mix eggs, flour, sugar, salt, and yeast in bowl. Add hot milk to flour mixture. Knead dough till smooth and elastic. Divide the dough in half. Set half the dough aside to rise.

Make 12 round balls from second half of dough. Roll each ball into a long pencil shape with hands. Tie dough into a knot. Set aside to rise for 2 hours. Mix filling.

Ingredients for filling:
1 apple
1 tablespoon margarine
½ cup sugar
2 teaspoons cinnamon
6 tablespoons melted margarine
½ cup Smucker's Caramel Flavor Topping
2 tablespoon applesauce
1 tablespoon sugar
1 teaspoon cinnamon

Filling: Cut the apple into quarters or bite-size chunks. Simmer in skillet with 1 tablespoon margarine for 5 minutes. This gives a baked-apple taste to the apple. Set aside to cool.

Mix ½ cup sugar, 2 teaspoons cinnamon, and 6 tablespoons melted margarine together in a bowl and set aside for filling.

Roll remaining dough into 8 balls about the size of your fist. Flatten each ball of dough and place 1 teaspoon caramel topping, 1 tablespoon cinnamon-sugar mixture, and 1 piece of cooked apple on the bread dough. Roll the bread dough around filling and place on buttered cookie sheet. Makes 8.

Spread 2 tablespoons applesauce over the tops of the round balls of dough. Sprinkle with 1 tablespoon sugar and 1 teaspoon cinnamon. Cover and let rise again for 2 hours.

Bake bread in oven at 325° for 30 minutes or until lightly browned.

Ingredients for icing:
4 tablespoons margarine
1 cup confectioners' sugar
1 tablespoon milk

Icing: Melt margarine with adult supervision. Add sugar and milk. Pour icing over warm apple bread fresh out of the oven. Drizzle remaining caramel topping over the icing.

Workstation 2: Affirmation of Faith

GETTING READY

Divide into work teams. Have one group measure ingredients.

<table>
<tr><td>

INSTRUCTION SIGN

In England in the 1600s, the church, as well as the government, was run by the king. The worship services were filled with organ music and choirs. The churches were often decorated with gold and elaborate stained-glass windows. The Pilgrims' church was very plain with absolutely no decorations, fancy windows, or organ music. Read 1 Peter 2:15-16.

In England, it was against the law at the time not to agree with the Church of England. The Pilgrims, or separatists as they were called, were often arrested for their beliefs.

Bake a chocolate cake for our dinner basket to remind us to give more than canned goods to those in need.

</td></tr>
</table>

FUDGY CHOCOLATE-CHERRY CAKE

Ingredients for cake:
    1 package (4 ounces) Baker's German Sweet
        Chocolate
    1 cup (2 sticks) margarine, softened
    2 cups sugar
    4 eggs
    2 cups all-purpose flour
    1 teaspoon baking soda
    ¼ teaspoon salt
    1 tablespoon vanilla
    1 teaspoon butter flavoring
    1 can (21 oz.) cherry pie filling

Preheat oven to 350°. Grease one 13" x 9" disposable aluminum cake pan with shortening and dust lightly with flour.

Melt chocolate with adult supervision. Set aside.

With an electric mixer or by hand, cream margarine, sugar, and eggs together until light and fluffy. Add flour, baking soda, salt, vanilla, melted chocolate, and butter flavoring. Mix well.

Stir in 1 can of cherry pie filling by hand. Mix well. Pour batter into prepared pan. Bake 40 minutes or until toothpick inserted in center comes out clean.

CHERRY BUTTERCREAM ICING

Ingredients for icing:
    ½ cup margarine
    ½ cup solid vegetable shortening
    2 teaspoons vanilla
    2 teaspoons butter flavoring
    4 cups confectioners' sugar
    2 tablespoons cherry juice

Cream margarine, shortening, flavorings, sugar, and cherry juice together. Cream till smooth. Spread over top of cake.

Workstation 3: Offering or Carpenter Shop

GETTING READY

Copy fruit recipe.

INSTRUCTION SIGN

The Pilgrims left England and lived in Holland for 12 years. The Dutch allowed the Pilgrims to worship as they pleased, but the Dutch celebrated Sunday as a holiday with family gatherings and joy. The Pilgrims solemnly spent most of Sunday in church, praying for hours. The Pilgrim children had to sit quietly during the long prayers while their Dutch friends played outside.

Do NOT make the salad; just put fruit and recipe in box. Cover box with paper. Then decorate box. Draw pictures of things you are thankful for. Make box look pretty. Read 2 Peter 1:5-8.

FRUIT SALAD

1 cantaloupe
1 jar (10 oz.) maraschino cherries
1 can (8 oz.) pineapple chunks
1 Delicious apple
1 orange, peeled
1 banana
1 kiwi
20 grapes

Recipe to be given with fruit. Do NOT cut fruit.

Cut cantaloupe in half. Scrape seeds out. With a melon spoon, scoop out the fruit from the cantaloupe and set aside.

Pour cherries and pineapple (with juice) into a bowl. Cut and core apple. Cut into bite-size pieces. Peel orange, banana, and kiwi. Cut into bite-size pieces. Add grapes and cantaloupe. Mix fruit together. Put fruit in cantaloupe shells.

Workstation 4: Sermon or Bible Study

GETTING READY

Boil potatoes ahead of time. This dish stores easily.

INSTRUCTION SIGN

On September 6, 1620, the *Mayflower* set sail with 102 men, women, and children, plus dogs, cats, birds, and other livestock. Food and water were in short supply. All cooking had to be done below decks on small iron trays filled with sand. A small fire was built on top of the sand. The food was not very good.

Family cabins were only five feet high and about the size of a twin bed. The entire family lived in the cabin for nine and a half weeks. The ship rocked and pitched so much that people tied themselves in their beds to keep from falling out. Life was very hard for the Pilgrims on this trip. Read Proverbs 22:9.

Then work together to make sweet potatoes for food basket.

SWEET POTATOES

8 medium-size sweet potatoes or yams
1 stick of margarine
½ cup brown sugar, packed
1 teaspoon cinnamon
1 pint of cream

(Cook potatoes in boiling water before session until done.)

Peel and mash potatoes in a baking dish. Add margarine while potatoes are hot or melt margarine. Stir in sugar and cinnamon. Gradually add pint of cream, stirring slowly until completely mixed. Spread into 13" x 9" disposable aluminum pan.

Sprinkle the top with brown sugar. Bake 40 minutes at 350° or until lightly browned on top. (Sweet Potatoes and Cake may be baked at the same time.)

Workstation 5: Witness to Faith

INSTRUCTION SIGN

During the long voyage on the *Mayflower,* the Pilgrim children studied lessons, read the Bible every day, and played word games. "Twenty Questions" was a favorite game.

Make Pilgrim and Native American Indian centerpiece dolls to go in our Thanksgiving basket. You may even make a doll to take home as a reminder of how difficult life was for the Pilgrim children and how difficult life still is today for many children around the world. Read 2 Peter 1:10-11.

Pilgrim

STEP 1:   Trace patterns for dress, sleeves, hat, apron, and collar. Use dark blue or black paper for dress. Make hat, apron, and collar from white paper for Pilgrim.

STEP 2:   Fold dress as you would to make a paper fan. Glue only side edges of skirt together to make a circular skirt. Make sure edges are level across the bottom so skirt will stand up.

STEP 3:   Roll sleeves on pencil. Glue edges to form a cylinder. Gather at neck of dress. Staple sleeves to neck. Leave opening for head. Roll scrap of stocking or sock into tight tiny ball. Glue ball in end of sleeve for hands.

STEP 4:   Glue top edge of apron to front of dress at neck.

STEP 5:   Stuff an old stocking or sock with cotton balls or stuffing. Make about a 1½" round head. Tie a knot in stocking to keep the head round. Gently stuff extra stocking through top of dress. Glue stocking in place inside dress or staple extra stocking to back of dress.

STEP 6:   Collar should fit neatly around neck. Glue down.

STEP 7:   Fold and glue hat together in back. Hair is not necessary but you may add if desired. Glue hat to head. Leave face plain as was the Pilgrim custom.

Native American Indian

STEP 1:   Follow same directions as before but use brown paper and fringe the edges of sleeves and collar. Glue Indian blanket around neck of doll. Glue blanket on last.

STEP 2:   Make a braided wig by cutting 30 strands of yarn the length desired. Place yarn evenly on masking tape. Glue masking-tape side of hair to top of Indian doll's head. Tape should not show. Hair should cover doll's head from front of face to back of neck. Braid. Tie off braids. Make headband.

Workstation 6: Prayer and Sewing Center

GETTING READY

Have one group make the pie crust while another group mixes the pie filling. You may also substitute a favorite pie recipe.

INSTRUCTION SIGN

The Pilgrims stood for hours praying during each worship service. All religious days were observed with prayer and fasting. Christmas and other religious holidays were spent in quiet, solemn prayer.

After the first winter, only 54 Pilgrims were still alive. Twenty-one were children sixteen years old or younger.

The First Thanksgiving was not a religious holiday for the Pilgrims. Thanksgiving was a harvest celebration. Read 1 Peter 5:6-7 and then make a pumpkin pie.

PUMPKIN PIE

Ingredients for pie crust:
⅔ cup shortening
2 cups flour
4 to 6 tablespoons ice water

Crust: Cut shortening into flour with pastry blender. Add water until mixture will hold together and form soft ball.

Roll out on floured board to desired size for pie pan. Line pie pan with dough. Make decorative edges for crust.

Ingredients for pumpkin pie filling:
4 eggs
1 can (16 oz.) solid pack pumpkin
½ cup sugar
¼ cup brown sugar
2 teaspoons ground cinnamon
½ teaspoon ground ginger
2 cups whipping cream
½ teaspoon vanilla

Filling: Preheat oven to 425°. Mix ingredients in mixing bowl. Pour into pie shell. Adult supervision for oven required.

Bake 15 minutes at 425°. Reduce oven to 350° and continue baking for 45 minutes or until knife inserted comes out clean.

Workstation 7: Benediction

INSTRUCTION SIGN

The Native American Indians who lived near Plymouth where the Pilgrims settled also celebrated a harvest festival called the "Green Corn Dance." Every year they burned their old clothes and made new ones for the festival. The festival lasted four days, food, games, and fun for everyone. The menu included such items as corn from the fall harvest, birds, ducks, geese, turkey, deer, eels, clams, lobsters, oysters, biscuits, corn bread, hoecakes, Indian pudding, and popcorn, which was popped in earthen jars over the coals. There's no mention of cranberries or pumpkin pie.

Make a card to send to someone special this Thanksgiving. Write a special message. Read Proverbs 3:27-31 for ideas.

STEP 1: Trace table and leg patterns. Decorate table by drawing or cutting pictures of food. Decorate outside of card.

STEP 2: Fold and glue table legs as indicated on pattern. When dry, your table will fold inside the card and pop up when you open the card. Write a message of love on your card.

The Worship Celebration

GETTING READY

Today's session is filled with cooking. Close with the Lord's Prayer.

ITEMS TO GO HOME TODAY: EXTRA CARDS AND CENTERPIECES

9

A Moment for Peace: An Advent Workshop

The Bible Lesson

The second chapters of both Luke and Matthew tell the story today.

What the Children Will Learn Today

Workstations tell how Christians around the world celebrate.

Time Needed

5 minutes for story
20 minutes for workstations
10 minutes for closing worship service

Supplies Needed (by Workstation)

1. 3" balloons, papier-mâché, and newspapers
2. 2-liter pop bottles, cloth for biblical clothes, black or brown yarn, skin-colored socks or stockings, and beads
3. Scrap wood, nails, and tools needed to build manger
4. Script and props needed for Christmas Eve Service
5. White tissue paper, 2-liter clear pop bottles, red ribbon, 14" white pipe cleaners, rubber bands, skin-colored socks or stockings for head and hands, and patterns
6. Purchase Darice brand #06101-5 yellow 8 mm beads, 340 #06101-5 clear beads, and 12-inch chenille stems
7. Copy "Church Advent Windows" and "Advent Take Home Worship Workbook" for each child.

Children's Meditation

STORY

Getting Ready for Christmas

It was a cold, dreary winter day. Megan sat at the kitchen table watching the rain splash against the windowpanes.

Megan hated winter. Winter spoiled everything. Snow was fun, but after a while even snow annoyed Megan.

Megan sat at a table covered with books. Mrs. Loftus, Megan's teacher, had told the class to research the origin of their family's Christmas celebration. There were lots of children from different countries. Raddika's family was from India, and she was planning to tell about the Diwali Festival of Lights. Jose's grandparents still lived in Mexico. One year Jose and his family visited and attended all nine La Posada celebrations. Rachel was Jewish and planned to tell about Hanukkah. Tuhun was doing his report on Kwanza. Megan couldn't think of anything.

Megan began to read silently to herself, " 'Advent began as a period of fasting for forty or fifty days before Christmas. Advent was a time of spiritual preparation.' " No cookies! No candy! That didn't sound like much of a celebration. Megan continued looking for something interesting. " 'Christmas was not always celebrated on December 25. For a time, Christ's birthday was celebrated on January 6, and some

Christians still celebrate on the sixth of January.'

"Jesus makes Christmas special," said Megan to herself. "After all, it is his birthday." Oh, Megan knew that December 25 wasn't the actual day Jesus was born, but that didn't matter. Christmas was a celebration of love.

Megan started to think about everything she enjoyed doing at Christmas. Lighting the candles on the Advent wreath, opening the windows on the Advent calendar, the tree . . . Suddenly Megan dropped the book she was holding.

"This'll be a great report," she said out loud. "I can make an Advent wreath and calendar to show to the class. I can also tell about the Christments we made. I even have pictures from last year's workshop." Megan began to write:

"Each year on the first Sunday in Advent, families meet at my church for an Advent workshop to make Christments. Christments are ornaments that tell the story of the life and teachings of Jesus. The Christment Tree is covered with tiny white lights to remind everyone of Christians around the world.

"The Christment Tree is beautiful when the lights are dimmed and everyone holds a candle while singing 'Silent Night' on Christmas Eve. Christmas is the most wonderful time of the year when we celebrate God's love and the birth of Jesus." Megan began to write faster as she became excited just thinking about Christmas.

Workstations

Workstation 1: Call to Worship

GETTING READY

Use cover-ups and covers for table. Mix papier-mâché.

INSTRUCTION SIGN

In the early sixteenth century, rich people in Italy played a game using a round clay cooking pot swung from a rope and pole. The clay pot would be hit with a stick until it broke. Everyone scrambled to gather the contents. The idea traveled from Italy to Spain where the first Sunday in Advent became known as "Piñata Sunday." Piñatas are still used the nine evenings before Christmas for the "posadas." "Posada" means "inn" and is a reenactment of Mary and Joseph's search for lodging.

Make a piñata lamb to help get ready for Christmas. Read the story of the Shepherds in Luke 2:8-10.

First Week of Advent

STEP 1: Blow up a small 3" balloon and cover the balloon with wet papier-mâché scrap paper strips.

STEP 2: Once balloon is covered, glue 4 tiny balls of dry paper UNDERNEATH balloon for feet.

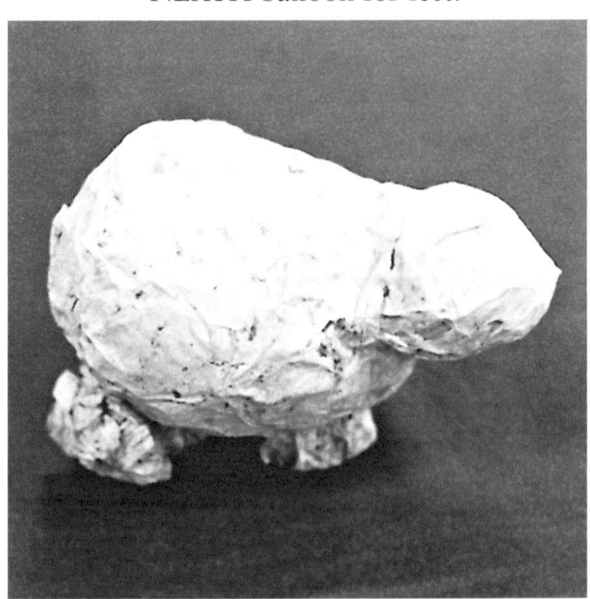

Go to Workstation 7 while lamb dries. Sign up to read Luke 2:1-3 for the service today.

Workstation 2: Affirmation of Faith

INSTRUCTION SIGN

"Nativity" means "birth." Create your own Nativity scene. Start today by making Mary. Read Luke 2:1-3.

STEP 1: Trace tunic pattern on cloth. Women often wore shades of blue in biblical times.

STEP 2: Gather tunic around pop bottle. Make sure hem covers the bottom of bottle. Fold edges under so that fabric does not ravel. Glue fabric to pop bottle.

STEP 3: Trace arm pattern from same cloth as tunic. Make 2 arms. Roll into a cylinder. Glue in place at neck of bottle. Rubber-band arms and neck of tunic to neck of pop bottle.

STEP 4: Trace and cut cloak. Cut diamond shape in center for neck opening. See pattern. Tie cloak loosely over tunic.

STEP 5: Roll sock or stocking into ball to form head. Glue to bottle cap. Decorate face with beads or sequins.

STEP 6: Flat-wrap yarn around a book 15 times for Mary's hair (no yarn should be bunched or overlapping any other strand). Tape down center with masking tape. Slide yarn off book. Cut hair in half. Glue to head. Drape cloth covering over head.

You are in charge of leading the opening Christmas carol for today's worship service. Sing "O Come, O Come, Emmanuel." Place Mary on the worship table today to remind us of HOPE.

Workstation 3: Offering or Carpenter Shop

INSTRUCTION SIGN

A manger is a clay feeding trough dug in the side of a limestone cave or stone wall as a place to feed animals. Wooden mangers were constructed from leftover scraps of wood.

Build a manger. Read Luke 2:12. Sign up to light candle.

Step 1: Cut four 2" x 2" boards 36" long for ends.

Step 2: Nail and glue boards together to form X shape.

Step 3: Cut eight 1" x 2" boards exactly 36" long or cut plywood board to fit. Glue 1" x 2" boards in place. Let dry.

Workstation 4: Sermon or Bible Study

GETTING READY

Have copy of Christmas Eve service for practice.

INSTRUCTION SIGN

St. Francis of Assisi, an Italian monk, reenacted the Christmas story with village participants to explain the meaning of Christmas to peasants who could not read. Read Luke 2:7.

During the four weeks of Advent, you will be practicing for our Christmas Eve Worship Service. Today's closing worship service is taken from the "Call to Worship" section of the Christmas Eve program. Read more slowly than you normally talk, emphasize phrasing, and work on reading with expression.

Sign up to read the first "Nativity Narrator" from the Christmas Eve service for our closing worship service today.

Workstation 5: Witness to Faith

GETTING READY

White tissue paper works best for this project.

INSTRUCTION SIGN

In Sweden, children begin their Christmas season on December 13 with "Santa Lucia Day." Lucia was a Roman Christian during the early days of the church and the time of persecution. She chose to die rather than deny her faith in Jesus Christ.

Later there was also a great famine and time of persecution for Christians in Sweden. The story is told that Saint Lucia came to the Swedish Christians who were meeting in underground caves to pray. The legend says that Lucia brought them food secretly so that they wouldn't starve. According to the legend, Lucia wore a crown with seven candles to light her way as she carried trays of food.

Saint Lucia has become a Christmas symbol for helping others. Read Luke 6:27-28. Work the next four weeks to make a pop-bottle Saint Lucia to take home as a reminder to help others. For today's service, you're the "1st Advent Candle Reader."

STEP 1: Roll skin-colored sock or stocking in a round ball for head. Glue head to bottle cap and rubber-band at neck.

STEP 2: Measure and cut three 16" x 13" pieces of white tissue paper for dress. Wrap all 3 pieces of tissue loosely around a clear 2-liter pop bottle. Dress is 13" tall. Gather around neck of pop bottle and secure with a rubber band at neck to hold in place. Do NOT glue tissue paper to pop bottle.

STEP 3: Braid 3 pipe cleaners together to form stiff arms (make 2). Twist in place around bottle cap.

STEP 4: Glue tiny ball of sock or stocking over end of pipe cleaner for hand. Rubber-band to hold in place.

STEP 5: Trace and cut 3 sheets of tissue for each sleeve. Roll around pencil to form cylinder. Slide sleeve onto pipe cleaner. Rubber-band sleeve in place at neck of pop bottle. Sleeve hangs loosely but completely covers pipe cleaner. Rubber band should not show.

STEP 6: Trace and cut cape. Tape cape over sleeves and around neckline to cover rubber bands at neck. Tie a wide red ribbon around neck and over cape. Tie a fancy bow in front. All rubber bands should be covered and not showing. Do NOT glue.

Workstation 6: Prayer and Sewing Center

GETTING READY

The Christment tree was first introduced in 1994. You do not have to make a Christment tree to use this workstation, but if you would like to know more about Christments, see: *The Christment Tree, How to Make Christian Ornaments for Your Christmas Tree, Pattern Book, Vols. I and II* (Meriwether Publishing, 1998).

The beads are inexpensive. Buy Darice brand #06101-5 yellow and #06101-5 clear 8 mm beads and 12" white chenille stems. You need 4 stems, 52 yellow beads, and 52 clear beads per person.

INSTRUCTION SIGN

We are making a Christment (ornament) that explains the meaning of Christmas. The TRIANGLE traditionally symbolizes the Trinity: Father, Son, and the Holy Spirit. A CIRCLE reminds us that God's love never ends. We add the early Christian sign of the fish and the Greek symbols for CHRIST (**XP**) to remind everyone that the birth of Jesus and the sharing of God's love are the reasons we celebrate Christmas. Read Luke 2:14.

STEP 1: String a combined total of 33 yellow and clear beads alternately onto a chenille stem. Shape into a circle. Twist ends tightly together. Trim excess stem. Set aside. See pattern.

STEP 2: String a combined total of 34 yellow and clear beads alternately onto a chenille stem. Shape into a triangle. The base will have 14 beads, and each side has 10 beads each. Shape to fit pattern. Twist ends tightly together. Trim excess stem. Set aside.

STEP 3: String a combined total of 10 yellow and clear beads alternately onto a chenille stem. Attach to triangle and to circle.

STEP 4: String a combined total of 5 yellow and clear beads alternately on stem. Twist into place to form the letter "P." See pattern.

STEP 5: String a combined total of 8 yellow and clear beads alternately on stem. Make "X" as shown on pattern.

STEP 6: String a combined total of 14 yellow and clear beads alternately on stem. Shape to make fish. Attach to circle as shown.

Sign up to lead the Lord's Prayer during worship.

Workstation 7: Benediction

GETTING READY

Copy "Church Advent Windows" page and an "Advent Take-Home Worship Workbook" for each child.

INSTRUCTION SIGN

The tradition of an Advent calendar originated in Norway. Families make a calendar and places candles each week in a window of their homes. In Germany, an Advent wreath is hung over or placed on the dining room table to count the weeks till Christmas.

STEP 1: Trace patterns and make a paper stand-up church to be your Advent calendar. Read Luke 2:1-4. Cut on solid lines.

STEP 2: Before assembling church, add wreaths to doors to symbolize peace, stained-glass windows, and other decorations.

STEP 3: Cut "Church Advent Window" page into 4 weekly strips. Cut evenly on solid line. Do NOT cut dotted lines. Glue or tape strips together in order: 1st week, 2nd week, etc.

STEP 4: Cut Advent slashes on roof. Trace pattern and cut exactly on the lines. Thread the "Church Advent Window" strip through the window as shown in example.

STEP 5: Assemble church by folding roof and gently pushing church front and back steeples through roof slits.

STEP 6: Take your Advent calendar home and use the calendar each day with the Advent Take-Home Worship Workbook.

Your job is to lead the closing Christmas carol after the Advent candle is lit. Sing "Let There Be Peace on Earth."

The Worship Celebration

GETTING READY

Use the "Call to Worship" portion of the Christmas Eve Worship Service for ten-minute worship time this week. Sing only first line of each carol. Make an Advent wreath to use each week.

SIGN-UP SHEET FOR TODAY'S WORSHIP CELEBRATION

Call to Worship (read Luke 2:1-3):
Affirmation (lead first line of "O Come, O Come, Emmanuel"):
Offering (light candle of hope):
Sermon (Nativity Narrator):
Witness (1st Advent Candle Reader):
Prayer (lead the Lord's Prayer):
Benediction (lead first line of "Let There Be Peace on Earth"):

ITEMS TO GO HOME TODAY: ADVENT CALENDAR AND ADVENT TAKE-HOME WORSHIP WORKBOOK

Advent Take-Home Worship Workbook

The children have made Advent calendars to help mark the days till Christmas. Set aside a special time for family worship during Advent. Bible passages and a narration are written for each day of the week. Make an Advent wreath. Read the passages for each day, light the Advent candle, sing a favorite Christmas carol, and close with the Lord's Prayer.

Making an Advent Wreath

Many different traditions are associated with Advent wreaths. First, decide on the type of wreath you want. Anything from a wire ring to a wooden circle to just a simple circle of evergreens can be used. Nonflammable artificial wreaths make an excellent choice. The evergreen circle reminds everyone that life is continuous.

Your second task will be to add four candles to the wreath for the four weeks in Advent and a white Christ candle in the center. There are many traditions surrounding the color of candles used at Advent. Many stores carry three purple candles and one pink as the traditional colors, but there is not one set color. Some churches believe all four candles should be purple or red while still others will have four blue candles to represent truth and honesty. One of the oldest traditions is to use all white candles.

Family Home Worship for the First Week of Advent

Add a Christmas carol and the Lord's Prayer to each day's worship.

First Sunday in Advent: The Candle of Hope

Narrator:	Advent is a time of spiritual preparation; a time spent getting ready to celebrate the birth of Jesus. A plain evergreen wreath is often used without ribbons or decoration. The circular wreath reminds us that God's love lasts forever. The simplicity of the wreath reminds us to be humble.
Bible Lesson: Symbols of Christmas:	Matthew 2:6 and Luke 2:4-6
	Look around your church each week and see if you can find the symbols of Christmas, perhaps on a tree or on a banner. Our first symbol is the CANDLE. Candles are used in church to represent the living light. The Advent candles are symbolic of the coming of Jesus. Jesus is often referred to as the "living light" (1 John 1:5).

Monday

Symbol of Christmas:	A rose is often used at Christmas as a sign of hope.
Narrator:	The Jewish people prayed and hoped for a Messiah. "Messiah" is Hebrew for "chosen one" or leader. The Jewish people wanted a leader to free them from harsh Roman rule.
Bible Lesson:	Isaiah 35:1-2

Tuesday

Bible Lesson:	Luke 2:7
Narrator:	The lower levels of houses were often dug out as caves. In Bethlehem, most simple limestone houses were built with a lower level or cave underneath.
Symbol of Christmas:	Many commercial Nativity scenes use a simple wooden stable to depict the place where Jesus was born. In Italy, the family often makes a cave. A cave would have been nothing more than a hole dug in the side of a limestone hill or a flat roofed clay house. The simple stable reminds us to be humble.

Wednesday

Narrator:	Jesus was called "the good shepherd" because he shows us how to

live a happier life—a life filled with love.

Bible Lesson: John 10:7-10

Symbol of Christmas: Shepherds were very poor and typically not invited to important happenings or events. The shepherd's crook reminds us that simple shepherds were called to the Nativity instead of the rich and important dignitaries of the time.

Thursday

Bible Lesson: Luke 1:50-53

Symbol of Christmas: The simple sign of the fish was used by early Christians. The Greek word for fish (ichthus) is often used at Christmastime to write the phrase IXOYC: I-Jesus, X-Christ, O-God, Y-Son, and C-Savior.

Narrator: If we follow the teachings of Jesus, we are his disciples. As followers, we are to go throughout the world and tell others about God's love.

Friday

Bible Lesson: Jeremiah 33:14-15

Narrator: Many Jews were waiting for a military leader such as King David had been to lead them into battle against the Romans. Jesus said he came instead to bring peace and lead his followers in humble service for God.

Symbol of Christmas: The crown is used to remind us that Jesus was not interested in riches or a position of importance; instead, Jesus lived his life as a simple teacher and encouraged others to "Come, Follow Me."

Saturday

Narrator: Lighting candles is a way of marking the days till Christmas and reminding us each week of the importance of peace and love. Throughout history, when coun-tries have been at war, often countries will cease fighting on Christmas Day. Christmas has traditionally been thought of as a day of Peace.

Bible Lesson: Romans 13:8-10

Symbol of Christmas: The dove is an international symbol of peace. The dove carries a single olive branch offering peace to all.

Home Worship for the Second Week of Advent

Add a Christmas carol and the Lord's Prayer to each day's worship. (Some traditions celebrate the candle of Joy on the third Sunday. Choose the tradition most appropriate for your denomination.)

Second Sunday in Advent: The Candle of Joy

Narrator: Today, we light the candle of Hope and the candle of Joy on the Advent wreath. The second candle is sometimes called the Shepherds' candle and represents the joy of the shepherds when they heard the good news of the birth of Jesus. Jesus said our Joy in life should come from serving God. We serve God when we help someone in need.

Bible Lesson: Matthew 25:37-40

Symbols of Christmas: The shepherds at the Nativity remind us to be humble servants. A simple Nativity scene, not made of gold or decorated with jewels, is a constant reminder that we too should focus on the humble and simple aspects of life. Each day this week, think of a way to help others for Jesus.

Monday

Narrator: Mary, Joseph, the shepherds, and a manger remind us that God is not necessarily seeking popular people or men and women of importance to convey his message of Peace and Love to the world. God sought humble, faithful servants.

Bible Lesson: Luke 2:1-6

Symbol of Christmas: It was most unusual for Joseph to walk while Mary rode the donkey on the trip from Nazareth to Bethlehem, for it was the custom of the time that men rode while the women walked. This simple act of kindness and humility is a reminder that Jesus calls us not to be proud or conceited but to follow him in thinking first of the needs of others.

Tuesday

Bible Lesson: Luke 2:7

Narrator: Many scholars believe that Jesus was born in a shepherd's cave called a "grotto." A shepherd's cave would have been nothing more than a hole dug in the side of a limestone hill. The cave could have been used as a stable for animals and would have provided a warm, dry place for Mary and Joseph to sleep and rest in private.

Symbol of Christmas: A simple stable reminds us that Jesus was not born into a life of luxury.

Wednesday

Symbol of Christmas: Shepherds were very poor and typically not invited to important happenings or events. Yet shepherds were called to the Nativity, not the rich and important dignitaries of the time.

Narrator: Jesus was called "the good shepherd" because he shows us how to live a happier life—a life filled with love.

Bible Lesson: John 10:7-10

Thursday

Bible Lesson: Luke 2:8-12

Narrator: Although we often say "Jesus Christ" as if it were his full name, Christ is a title. Christ means "anointed or chosen one" in Greek. We are actually saying, Jesus is the chosen one or one chosen to lead us. The Hebrew word for Christ is "Messiah."

Symbol of Christmas: The early Greek Christians used the CHI and RHO (X and P), the Greek initials for Christ, to remind Christians everywhere to follow the teachings of Jesus.

Friday

Bible Lesson: Luke 1:31

Symbol of Christmas: The early Greek Christians told others that they believed in Jesus by decorating their places of worship with the first three letters of his name (Iota Eta Sigma or IHS).

Narrator: Our celebration of the birth of Jesus often gets lost in the middle of busy shopping schedules and parties. What can you do in your family this week to honor Jesus?

Saturday

Bible Lesson: Micah 5:2-5

Narrator: As followers of Jesus, we must continually look for ways to share the simple joys and pleasures of God's love. You do not need fancy gifts to make someone happy. Joy comes from showing someone you care.

Symbol of Christmas: We still use the ancient Greek symbols (IHS and XP) to tell others that we too are followers of Jesus. Look in your church on Sunday morning and see if you can find these symbols on the Communion table or on a banner.

Home Worship for the Third Week of Advent

Add a Christmas carol and the Lord's Prayer to each day's worship.

Third Sunday in Advent: The Candle of Love

Narrator:
This week we light the candles of Hope, Joy, and Love on the Advent wreath. Jesus came to tell everyone that Love, not fear, should lead them to worship God. The emphasis that Jesus placed on God's love for us, rather than the Jewish tradition of sacrifice, obedience, and anger from God, was to become the cornerstone of Christianity.

Bible Lesson: Mark 12:33

Symbol of Christmas:
The humble but trustworthy loyalty of a shepherd tells us to concentrate not on riches but on our faith. The small fuzzy lamb that is placed by the manger each Christmas reminds us to read, learn from, and follow the teachings of Jesus.

Monday

Narrator:
Magi means "wise men," and it is believed that the Magi who came to worship Jesus were Persian priests and astrologers who studied the stars and heavens every night to foretell upcoming events.

Bible Lesson: Matthew 2:1-2

Symbol of Christmas:
The Persian astrologersgave names and significance to the constellations. The Greeks later redefined the constellations into their present meaning. "Pisces" or the fish was believed to hold special significance for Israel. The simple sign of the fish later became an important symbol to the early Christians. Often the sign of the fish is hidden in patterns on a cross. Look for the sign of the fish in church. Make a simple fish to hang on your Christmas tree at home.

Tuesday

Narrator:
The Star of Bethlehem has been the topic of study by many scholars. One theory is that the star was the conjunction of Jupiter and Saturn. This would have been important to the Persian astrologers or Magi because it would announce the coming of the Messiah.

Bible Lesson: Matthew 2:3-6

Symbol of Christmas:
The first Greek letter in Jesus (I) and the first Greek initial for Christ (X) are often used at Christmas to form a star and remind us of the Bethlehem Star that led the Magi to Jesus.

Wednesday

Narrator:
Planets do appear to move across the sky as the earth revolves and rotates around the sun. Scientific calculations do indicate that a triple conjunction or appearance of the two planets together did occur three times with Saturn and Jupiter in the year 7 B.C. This is a rare occurrence and happens only every 125 years, so the Magi would have been watching for something special.

Bible Lesson: Matthew 2:7-8

Symbol of Christmas:
The Magi are usually depicted in elegant costumes with fancy gifts, a dramatic contrast to the humble, obedient shepherd and a simple manger filled with straw. The Magi remind us that Jesus came for all people.

Thursday

Bible Lesson: Matthew 2:9-10

Narrator:
According to Jewish tradition, Jupiter was considered to be a lucky or royal star and Saturn was

supposed to protect Israel. Astrologers equated the two passing so closely together in the constellation of "Pisces" as the ending of an old age and the dawning or beginning of a new era for Israel.

Symbol of Christmas:
The gift of gold brought by the Magi symbolized virtue or moral goodness. It is a reminder that we too as followers of Jesus are called to live by his example.

Friday

Bible Lesson: Matthew 2:2

Narrator:
"We have seen his star in the East" translates as "We have seen his star appear in the first rays of dawn." The star is shown in many shapes by artists and is often placed above the Nativity to remind us that Jesus is the Light of the World. Candles or eternal flames are often found in places of worship or prayer to remind us that God is always with us.

Symbol of Christmas:
Frankincense is a white resin found underneath the bark of Boswellia trees in Arabia and Africa. The resin was collected and burned. Frankincense symbolized prayer.

Saturday

Symbol of Christmas:
The third gift of the Magi was myrrh. Myrrh is an aromatic gum like substance taken from a shrub or small tree from the species of *Commiphora*. It was rather strong smelling and used in perfumes. Myrrh symbolized suffering.

Bible Lesson: Matthew 2:11

Narrator:
Writing the words "I Love You" or telling someone you love them can seem very simple but be very important. Take the time to tell those in your family how important they are to you. This

week do a simple act of kindness that doesn't cost any money for each member of your family. Gifts of love cannot be bought, but they are yours to freely give away.

Home Worship for the Fourth Week of Advent

Add a Christmas carol and the Lord's Prayer to each day's worship.

Fourth Sunday in Advent: The Candle of Faith

Narrator:
On this the fourth Sunday in Advent, we light the candle of Hope for a better world to come, of Joy for the simple humble pleasures we share in life together, of Love for family, friends, and neighbors everywhere, and of Faith.

Bible Lesson: Luke 2:6-7, 14

Symbol of Christmas:
The children have made a simple Christment to take home and hang on their Christmas tree as a symbol of their faith and commitment to follow Jesus. The Christment is comprised of several symbols that form an Affirmation or statement of faith.

Monday

Narrator:
The humble shepherds remind us that everyone is welcome in God's church. You do not have to be rich, popular, or famous. God loves everyone.

Bible Lesson: Luke 2:15-16

Symbol of Christmas:
The first symbol on the children's Christment is a simple shepherd's crook to remind us to be humble servants and followers of Jesus.

Tuesday

Narrator: The Bethlehem Star was also a symbol of faith for early Christians. They drew a simple eight-pointed star as a secret sign of their commitment to follow Jesus.

Bible Lesson: Luke 6:37-38

Symbol of Christmas: The second symbol on the children's Christment is the early Christian sign of the fish. The fish tells others of our decision to be a disciple or follower of Jesus.

Wednesday

Narrator: Christians all around the world are called together at Christmastime to celebrate, renew faith, and strengthen our commitment to follow the teachings of Jesus.

Bible Lesson: Matthew 5:43-47 and Luke 6:32-36

Symbol of Christmas: The Greek monograms for CHRIST (X) and (P) are placed on the shepherd's crook Christment to remind everyone that the birth of Jesus and the sharing of God's love are reasons we celebrate at Christmas.

Thursday

Narrator: Christmas brings new life, a new beginning.

Bible Lesson: Matthew 7:12

Symbol of Christmas: Jesus taught that God is a God of love. The butterfly is a symbol of that love and the new life that is offered us.

Friday

Narrator: Just as the Magi came to Bethlehem to worship Jesus, we are called to God's church to worship and celebrate.

Bible Lesson: Matthew 5:14-16

Symbol of Christmas: Without people, the church is but a building. It is when the church is filled with people loving and caring for one another that the building becomes a church.

Saturday

Narrator: The four candles of Advent and the center Christ candle, which is lit on Christmas Eve, remind us that Christmas is not a one-day event. Christmas is a celebration of love.

Bible Lesson: Matthew 22:37-40

Symbol of Christmas: The candles of the Advent wreath may be lit throughout the twelve days of Christmas.

Christmas Eve Worship Service

(Note: The children will practice and use this service for their weekly worship time during Advent.)

Prelude
[Have children play music before service starts. This is an excellent time to have children who take private lessons play. Keep all songs religious in nature, telling of the birth of Christ, to set the mood for the worship service.]

Call to Worship
BIBLE READER: [Read Luke 2:1-3.]

NATIVITY NARRATOR: Life was very difficult for the people in the little town of Nazareth in the year 7 B.C. The Romans were very harsh rulers and demanded high taxes from people who barely had enough food to eat. Life was simple.
[Mary and Joseph enter sanctuary and begin walking slowly up and down the aisles as if traveling. They do not arrive at the manger until the singing of "Away in a Manger."]

CAROL: [Sing "O Come, O Come, Emmanuel."]

1st ADVENT CANDLE READER, CANDLE OF HOPE: We light the first candle on the Advent wreath to remind us to continue to *hope* for peace. Christmas is often celebrated as a day of peace, even during times of war. As we light our first candle, we pray for peace in every land and home throughout the world. Peace between countries! Peace among family members! Peace with every neighbor! [Light candle.]

CAROL: [Sing "Let There Be Peace on Earth."]

Affirmation
BIBLE READER: [Read Luke 2:4.]

CAROL: [Sing "O Little Town of Bethlehem."]

BIBLE READER: [Read Luke 2:5-7.]

CAROL: [Sing "Away in a Manger."]

NATIVITY NARRATOR: His life began in a humble shepherd's cave. No castles! No velvet robes! No crowns with rubies and diamonds! Nothing more than a simple cattle trough for a bed. Throughout his life, Jesus would continue to teach that it is the simple, humble way of life that leads to God eternal.

BIBLE READER: [Read Luke 2:8-14.]

CAROL: [Sing "It Came Upon the Midnight Clear."]

2nd ADVENT CANDLE READER, CANDLE OF JOY: We light the second candle of *joy* on the Advent wreath to remind us of life's simple gifts and pleasures.

Witness to Faith
BIBLE READER: [Read Luke 2:15-16.]
[Shepherds arrive at Nativity.]

CAROL: [Sing "The First Noel."]

NATIVITY NARRATOR: Shepherds have never been thought of as important people. Yet Jesus is often called the "Good Shepherd." The shepherd calls and the sheep come to the sound of the shepherd's voice. "Come," he said, "and follow me."

CAROL: [Sing "Go, Tell It on the Mountain."]

BIBLE READER: [Read Matthew 2:1-2.]

NATIVITY NARRATOR: The Magi, or wise men as they are often called, were astrologers who studied the stars and configurations of the planets to foretell the future. They traveled from Persia on slow, plodding camels, following the belief that a new leader was to be born in Bethlehem. [Wise men begin journey.]

CAROL: [Sing "Joy to the World!"]

3rd ADVENT CANDLE READER, CANDLE OF LOVE: We light the candle of *love* on the Advent wreath for those we love and hold most dear in our lives. We also remember that Jesus said to show love to everyone, even those who have been mean and cruel to us.

CAROL: [Sing "Love Came Down at Christmas."]

Prayer
4th ADVENT CANDLE READER, CANDLE OF FAITH: We light the fourth candle of *faith* to remind us to be humble servants and followers of Jesus Christ.

BIBLE READER: [Read Matthew 2:9-11.] [Wise men arrive at Nativity.]

CAROL: [Sing "What Child Is This?"]

Benediction
LIGHTING OF THE CHRIST CANDLE: We light the *Christ* candle to remind us that Christmas is truly the Lord's day. As we depart this evening, may we go in peace with renewed faith to follow Jesus.

Help us, we pray, O Lord, to follow in your footsteps and to seek those in need at home and around the world.

CAROL: [Sing "Silent Night, Holy Night."]

Postlude
[Music provided by the children.]

Session 20
The Second Sunday of Advent: Joy

The Bible Lesson

Lesson comes from the shepherds in the second chapter of Luke.

What the Children Will Learn Today

Learning about Christmas customs around the world.

Time Needed

5 minutes for story
20 minutes for workstations
10 minutes for closing worship service

Supplies Needed (by Workstation)

1. Papier-mâché, tape, rubber bands, directions from last week (Step 1), and white scrap office paper or plain newsprint
2. 2-liter pop bottles, cloth scraps for shepherd's clothes, black or brown yarn or fake-fur scraps, skin-tone socks or stockings, pattern and stuffing for lamb, and beads or sequins
3. Scrap wood, nails, and tools needed to build manger
4. Christmas Eve script and props needed for Nativity
5. Yellow yarn, fake doll hair or yellow paper for hair and green pipe cleaners for wreath, and paper for candles and flame
6. Christment supplies and stockings or socks, embroidery thread, needles, cloth scraps, white cloth, and ribbon
7. Construction paper supply basket and house pattern

Children's Meditation

STORY

The Christmas Tree That Didn't Sell

It was almost Christmas, and a local hospital in town was holding a Christmas tree decorating contest. Everyone was encouraged to enter. The trees would be auctioned off the week before Christmas to raise money to build a new children's wing.

The children decided to make ornaments to tell about the life and teachings of Jesus and worked for weeks stringing beads. The day before the contest, the children worked late into the night. A tired and exhausted cheer rose through the room as the last sparkling beaded ornament, the church, was hung on the tree.

At the contest, the children were in awe and a little worried that their handmade tree wouldn't compete very well. There were many magnificent, professionally decorated trees. There was a tree that wasn't even a tree at all; it was chicken wire covered with paper flowers, another tree was cut and shaped into a snowman, and a third tree was covered with baby dolls.

"Well, at least our tree will sell," said Sarah. "It would have been nice to win a ribbon, but our main objective was to raise money for the hospital and tell others about Jesus."

As the judges stepped forward to announce the winners, a hushed silence fell over the room. The Best of Show, Most Original, Best Decorated . . .

"For our final award," the judge continued, "we present this 'Special Merit' award to the seven children who worked hard and decorated their very own tree."

The children squealed with delight and ran forward to receive the award. Then they settled back for the auction. Tree after tree sold, but the children's tree didn't sell. The children were in tears.

"We worked so hard. We even won a ribbon. Why didn't it sell?" said Brian.

"No one saw our little tree with the house

lights off," said Sarah. "It wasn't as pretty sitting here in this big empty room with the bright lights shining on it."

"Remember how it glowed when we turned the chapel lights off last night?" Marsha added.

"It didn't have a chance," said Jack.

"I'll never make another tree," moaned Linda. "All our hard work was wasted."

"No, it wasn't," said Mrs. Jenkins, their teacher. "It was just that no one could see the simple beauty of the handmade ornaments amid the glittering elegance of the fancy decorated trees. Sometimes we miss the true meaning of Christmas when our lives are cluttered and overwrought by hectic schedules. It is, after all, the simple things in life that are the most meaningful."

The children didn't talk much about the tree for the remainder of the week. On Christmas Eve before the closing hymn, the minister stepped forward. "I'd like to take a moment to read a note I received this week in the mail," he said as he opened a card and began to read.

Dear Children,

I purchased your tree from the tree contest. I had looked at the tree several times that day, but did not decide to buy the tree until right before the doors closed. I am so glad I did.

I'm very elderly and cannot decorate my own tree anymore. I'm spending Christmas with my children. This was going to be my first year not to have a Christmas tree in my house.

Your tree has brought me such joy. I turn out the lights and sit for hours in my rocking chair, singing Christmas carols, and remembering the story of a baby born in Bethlehem. Thank you for my tree. Thank you for helping me celebrate Christmas.

Love,
Miss Judy

Workstations

Workstation 1: Call to Worship

GETTING READY

Have cover-ups, last week's sign, and papier-mâché ready.

INSTRUCTION SIGN

In Mexico, priests used the simple game of the piñata to teach the Indians about Christmas. The priests would read the Christmas story and then use the piñata game to give gifts to all. Children in Mexico say "Feliz Navidad" (Merry Christmas) to everyone they meet on Christmas Eve. Read Luke 2:20.

Second Week of Advent

If you did not start a piñata last week, start with Step 1.

STEP 2:   Shape paper into a round ball for head. Tape head in place on body from last week. Papier-mâché entire body of lamb with a layer of white paper. Let dry.

Sign up to read Luke 2:4 for the worship service today and lead the carol "O Little Town of Bethlehem."

Workstation 2: Affirmation of Faith

INSTRUCTION SIGN

In France, they call the manger scene a "créche" and each créche has not only the traditional figures but also little painted clay figures called "santons" or little saints. The santons are people from everyday life who go out of their way to help others. Read Luke 2:5-7, 8-14. Sign up to read Luke 2:5-7 for worship. Add a shepherd and a lamb to your Nativity.

STEP 1: Make shepherd from rough, scratchy cloth. Shepherds were very poor. You may add fake fur, polyester stuffing or cotton balls pulled apart, or scraps from a blanket for a cloak to represent lamb's wool to keep the shepherd warm. Use patterns from last week. Glue a cloth across the top of shepherd's head and secure with string.

STEP 2: Make a lamb. Trace pattern on white poster board. Color black markings with marker. Tape interior braces in place as marked on pattern. Glue white cotton or stuffing to body of lamb. Read Luke 2:15-16.

Workstation 3: Offering or Carpenter Shop

INSTRUCTION SIGN

A wooden Noah's ark was the only toy children were allowed to play with on Sunday in the 1600s in Germany. Some of the arks were large; others were small. Children played with wooden or clay animals. Some children had only two animals. Read Luke 2:16 and continue working on the manger for Christmas Eve.

Sign up to lead the group in singing "Away in a Manger."

Workstation 4: Sermon or Bible Study

INSTRUCTION SIGN

The Roman Empire celebrated the "Birthday of the Sun" on December 25. The celebration was one long, continuous festival from December 17 till January 3. It was a time of peace. Soldiers didn't fight. People didn't go to work. Families spent time together and decorated their houses with evergreens. Trees were decorated with candles and carried in parades up and down the streets. Bonfires and candles were lit to welcome all. In England and Sweden, this same festival was called "Yule."

The first Christian Christmas services were solemn and filled with prayer and meditation. The early Christians spent more time getting ready for the sun festival than they did for Christmas. The church therefore decided to transform some of the traditional festivities and give them religious significance. We use many of these traditions today. Candles are placed in the windows as a symbol of welcome and to remind everyone to welcome Jesus into their homes. We decorate evergreen trees with lights to remind us that there are Christians all around the world, and we decorate our homes with evergreen wreaths to symbolize God's never-ending love. Read Luke 2:14.

Continue practicing for our Christmas Eve service. Practice the Affirmation portion. Read the "Nativity Narrator" section.

Workstation 5: Witness to Faith

INSTRUCTION SIGN

In many Scandinavian countries, people hang sheaves of wheat on their houses as part of their Christmas decorations and also for the birds. Put out food for birds at your house this week.

Read Luke 2:8-14 and continue working on Saint Lucia.

STEP 1: Decorate face with beads and sequins, or leave plain. Tiny buttons also work nicely.

STEP 2: Make hair from strips of yellow paper, ribbon, yarn, or use fake doll curls if available. For paper curls, cut thin strips of yellow paper. Curl on end of pencil. Glue in place on head.

STEP 3: For yarn hair, glue yellow yarn to paper head. Cut evenly. Let hair hang loose or braid.

STEP 4: Braid 3 green pipe cleaners and fasten around head for wreath. Roll white paper to make 7 candles or use white pipe cleaners. Roll paper tightly and glue. Hold each candle till glue dries. Glue candles in place on wreath. Cut and glue paper flames for tops of candles. Glue wreath to Saint Lucia's hair. Sign up to read Luke 2:8-14 and lead "It Came Upon the Midnight Clear."

Workstation 6: Prayer and Sewing Center

GETTING READY

Keep pattern for Christment posted. Some children will finish their Christment the first week; others will take longer. Leave patterns and instructions all four weeks so that everyone will have an opportunity to make a Christment.

INSTRUCTION SIGN

When baby Jesus was born, he was washed and salt was rubbed over his skin to toughen the skin and prevent infection. Then he was wrapped tightly in 6 yards of continuous white cloth called swaddling clothes, as was the custom. The Hebrew people believed that wrapping the baby's arms and legs tightly would help them grow straight. Read Luke 2:7. Make a baby Jesus doll for the manger or to take home.

STEP 1: In early American colonial days, families could not afford to buy special stuffing just for toys, so dolls were handmade and stuffed with rags. Thus, the name "rag doll." Take an old skin-colored stocking or sock. Stuff with scraps of cloth, yarn, and felt. Pack tightly and tie closed. Cover with an extra sock or stocking(s) so that scraps do not show through and so that face has a skin color.

STEP 2: Sew eyes, nose, and a mouth for baby Jesus. Closed eyes are the easiest to make.

STEP 3: You do not need to make arms and legs because the baby will be wrapped in swaddling clothes from head to toe.

Your job for today's service is to read the "2nd Advent candle reader, candle of joy" portion from the Christmas Eve service and to light the 1st and 2nd Advent candles.

Workstation 7: Benediction

> ## INSTRUCTION SIGN
>
> In the Ukraine, children celebrate Christmas on January 6. The children say *"Srozhdestvom Kristovym"* (Merry Christmas).
>
> On Christmas Eve, the Feast of Nativity begins when the children sight the first star of the evening. The mother prepares a 12-course meatless meal in memory of the 12 apostles. Straw under the table and table-cloth reminds everyone of the lowly stable where Jesus was born. Sometimes farm tools are brought inside and placed under the table, too, because Ukrainians have tra-ditionally been farmers. Everyone speaks in soft, low voices during dinner. They believe that if there are peace, order, love, and affection in the home on Christmas Eve, they will last throughout the year till next Christmas. Dessert is a favorite of the chil-dren and is called *kutya*. After dinner, the children receive gifts of nuts and apples and attend a midnight church service.
>
> Read Luke 2:8-14. Make a house card and show how your house is decorated for Christmas. Make a list on your card of favorite traditions in your home. Trace pat-tern and tell something special that you do in your family to celebrate the birth of Jesus.
>
> Your job for today's closing worship service is to lead the Lord's Prayer.

SIGN-UP SHEET FOR TODAY'S WORSHIP CELEBRATION

Call to Worship (read Luke 2:4; lead first line of "O Little Town of Bethlehem"):

Affirmation (read Luke 2:5-7):

Offering (lead first line of "Away in a Manger"):

Sermon (Nativity Narrator):

Witness (read Luke 2:8-14; lead first line of "It Came Upon the Midnight Clear"):

Prayer (2nd Advent candle reader; light first and second Advent candles):

Benediction (lead the Lord's Prayer):

ITEMS TO GO HOME TODAY: HOUSE CARD; POP-BOTTLE NATIVITY FIGURES

The Worship Celebration

GETTING READY

Today's service is taken from the "Affirmation" portion of the Christmas Eve service. The candle of joy is celebrated by some churches during the third week of Advent instead of the second week as listed here. Adjust to fit your church tradition.

Session 21
The Third Sunday of Advent:
Love

The Bible Lesson

The Christmas story (Luke 2:15-16; Matthew 2:1-2).

What the Children Will Learn Today

Continuing projects and learning to share God's love.

Time Needed

5 minutes for story
20 minutes for workstations
10 minutes for closing worship service

Supplies Needed (by Workstation)

1. Black paint and white polyester stuffing
2. Pop bottles, cloth, black or brown yarn or fake fur, old socks or stockings for faces, and beads, or sequins for face
3. Scrap wood, nails, and tools needed to build manger
4. Script and props needed for play
5. Wood or cardboard, paper, salt dough from appendix
6. Christment and baby Jesus supplies
7. Construction paper supply basket and stapler

Children's Meditation

STORY

The Handmade Teddy Bear

Christmas was approaching and Sandy's church was dressing teddy bears to donate to needy children for Christmas. The excitement started every year on the third Sunday of Advent. Tables were set up for making tree ornaments.

The idea was to make two ornaments. One ornament you would take home to put on your tree. The other ornament was for the tree that was being decorated for a needy family.

There was also a gift exchange table where you could buy kits from the sewing circle to make a present for the Christmas Store. Sandy had been saving her allowance for weeks because she wanted to buy one of the bear kits and learn how to dress a bear.

Sewing machines lined the wall. Mrs. Jorgensen let Sandy sit in her lap while she showed Sandy how to sew lace on the bear's dress. Sandy only had time to make one flower at the workshop, so she took the bear kit home to finish. Sandy wanted to sew flowers all around the hem of the dress, on the hat, and maybe even put one on the drawstring purse.

Sandy held the little bear in her lap while she sewed. Sandy named her bear "Scarlett." Sandy wanted whoever received "Scarlett" to think she was the most beautiful bear in the world.

On the Sunday before Christmas a big luncheon was served. Afterward, those in need could go to the Christmas Store to shop. Families didn't need money because everything in the Christmas Store was free, which was fortunate for Jody because this year Jody's family didn't have any money. Their house had burned down two weeks ago and they were living at the shelter. Jody's mom had said Christmas would have to be a lot different this year. There'd be no toys, no new clothes, no fancy dinner. Christmas dinner would be whatever was served at the shelter.

Jody's mom was hoping to find some warm mittens and maybe a coat to fit Jody today at the Christmas Store. Each family was given a box of groceries and allowed to fill a bag with clothes. Each child was invited to select one toy from underneath the donation tree.

Jody couldn't take her eyes off the tree. As she followed her mother around the room, Jody stared at the bear in the beautiful burgundy and pink dress with the puffy embroidered flowers. It was the most beautiful bear Jody had ever seen; it was even more beautiful than her sweet

Miss Fluffy bear that had been destroyed in the fire. Oh, how Jody longed to hold the bear for a moment.

Sandy, who was at the Christmas Store helping her mother, bounced over to give Scarlett a quick hug. As Sandy wrapped her arms around Scarlett, Jody's and Sandy's eyes met. There was something special about the way Jody looked at Scarlett.

"Have you received a toy from the donation tree?"

"No," Jody said very shyly.

"Everyone gets to pick a toy. You may select any toy you want. Would you like to have Scarlett?" Sandy asked as she held the bear out to Jody.

"Is she yours?" Jody asked.

"Yes, I made her for someone special like you," Sandy said as she handed Jody the bear with the note still attached. "Scarlett needs someone nice like you to love her."

Workstations

Workstation 1: Call to Worship

INSTRUCTION SIGN

The Mexican posadas are plays that reenact the search by Mary and Joseph for a place to sleep. The posadas last for the nine evenings before Christmas Eve. Families and friends walk through the streets going from house to house carrying candles, singing, and carrying small Nativity figures of Mary and Joseph on a tray. Those chosen to play Mary and Joseph for the evening knock on door after door, but each time they are refused lodging until they come to the house where the party is to be held that evening. The party ends with the piñata game. On Christmas Eve the posada ends at the church.

Complete all papier-mâché work and make sure it is dry before proceeding to STEP 3. Read Luke 2:7.

Third Week of Advent

STEP 3:   Paint feet and face of lamb piñata black. Let dry.

When completely dry, cover lamb with polyester stuffing. Glue eyes in place. Sign up to lead the "The First Noel" today.

Workstation 2: Affirmation of Faith

> **INSTRUCTION SIGN**
>
> Christmas is a celebration of love, especially the love we share with our family. Make Joseph today. Read Luke 2:4.
>
> STEP 1: Trace tunic pattern on cloth. Use earth-tone colors or stripes. Joseph was a carpenter and would have dressed in better-made garments than a shepherd, but not in anything fancy.
>
> STEP 2: Gather tunic around pop bottle. Make sure hem covers the bottom of pop bottle. Fold edges under so fabric doesn't ravel. Glue fabric to pop bottle.
>
> STEP 3: Trace arm pattern from same cloth as tunic. Make two arms. Roll into a cylinder. Glue in place at neck.
>
> STEP 4: Trace and cut cloak. Cut diamond shape in center for neck opening. See pattern. Tie cloak loosely over tunic.
>
> STEP 5: Roll sock or stocking into ball to form head. Glue to bottle cap. Decorate face with beads or sequins.
>
> STEP 6: Trace patterns. Make Joseph's hair and beard from fake fur. Use fabric glue. Place Joseph on worship table as a reminder to be humble. Sign up to read the "3rd Advent Candle Reader" statement from Christmas Eve service.

Workstation 3: Offering or Carpenter Shop

> **INSTRUCTION SIGN**
>
> In Poland, the Christmas celebration begins when children see the first star of the evening. Hay is placed underneath the table and tablecloth in remembrance of the straw in the manger, and a plate is always set for the Christ child at the dinner table. Read Matthew 2:1-2. Continue building the manger. Sign up to lead the singing of the carol "Joy to the World."

Workstation 4: Sermon or Bible Study

> **INSTRUCTION SIGN**
>
> Chinese Christians make lanterns at Christmastime. The Chinese call their Christmas tree the "Tree of Life." They make elaborate paper characters to represent "Peace" and "Joy."
>
> Read Matthew 2:9-10 and practice the Christmas Eve service. Sign up to read the Bible verses, Luke 2:15-16, for worship time.

Workstation 5: Witness to Faith

INSTRUCTION SIGN

Sheaves of grain are often used as Christmas decorations to remind us of the needs of others. The grain symbolizes the staff of life, bread. In Sweden and Mexico handmade straw ornaments are hung on the tree. Make the bread and serving tray today for Saint Lucia.

STEP 1: Trace pattern and make cardboard tray. Shape Lucia's arms and glue tray to hands. Hold in place till dry.

STEP 2: You can also make a coffee pot, cups, and plates if you choose. Read Luke 6:30-33 and think about what you have to give.

STEP 3: Mix salt dough and make small loaf of bread. Bake. Glue onto tray when dry. Sign up to light Advent candles today.

Workstation 6: Prayer and Sewing Center

INSTRUCTION SIGN

Christmas is celebrated in many countries around the world. It is truly a joyous celebration of love for everyone. You may have heard someone speak of Christmas in a different language: Italians celebrate "Natale," the Spanish "Navidad," and the French "Noel."
Make swaddling clothes for baby.

STEP 1: Use pattern and cut cloth into strips. If you can make one long, continuous bandage, fine. If not, sew or glue strips together.

STEP 2: Wrap doll from head to toe in swaddling clothes.

STEP 3: Wrap ribbon around baby to hold swaddling clothes in place. You may even sew embroidery flowers on your ribbon as Mary would have done. Sign up to lead the Lord's Prayer.

Workstation 7: Benediction

INSTRUCTION SIGN

STEP 1: Trace pattern and cut 3 green trees.

STEP 2: Staple trees together on middle fold. Open and stand up. Use pattern and cut a circle. Glue bottom of trees to circle. Read 1 Corinthians 13:4-7. Write verse on circle.

STEP 3: Trace pattern and decorate tree with teddy bears, little circles of paper punched from scraps, or other supplies available. Sign up to read Matthew 2:1-2 for worship today.

The Worship Celebration

GETTING READY

Today's worship time is taken from the "Witness to Faith" portion of the Christmas Eve service.

SIGN-UP SHEET FOR TODAY'S WORSHIP CELEBRATION

Call to Worship (lead first line of "The First Noel"):

Affirmation (3rd Advent Candle Reader):

Offering (lead first line of "Joy to the World!"):

Sermon (read Luke 2:15-16; Nativity Narrator):

Witness (light Advent candles):

Prayer (lead the Lord's Prayer; lead first line of "Go, Tell It on the Mountain"):

Benediction (read Matthew 2:1-2; lead first line of "Love Came Down at Christmas"):

Session 22
The Fourth Sunday of Advent: Peace

The Bible Lesson

The Christmas story is linked today with the words of Jesus and his directives on how we are to live our lives for God.

What the Children Will Learn Today

God wants us to return his love—through service to others. Christmas is a time of giving to those in need—the gift of love.

Time Needed

5 minutes for story
20 minutes for workstations
10 minutes for closing worship service

Supplies Needed (by Workstation)

1. Black paint and white polyester stuffing or cotton balls
2. White cloth, small bottle or jar, sock or stocking for face, needle and embroidery thread or sequins for face, shoe box for manger, papier-mâché or salt dough mixture from appendix for manger, yellow construction paper scraps, and cloth scraps
3. Scrap wood, nails, and tools needed to build manger
4. Script and props needed for Christmas Eve
5. White tissue paper, red ribbon, scrap of wood paneling or cardboard, salt dough for bread, green pipe cleaners for wreath, yellow yarn, and light-colored stockings or socks
6. Christment and swaddling cloth baby supplies
7. Construction paper supply basket

Children's Meditation

STORY

A Patchwork Christmas

It was early morning on Christmas Eve. The city slept. A powdery dusting of snow covered the grass. The streets were dressed in their Christmas finery.

The downtown buildings were outlined with white lights. Blue banners lined the streets. "Peace to All" was stamped beneath the fluttering white dove.

The store windows were filled with enchanting scenes of Christmas joy. A family of dolls decorated a Christmas tree as they moved their heads from side to side. A motorized kitten lay next to the flickering pretend fire and rolled its head in a circular motion.

The streetlights clicked off automatically. The sun began to peek over the edge of the old stone bridge.

Helga pushed open the end of the refrigerator shipping box. Helga had not always lived alone on the street. She was once the proud mother of five lively children and had lived with her husband in a small white house with a picket fence. There had been a swing, a sandbox, and Helga's little sewing shop built onto the back of the garage.

Today, Helga lives under a bridge, poor, cold, and lonely. Her children live faraway, busy with their own lives and unaware of the cardboard box she now calls home.

Helga spends each day gathering fabric scraps from trash cans and sewing patchwork quilts to sell for food and medicine. In good weather, Helga can be found sitting in the park. In the winter, she walks to the mall and sews till closing time when she once again returns to her home beneath the bridge.

A free lunch is offered every day at noon by the church on the town square. Helga and her friends gather for food and the warmth of friendship every noon.

Helga's been hurrying to finish her latest quilt. She plans to give it away tonight as her gift for the poor.

Every Christmas Eve at midnight the entire town gathers in front of the little white church to watch the children reenact the Christmas story. As carols are sung everyone comes forth in turn to bring a gift. The gifts are placed in front of the manger. The residents form long lines stretching around the square as they wait their turn to present their gifts.

Some people dress in their absolute finest and bring big glittering, impressive gifts. The gathering can become quite a spectacle. Unfortunately, some of the gifts, although they look very impressive, are not of much use to the poor. Silver tea sets make a nice show but are not very useful to someone living in a cardboard box, particularly if the tea set can't even be sold for enough money to buy a pair of shoes or a coat.

Helga has always made her Christmas Eve gift. Over the years, she's made ruffly dresses, warm coats, and even quilts. This year, Helga didn't have much cloth to work with, but with what she could find, Helga stitched together a beautiful quilt. Helga herself covers up with newspapers each night to stay warm.

When it was Helga's turn, she hobbled forward. It was hard for Helga to walk these days, but she cradled the handmade quilt and proudly placed it at the foot of the manger.

As Helga turned to walk away the church bell rang. Some said it was boys playing in the church tower, but to Helga it was but a simple thank you.

Workstations

Workstation 1: Call to Worship

INSTRUCTION SIGN

Advent is a time of getting ready for Christmas. Christmas is a celebration of God's love. We are to go out and share God's love with others by how we act. Read Galatians 5:22. We often think of Christmas as a time of gift giving. The most important gift you can ever give is love. Go home and tell your parents "I love you" today. It's the simple things in life that count the most.

Finish adding the polyester stuffing to your lamb. We'll use our lambs on Christmas Eve.

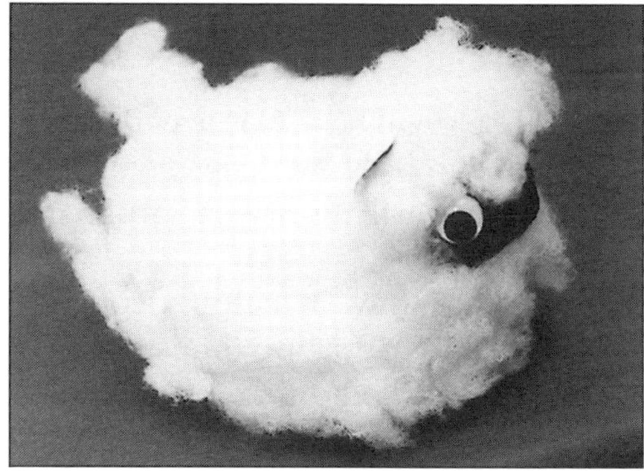

Sign up to lead "Silent Night, Holy Night" for worship.

Workstation 2: Affirmation of Faith

GETTING READY

If you're using salt dough, have ready before session.

INSTRUCTION SIGN

Children all around the world make Nativity scenes. The word "presepio" means "Nativity" in Italian. The French refer to the manger scene as a "créche." In Germany the Nativity is called a "Krippe or crib." The Spanish carry a Nativity scene called a "nacimiento" throughout the town in a special parade on Christmas Eve.

Continue working on your Nativity today by making baby Jesus. Read Luke 2:1-7. Think of ways that you can share God's love with others.

STEP 1: Use small box. Cover with salt dough or brown paper. Salt dough will air-dry on cardboard box.

STEP 2: Make straw by cutting scraps of yellow paper into thin strips. Place a cloth inside manger for baby Jesus.

STEP 3: Use a small jar or bottle with a cap. Make sock or stocking head. Place on cap of bottle. Draw or embroider sleeping baby's face on stocking head.

STEP 4: Wrap strips of white cloth around bottle for swaddling clothes. Wrap head to toe. You do not need arms or legs for baby because they were wrapped inside the swaddling. Stitch or glue to hold swaddling in place.

Place baby in manger and put on worship table today. Sign up to lead singing of "What Child Is This?" for today's service.

Workstation 3: Offering or Carpenter Shop

INSTRUCTION SIGN

Christmas Eve is a special evening in the church when we pause from our hectic schedules to remember the birth of Jesus and the wonder of God's love. Do you have a special tradition in your family for celebrating the birth of Jesus?

On Christmas Eve in Austria, the family living farthest from the church starts out with torches, singing carols and adding new families as they walk along carrying a manger. They finally end up on the steps of the church for the Christmas Eve service. Read Luke 2:20. Today, work on the manger for Christmas Eve.

Sign up to light the candles on the Advent wreath and read the 4th Candle reading from the Christmas Eve service. Place manger in front of worship table for service today.

Workstation 4: Sermon or Bible Study

GETTING READY

The children have practiced the readings for Christmas Eve. If you need extra rehearsals before Christmas Eve, announce time and date today. Make sure everyone is ready for the service.

INSTRUCTION SIGN

Many families around the world make Advent calendars to help count the days till the celebration of Christ's birth. The number of days in the fourth week will vary depending upon which day of the week December 25 falls that year. If Christmas Day happens to be on Monday, then Christmas Eve is the only day in the fourth week of Advent. Continue practicing today. Make sure you are ready for Christmas Eve. Sign up to read the Bible verses for today's service: Matthew 2:3-11.

Workstation 5: Witness to Faith

GETTING READY

Everyone should be able to finish today, but if children need more time, they can finish during the 12 Days of Christmas.

INSTRUCTION SIGN

In Sweden on December 13, the oldest daughter rises very early to take a special breakfast to her parents. She wears a simple, long white dress with a red sash and a crown of evergreens with 7 candles. Sometimes her brothers and sisters follow carrying candles and singing carols. They also dress in white. This celebration is called "Luciadagen" or Santa Lucia Day. Do you have a special way of saying "thank you" to your parents at Christmas? Read Matthew 25:35-36. Start a new family tradition.

You have worked very hard. Finish Saint Lucia today by gluing salt dough bread made last week in place on the tray. Place Saint Lucia on worship table as a reminder to help others. Sign up to light the Christ candle in today's service.

Workstation 6: Prayer and Sewing Center

GETTING READY

Keep one baby doll to be used for Christmas Eve service.

INSTRUCTION SIGN

Christmas is a season of love. The gifts we give to others have no meaning unless we remember to show others that we love them through our words and actions.

Take the baby wrapped in swaddling clothes home to place beneath your Christmas tree as a reminder of the true meaning and purpose of Christmas. Read Matthew 2:1-2. Lead prayer today.

Workstation 7: Benediction

GETTING READY

The only trick to this little box is cutting on the solid lines and folding on the dotted ones.

INSTRUCTION SIGN

The reason for Christmas is love. We celebrate God's love for us by showing love to one another. Make a package filled with love. Give it to someone special. Read 1 Corinthians 13:4-7.

STEP 1: Trace pattern. Cut on solid lines. Write "I love you" in center square along with today's Bible verse.

STEP 2: Fold on dotted lines. Fold box and glue flaps together. Remember to leave lid so that it will open.

STEP 3: Make a ribbon by folding and gluing flattened paper circles. Trace pattern. Glue paper to make a circle. Glue one circle on top of the other, arranging paper circles in a crisscross pattern. Flatten and glue circles ONLY in the middle. Glue ribbon when complete to top of lid. See examples.

Place finished gift box on worship table today and sign up to provide music for the postlude of service.

The Worship Celebration

GETTING READY

Today's worship time is from the "Prayer" and "Benediction" portions of the Christmas Eves service.

SIGN-UP SHEET FOR TODAY'S WORSHIP CELEBRATION

Call to Worship (lead first line of "Silent Night, Holy Night"):

Affirmation (lead first line of "What Child Is This?"):

Offering (4th Advent Candle Reader; light the Advent candles):

Sermon (read Matthew 2:3-11):

Witness (light Christ candle):

Prayer (lead the Lord's Prayer):

Benediction (provide music for postlude):

ITEMS TO TAKE HOME TODAY: PIÑATA LAMB; BABY DOLL; SAINT LUCIA; "I LOVE YOU" PACKAGE

10

From Christmas to Epiphany: The Twelve Days of the Christmas Season

Children's Meditation

STORY

The Christmas Spider

The Bible Lesson

The story of the Magi from Matthew 2 tells of God's love.

People tell many legends and stories at Christmastime. Some of the legends are stories based on true events that actually happened, but many of them are simply stories that teach a moral lesson. I'd like to share a special legend with you today. No one knows whether it's true or not, but the story lives on in the memories of children.

What the Children Will Learn Today

Christmas traditions from around the world.

There was once, a long time ago in the Ukraine, a woman with nine children and no money. Potatoes were the only food the old woman and her children had to eat.

Time Needed

5 minutes for story
20 minutes for workstations
10 minutes for closing worship service

As January 6 grew closer, the old woman worried and fretted over what she would do for Christmas this year. It was the custom to prepare a twelve-course meatless meal called the "Holy Supper" for the family before going to midnight Mass.

Supplies Needed (by Workstation)

The oldest son found twelve pieces of wood for the stove, and he carefully dried the wood for twelve days in memory of the twelve apostles, as was the custom. Still there was no food.

1. Leftover wrapping paper, tissue, and craft supply basket

As Christmas Eve arrived, all of the children rose early to clean house, for the entire house must be spotlessly clean before the first star was sighted and the "Feast of the Nativity" began. No one quarreled or argued, for it is believed that if "peace, order, love, and affection are abundant in your home on Christmas Eve, they will last all year long till the next Christmas." So the children spoke in hushed, quiet voices.

2. 2-liter pop bottles, tiny boxes, fancy cloth scraps (velvets, silky fabrics, brocades, corduroy, or sequin cloth), black or brown yarn or fake-fur scraps, socks or stockings for faces, beads, glitter, sequins, Nativity patterns from Session 19

3. 2" x 2" wooden scraps from puppet stage and ruler

4. Church hymnal

5. Lightbulbs, newsprint, Styrofoam cups, papier-mâché

6. Black construction paper, 4" x 4" cardboard squares or scrap paneling squares, tacks or pins, silver or white thread

7. White paper and craft supply basket

Two of the children found a tiny evergreen tree and placed it in the corner of the room. A more pitiful-looking tree had never been seen. This poor tree was half dead from the cold, hard winter.

Only a few green sprigs were left on the branches.

It was the custom for the parents to decorate a tree on Christmas Eve after the children went to bed. The old woman had no idea what she could do, for she didn't have decorations or money to buy any.

Dinner began when the youngest child spotted the first star of the evening. Everyone gathered around the table. Clean straw from the barn had been placed in the center of the table and underneath to remind the family of the lowly stable where Jesus was born. The old woman put the hoe from her garden under the table because it was with the potatoes from her garden that she was able to feed her children tonight.

There was no *kutya*, the traditional Ukrainian dessert, and the children did not receive gifts of fruit and nuts, which was the custom after dinner, but the children didn't complain. They hugged their mother and said "I love you" before going off to bed still hungry.

At dawn, the old woman and her children awoke to the most beautiful sight. They couldn't believe their eyes. How could this have happened?

The sun came streaming in through the window. The little tree sat sparkling in the corner, a silver cascade of beauty.

The children were delighted, hugged their mother, and said it was the most beautiful tree ever. The old woman smiled as she watched a tiny spider spin its web from branch to branch on the little tiny tree.

In the Ukraine, to this day, a spiderweb is a sign of good luck and many children make spiderwebs to place on their Christmas trees to remind them of the old woman and her little tree. In the United States, the tradition of using silver tinsel or icicles was started to re-create the beautiful silvery effect of the spiderweb-covered tree.

Workstations

Workstation 1: Call to Worship

GETTING READY

Have candy or small toys for the children to place in their crackers or have the children write messages.

INSTRUCTION SIGN

December 26 is the first day of Christmas and is also known as "Boxing Day" in Great Britain, Australia, and Canada. In the Middle Ages it was the custom for people who were wealthy to share with those who were poor. In your own house, you might put together a family donation box of canned goods or used but usable toys or clothes.

Perhaps you could buy two of something new that you buy for yourself this week. Then donate one.

Another old English custom is making "crackers." They became popular because of the distinctive snapping sound they made when pulled apart at parties. The Viennese wrapped candy or toys inside and covered the entire Christmas tree with tiny white and silver crackers for children and guests to take off and eat when they visited. This was a way of saying "Welcome and Merry Christmas." By the end of Christmas, the tree was bare.

Make crackers to pass out at home.

STEP 1: Cut out three 5" square pieces of white tissue paper. Fringe ends by cutting thin strips up toward the middle.

STEP 2: Place the candy or small toys in the middle of the tissue that was not cut. You may also include a wish or message for the new year. For example, "I hope more people take the time to say 'I love you' to family and friends during the new year."

STEP 3: When you have placed your message and gift inside, roll up the tissue. Cut a strip of wrapping paper or silver foil just large enough to cover the middle. Glue in place.

Make a cracker to snap open for the Call to Worship. Write a message inside. Read Psalm 66:1-2 for help.

Sign up with a friend to lead the Call to Worship today. Start by pulling cracker apart, then read message.

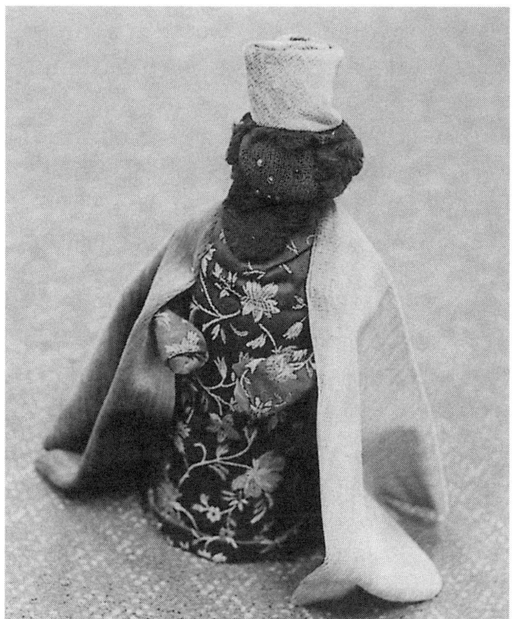

Workstation 2: *Affirmation of Faith*

INSTRUCTION SIGN

December 27 is the second day of Christmas. During the twelve days of the Christmas season, we remember the wise men or Magi from Persia who followed the star. Read Matthew 2:1-2.

Some families do not add the Magi figures to their Nativity scene until after Christmas Day to remind them of the wise men's long journey. Make 3 wise men to add to your Nativity.

STEP 1: Make basic tunic and sleeves using same patterns as before (Session 19) but use much fancier fabrics. Use shiny or silky fabrics. Velvet scraps or sequins work nicely.

STEP 2: For the cloak, wrap fabric around shoulders of pop-bottle figure as you would a cape. See picture. Glue or pin in place. Cloak should drape to floor.

STEP 3: Make heads and faces as before. Add fake-fur hair and beards. Make turbans by wrapping scraps of fabric in a circle on top of head. See picture. Glue and pin in place.

STEP 4: Make gifts for wise men to carry from small boxes or paper. Remember, you can cut a cereal box into squares and make a tiny box. Decorate with glitter, sequins, or shiny paper.

Place your Magi figures on the worship table to remind us to always put Jesus first in our lives. Sign up to read Matthew 2:1-2 in the service today.

Workstation 3: Offering or Carpenter Shop

GETTING READY

Use 2" x 2" scraps from building puppet stage.

INSTRUCTION SIGN

December 28 is the third day of Christmas. Christmas is celebrated around the world as a time of peace. Jesus is often called the "Prince of Peace." Read Isaiah 9:6 and sign up to read this verse in the service today.

Cut five 2" wooden PEACE building blocks from leftover 2" x 2" scraps to place on our worship table. Cut blocks today. Sand each block until smooth. Paint blocks next week.

You may also make wooden PEACE blocks to take home. Make sure everyone has a turn to saw today.

Workstation 4: Sermon or Bible Study

INSTRUCTION SIGN

December 29 is the fourth day of Christmas. Our worship service today will be a service in song. You will select several of your favorite Christmas carols to sing for the service. Select 5 songs that tell the story of the birth of Jesus. Select: (1) a song that tells of Mary and Joseph going to Bethlehem, (2) a favorite song about baby Jesus, (3) a song about the shepherds, (4) a song about the Magi or the Star of Bethlehem, and (5) a happy song that tells about God's love.

Read Luke 2:14. Sign up and be ready when service starts.

Workstation 5: Witness to Faith

GETTING READY

It will take two weeks to finish this project. Do papier-mâché this week. Paint face next week. Lightbulbs can be safely used if completely covered with 3 layers of papier-mâché. When using lightbulbs, always have adult supervision and have an adult check to make sure lightbulb is completely covered. For younger children, Styrofoam balls may be substituted.

INSTRUCTION SIGN

December 30 is the fifth day of Christmas. Make a lightbulb caroler to take home as a reminder to keep the spirit of Christmas, which is love, alive in your heart all year long.

STEP 1: Mix glue and water in a large bowl to make a thick paste for papier-mâché.

STEP 2: Carefully cover an old burned-out lightbulb, (remember, lightbulbs are breakable) with strips of newsprint soaked in papier-mâché. Completely cover the lightbulb with AT LEAST 3 layers of smooth paper strips. The lightbulb will form the face, so make sure it is nice and smooth. Every square inch of the lightbulb must be covered completely, even the base.

STEP 3: Select a Styrofoam cup to use as the body. Do not use paper. Turn the cup upside down. Place the papier-mâché lightbulb through the bottom of the cup. Cover the lightbulb and cup with papier-mâché. Fill inside of cup with papier-mâché. Lightbulb must be completely covered.

STEP 4: Roll 2 pieces of paper-mâché to attach as arms. Make a hymnal to place in caroler's hands if desired. Sign up to help Workstation 4 with the songs about the birth of Jesus.

Workstation 6: Prayer and Sewing Center

GETTING READY

Use pins or tacks with squares of cardboard.

INSTRUCTION SIGN

December 31 is the sixth day of Christmas. "We have seen his star in the East" translates as "We have seen his star appear in the first rays of dawn." The star is shown in many shapes by artists and reminds us that Jesus is the Light of the World.

Make a star or a spiderweb. Read Matthew 25:35, 40.

STEP 1: Glue black paper onto cardboard square. Place 8 tacks equally spaced around the outside edges.

STEP 2: Measure with a ruler and place 9th tack exactly in the center of board. Tie silver or white thread to 9th tack.

STEP 3: String thread from center tack to each of the outside tacks. Return to center and weave out to each corner. Tie off ends when complete. Glue a black bead or wad of black construction paper in center of web for spider.

Sign up to lead the Lord's Prayer for today's service.

Workstation 7: Benediction

INSTRUCTION SIGN

January 1 is the seventh day of Christmas. January 1 is also called "Jesus Day."

In some countries, Christians celebrate Christmas on December 25 and others on January 6. It doesn't matter which day we celebrate as long as we remember that Jesus should always be the central focus of our Christmas celebrations.

Every Sunday is a day of celebration for Jesus. Make New Year's Day a day to celebrate Jesus in your family too.

In Sweden, the children make paper snowflake baskets to hang on their Christmas trees. Make a snowflake basket.

STEP 1: Trace something round to make a circle, then fold and cut 2 snowflakes. Glue circles together to make a "V" shape.

STEP 2: Cut handle and glue in place.

STEP 3: Read Matthew 2:9-11. Write a wish you have for the new year. Place it in your basket. Sign up to read for Benediction.

The Worship Celebration

SIGN-UP SHEET FOR TODAY'S WORSHIP CELEBRATION

Call to Worship (read message enclosed in cracker):

Affirmation (read Matthew 2:1-2):

Offering (read Isaiah 9:6):

Sermon/Witness (sing 5 songs about the birth of Jesus):

Prayer (lead the Lord's Prayer):

Benediction (read Matthew 2:9-11):

ITEMS TO GO HOME TODAY: POP-BOTTLE MAGI; SPIDERWEBS; SNOWFLAKE BASKET

Session 24
Celebrating Christ's Birthday in Many Lands

The Bible Lesson

The story of the Magi is our lesson today.

What the Children Will Learn Today

Children continue to learn about customs of Christians around the world. Story of the Bethlehem star is also retold.

Time Needed

5 minutes for story
20 minutes for workstations
10 minutes for closing worship service

Supplies Needed (by Workstation)

1. Black thin, silky-type fabric, craft supply basket, assortment of colored beads, black pipe cleaners, needle and embroidery thread, old stocking or socks, pattern for Zulu, and hole punch
2. 2-liter plastic pop bottles, fancy cloth scraps for wise men, black or brown yarn, brown, black, or tan fake-fur scraps, old socks or stockings for faces, and beads, glitter, or sequins
3. 2" x 2" blocks, brushes, cover-ups, and paint for blocks
4. Skit, 3 puppets (including Sunshine), and paper-towel rolls
5. Caroler (last week), skin-tone paint, cloth, and yarn
6. Yarn and small hardback books to wrap yarn around
7. Yellow, orange, and assorted colors of paper

Children's Meditation

STORY

Three Gifts

Johnny had to get his mother a present. He had sort of forgotten to give his mother anything for Christmas. Well actually, he didn't forget. Johnny didn't have any money. Johnny never seemed to have any money.

Mrs. Jones, Johnny's teacher at school, had been talking all week about how Christmas wasn't really over yet. Mrs. Jones explained that there were twelve days of Christmas. Tomorrow was going to be the twelfth day, Johnny's last chance. So Johnny figured he'd make up for not giving his mother a present on Christmas Day by giving her something nice now.

Johnny had worked on a card and a caterpillar refrigerator magnet at school all week. Johnny's caterpillar had not turned out so well. He sort of threw it together.

Johnny asked his mom three times for gift ideas. Johnny's mom replied that she'd love to have a simple "thank you" once in a while when she finished his laundry or made his lunch for school. "Yes, a simple thank you would be nice," she had said.

When Johnny explained about the twelve days of Christmas, his mother had said, "a hug and a kiss would be great. Yes, a thank you, a hug and a kiss each day, and a simple 'I love you' in the morning or evening would be perfect."

If his mother thought he was going to give her a hug and a kiss every day, she was wrong. Johnny hated being hugged, and he hated kisses even more.

When Aunt Betty visited, she always insisted on hugs and kisses. When Aunt Betty hugged you, she squeezed the life out of you.

A ten-year-old couldn't go around giving hugs and kisses, certainly not to his mother. What would the guys think? Why hadn't she said something like to get straight A's or to clean his room?

The school day came and went with no solution to Johnny's problem. Johnny placed the caterpillar magnet and card at his mother's place at the dinner table. After the blessing, Johnny's mother opened the card and went on and on about how nice his caterpillar had turned out.

As his mom was about to start clearing the dishes, Johnny said, "Thanks for the muffin you baked for my lunch this morning, and by the way, I really do love you, even though I don't say it very often. You're actually not so bad, for a mom."

Slowly, ever so slowly, Johnny got up out of his chair and gave his mom a hug and a tiny kiss.

"Thank you," his mother said. "That's the nicest present I've ever received."

Workstations

Workstation 1: Call to Worship

GETTING READY

A silky, thin black lining-type fabric works best for doll.

<table>
<tr><td colspan="2" align="center">INSTRUCTION SIGN</td></tr>
<tr><td colspan="2">

January 2 is the eighth day of Christmas. For the Zulu people in Natal, South Africa, Christmas is in the summertime. It's very hot, so the family has a picnic dinner on the lawn at sunset on Christmas Day. The Christian families decorate a gum or eucalyptus tree instead of an evergreen tree and say *"Werkamal"* or *"Be duoth ka mal,"* meaning "Go Well!" or "Stay Well!" instead of our traditional "Merry Christmas."

Make a Zulu mother carrying her baby on her back. Read Luke 18:15-17 and remember that you are important to God.

</td></tr>
<tr><td>STEP 1:</td><td>Punch 2 holes for arms in top of tissue holder. Push a black pipe cleaner through holes for arms.</td></tr>
<tr><td>STEP 2:</td><td>Take an old stocking or sock and form a ball to place on top of the tissue holder for the head. Tie or tape sock or stocking to pipe cleaner to hold head in place.</td></tr>
<tr><td>STEP 3:</td><td>Trace dress pattern onto black cloth. Slit cloth and slip over head of doll. Make hole small. Cut holes for the arms. Make sure cloth touches the bottom of the tissue holder.</td></tr>
<tr><td>STEP 4:</td><td>String beads onto pipe cleaners. Wrap beads around the cloth to form head of doll. Make a wad of fabric on top for the hair topknot. Secure in place with beads. Wrap beads around pipe-cleaner arms for bracelets and decoration.</td></tr>
<tr><td>STEP 5:</td><td>Roll a small piece of fabric into a tight roll for baby. Glue or sew a little round ball of old stocking on top of roll for baby's head. Sew baby in place on mother's back.</td></tr>
<tr><td>STEP 6:</td><td>Sew embroidery eyes or glue sequins on for face. Sign up to lead your favorite Christmas carol for worship.</td></tr>
</table>

Workstation 2: Affirmation of Faith

INSTRUCTION SIGN

January 3 is the ninth day of Christmas. Flowers are in full bloom at Christmastime in Costa Rica, so the Nativity scenes are decorated with beautiful flowers. Spanish Nativity scenes always include a small stream with a woman kneeling as she does the family laundry, small candles, and a hillside for the shepherds. In Bolivia, people make figures of friends and pets out of clay to add to their Nativity scenes.

Read Matthew 2:1-6. Finish making 3 wise men for your Nativity scene. Sign up to read the Bible verse today.

Workstation 3: Offering or Carpenter Shop

INSTRUCTION SIGN

January 4 is the tenth day of Christmas. Read Matthew 2:5-6 and finish PEACE blocks.

Workstation 4: Sermon or Bible Study

INSTRUCTION SIGN

January 5 is the eleventh day of Christmas. Our Bible lesson today comes from the story of the Magi who came by camel caravan across many miles following a star to worship Jesus. Read the story in Matthew 2:1-12. Then, prepare today's sermon. You need Sunshine Share-a-Lot and 2 other puppets. You need 3 puppeteers and 3 readers today. Remember to read slowly and clearly.

PUPPET PLAY FOR SERMON:

I Don't See a Star

[Puppets use telescope or rolled-up piece of paper and pretend to be looking at stars as puppet play begins.]

ERIN:	I don't see a star. There aren't any stars out here.
SUNSHINE SHARE-A-LOT:	There are always stars. We can't always see them. On a cloudy night, the stars are still there. The stars are there during the daytime too.
JORDAN:	How can there be stars in the daytime? You can't see stars in the daytime!
SUNSHINE:	A star is merely a ball of hot gas that gives off heat and light. It's always there. As a matter of fact there are about 100 billion stars. Even in ancient times, people studied the stars.
ERIN:	The Magi were astrologers who studied the stars.
SUNSHINE:	That's right! People of ancient times were very superstitious. They gave different meanings to the different stars. The Magi believed they could tell the future by watching the stars and charting their movements.
JORDAN:	Magi? I thought they were wise men.
SUNSHINE:	*Magi* means "wise men," and it's believed that the Magi were Persian priests, astrologers who studied the stars. The Star of Bethlehem is believed by many scholars to have been a star that was formed by the conjunction of the planets Jupiter and Saturn in the constellation of Pisces. This conjunction only happened about every 125 years and would have been very important to the Persian astrologers. The Magi would have been watching and following the movement of Jupiter and Saturn across the sky.
JORDAN:	I don't understand how you follow a star.
ERIN:	Homing pigeons use the sun and stars to find their way home. Scientists believe they recognize star patterns.
JORDAN:	How do you know that?
ERIN:	I read it in a book. If you'd spend more time reading instead of watching TV, you could learn about homing pigeons too.
SUNSHINE:	The Magi recognized star patterns, too, and plotted each day's movement. If you use a star map or chart, the planets and stars do appear to move.
JORDAN:	This is getting too complicated for me. What does all of this plotting of stars have to do with Christmas?
SUNSHINE:	Well, it's the records of ancient astrologers that researchers have used to try to determine the birth date of Jesus. Jewish tradition says that Jupiter was considered to be a lucky or royal star and Saturn was supposed to protect Israel. When astrologers saw the two passing so closely together in the constellation of "Pisces" they thought it meant the ending of an old age and the beginning of a new era for Israel, or as a sign of the coming of the Messiah. So, the star was like a birth announcement sent out to everyone to tell all believers that the "King of kings and Prince of Peace" had been born.
ERIN:	Wow! A star for a birth announcement!
JORDAN:	There are too many stars. I can't tell one from the other. [Puppet puts down telescope.]
SUNSHINE:	If you get confused, read about the birth of Jesus in the Bible. It's one of the greatest stories ever told.

Workstation 5: Witness to Faith

GETTING READY

Have papier-mâché carolers from last week.

INSTRUCTION SIGN

January 6 is the twelfth day of Christmas or the "Day of Epiphany." "Epiphany" means "appearance" and celebrates the coming of the Magi to worship Jesus. The season of Epiphany lasts until Lent and is a season of great joy. Read Matthew 2:9-11.

STEP 1: If lightbulb is not COMPLETELY COVERED with 3 layers of papier-mâché, you must START OVER. It is not safe to use a lightbulb that is not completely covered.
Paint caroler's face a skin-tone color. While paint is drying, make dress, hymnal, and hair.

STEP 2: Make a paper hymnal for caroler.

STEP 3: Wrap fabric around cup for dress. Glue dress to papier-mâché cup for caroler. Add lace or decorations. Cover arms with same fabric as dress. Glue in place.

STEP 4: Cut yarn for hair. Make long hair to cover where arms attach to doll. Glue hair to head.

STEP 5: Paint hymnal. Add tissue-paper pages from scrap paper. Place caroler on worship table to sing to the Lord.

Workstation 6: Prayer and Sewing Center

INSTRUCTION SIGN

Make a yarn doll to remind you of the many Christians around the world who gather to worship at Christmastime.

STEP 1: Wrap 40 strands of yarn around a book. Put a pencil underneath your first wrap to work as a spacer and make the yarn easier to slip off later.

STEP 2: Tie a piece of yarn around the 40 strands. This will hold yarn in place. Tie ends together to make a hanger.

STEP 3: Tie a piece of yarn about one-third of the way down from the top to form the head. Tie this yarn tightly so that the head will be rounded.

STEP 4: Two-thirds of the way down from the top tie another piece of yarn tightly to form the waist.

STEP 5: To make a girl, cut the bottom of the yarn off evenly. Do not cut the end where you placed your yarn hanger.

STEP 6: For a boy, divide the loose bottom yarn in half. Tie each section to form separate legs. Cut ends or leave in loops.

STEP 7: Wrap 10 strands of yarn (length of pattern) to make the arms. Tie at each end for hands. Cut ends or leave looped. The loops make nice fingers. Push arms through middle of doll. Keep arms even. Read Matthew 2:11 and sign up to lead the prayer for service.

Workstation 7: Benediction

INSTRUCTION SIGN

In India, Christians use small saucers or clay oil lamps with tiny cotton wicks to outline the roofs, doors, and windows of their houses for the Diwali Festival of Lights. Christians in India light their lamps on Christmas Eve.

Candles are a universal symbol of peace and love. Candles are often placed in the windows of houses and churches at Christmastime to symbolize our faith in Jesus Christ. Make a candle to remind you that "Jesus is the Light of the World."

STEP 1: Take any color of construction paper and fold the paper as if you are making a paper fan.

STEP 2: Cut the paper fan evenly in half. See example.

STEP 3: Staple and/or tape the 2 paper fans together to make a circle candle stand.

STEP 4: Trace candle pattern. Decorate with markers. Cut slashes on one end of candle pattern. Glue candle to make a cylinder. Bend slashes inside and glue to candle fan stand.

STEP 5: Trace and cut flame pattern from yellow or orange paper. Glue flame inside top of candle.

Sign up to read for the benediction today.

The Worship Celebration

SIGN-UP SHEET FOR TODAY'S WORSHIP CELEBRATION

Call to Worship (lead favorite Christmas carol):

Affirmation (read Matthew 2:1-6):

Sermon (3 puppeteers and 3 readers for "I Don't See a Star"):

Prayer (lead the Lord's Prayer):

Benediction (read Matthew 2:9-11):

ITEMS TO GO HOME TODAY: ZULU DOLL; MAGI POP-BOTTLE FIGURES; PEACE BLOCKS; CAROLER; YARN DOLL; CANDLE

11

Learning to Say "Thank You"

The Bible Lesson

The Bible lesson comes from 1 John 3:11, 17-18; 2 John 1:5-6; and 3 John 1:11.

What the Children Will Learn Today

This special program for Mother's Day emphasizes what it means to say "I love you" through your actions.

Time Needed

6 minutes for story
28 minutes for workstations
1 minute for Bible reading for closing

Supplies Needed (by Workstation)

Story: Scissors, glue, green, red, black, and pink construction paper, a pencil, an old bent paper clip, tape, two crumpled pieces of aluminum foil, and markers or crayons in shoe box. If children are to cut a card as you talk, they will each need scissors, a pencil, and green, black, red, and pink construction paper.

1. Construction paper, patterns, and frozen juice cans

2 and 3. Yellow and green paper and yellow crepe-paper streamers, leftover tissue rolls, patterns, and craft supply basket

4 and 6. Construction paper, patterns, and sharp scissors

5. Construction paper, sharp scissors, and patterns

7. Construction paper supply basket and patterns

Children's Meditation

GETTING READY

Today's action story invites the children to cut a card as you talk. If children cannot follow action, patterns and instructions are provided at Workstation 4: Sermon or Bible Study.

Have an old shoe box with items inside: scissors, glue, green, red, black, and pink construction paper, a pencil, an old bent paper clip, tape, two crumpled pieces of aluminum foil, and markers or crayons. Trace handprints ahead of time.

STORY

A Gift for Mother

Tomorrow would be Mother's Day and the girls were buzzing around the house with excited whispers and plans. Jessica, a senior in high school, had worked for weeks to make Mother a new dress. Jennifer saved her baby-sitting money and bought Mom a pink necklace to match the dress. Dad ordered a corsage, and even Megan joined in. Megan planned to make a breakfast tray and serve Mom breakfast in bed. Everyone had something for Mom but Joey. Oh, the girls remembered to have Joey sign their card and he had copied a poem in school, but somehow it wasn't the same. Joey wanted to do something special for Mom this year.

Joey pulled out the box [show shoe box] where he kept all his special treasures. Joey dumped the contents on the bed [dump shoe box].

An old bent paper clip sure wouldn't make much of a present, but as Joey sorted through his box, an idea came to mind.

Joey folded the green construction paper in half, traced around his hands, and cut out two handprints. On each finger, Joey wrote down a job, task, or just something his mom had been asking him to do for the last several weeks.

Next, Joey folded the red paper in half. Joey cut rectangles for doors down at the bottom and then cut the corners off a scrap of black paper for the roof. Joey added windows and flowers and glued the hands on the back so that the hands helped the card stand up. Not bad, a house card that stands up [show outside of finished card].

Now, what was he going to put inside? This couldn't be like just any other old Mother's Day card that you would buy at the store. This card had to be something special. But what?

Slowly, Joey folded the pink piece of paper in half. With his scissors, Joey began to cut very slowly and carefully. First across the top and then the bottom. Joey was careful not to cut through the sides because he didn't want his surprise to fall apart.

Joey wrote "I Love You" in the center. Then, he glued just the corners of the pink paper inside the red house. Joey gently closed the card and flopped back on his bed with a definite feeling of satisfaction. Now all he had to do was wait till morning.

Joey woke up early on Sunday morning, raced downstairs, and placed his card on Megan's breakfast tray with the poem from school on top. Then Joey flew back upstairs, leaped into bed, and pulled the covers over his head. Joey waited in silence.

Finally, he heard the girls come upstairs and yell "Surprise!" as they entered Mom and Dad's room with the breakfast tray and packages. Joey listened as he heard his mother say over and

over how pretty the dress and necklace were and how scrumptious the breakfast was. Then he slowly crept out of bed, tiptoed across the hall, and stood peeking in from the doorway as he heard his mother say, "What a beautiful card! This must be from Joey."

At the very instant that his mother opened the card to read inside, Joey sprang into the room with a loud, "Happy Mother's Day," as the series of hearts sprang forward [open finished card].

Joey had done it. From a pile of leftover junk, Joey had created a Mother's Day card fit for the occasion. You can too. You don't have to have any money or fancy supplies. All you need is love.

Each of our workstations has a special gift or card for you to make and take home to give to your mom today. All you need to add is love. After all, a gift you make yourself is the best gift of all.

Workstations

Workstation 1: Call to Worship

> INSTRUCTION SIGN
>
> Give Mom a cupful of love. This is a very easy project made special by what you put inside. First, read 1 John 3:17-18.
>
> STEP 1: Trace around cup and handle pattern. Glue to an empty frozen-juice container. Glue handle in place as indicated on pattern. Decorate cup for Mom.
>
> STEP 2: Trace pattern and cut one or more clouds of steam to go in your cup. Write three acts of kindness on your steam card that you will do for Mom this week or write a poem or letter to Mom. Our sermon this week is a sermon of action. Your job is to show how God's love can be shared at home by the way you share love with others in your family. Make sure you follow through on your acts of kindness. Give your cup to Mom with a special hug. Sign up to read for service.

Workstations 2 (Affirmation of Faith) and 3 (Offering or Carpenter Shop) Combined

> INSTRUCTION SIGN
>
> Jesus says that we should never judge other people, just as you should never judge how hard a project will be to make by first glance. God loves us even when we make mistakes. Read Matthew 7:1-5.
>
> Mom loves you, even when she has to say "No" or enforce a rule. Make a daffodil to give to your mom to brighten her day. You may also write a poem or special statement of love on your daffodil. Read 3 John 1:11 for help. If you can't think of anything special to write, just say "I Love You."
>
> STEP 1: Cut stem and roll on a pencil. Glue in place on green paper. Write a special message to Mom on green paper.
>
> STEP 2: Cut green leaves on fold. Glue only tips underneath stem. Leave leaf loose to stand away from paper.
>
> STEP 3: Cut 6 yellow daffodil petals on the fold using pattern. Folding petals give flower a 3-dimensional look. Arrange petals on paper in a circle. DON'T glue yet.
>
> STEP 4: Cut a cardboard toilet-tissue roll into 3 sections. You will need 1 section. Share other 2 sections with friends. Cut yellow crepe-paper streamer to wrap around the outside of the tissue roll. Fringe top edge of streamer. Glue streamer to tissue roll.
>
> STEP 5: Wrap yellow crepe-paper streamer around your hand about 10 times. Fringe top edges. Glue fringed, rolled streamer inside tissue roll. Fluff edges of fringe. Glue tissue-roll center on top of center of flower petals. Set aside till dry. Give to Mom with a special hug when she arrives. Sign up to read Bible verse for service.

Workstations 4 (Sermon or Bible Study) and 6 (Prayer and Sewing Center) Combined

GETTING READY

Have example from story and patterns for children.

INSTRUCTION SIGN

You can make a card exactly like the one Joey made in today's story.

Read 1 John 3:11. Use the patterns and make a special card for Mom.

STEP 1: Fold a piece of paper in half to make a house. Trace pattern for roof and cut doors on front of house as shown on pattern. Use aluminum foil and add windows and other trim that you would like.

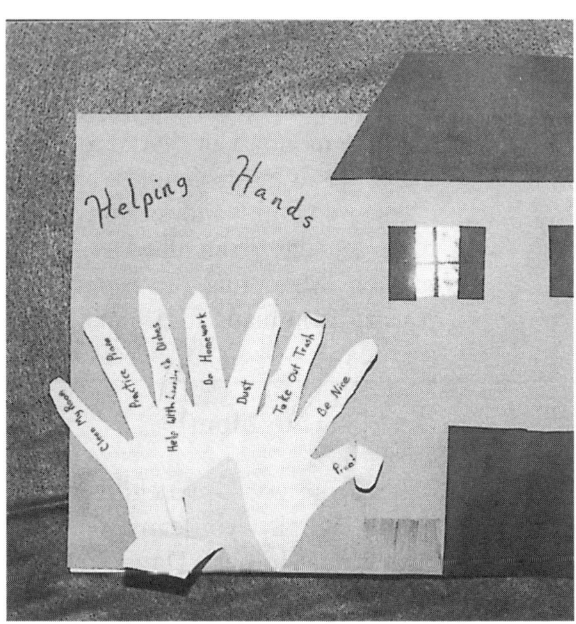

STEP 2: Fold a second contrasting color of paper in half. Trace inside heart pattern on folded paper. Carefully, cut out heart shapes. Remember, hearts must stay connected to make card open and stand up. Write "I Love You" on inside heart.

STEP 3: Trace both hands with fingers spread apart on a separate piece of paper. Write a job on each finger that you will do for your mother this next week or month. Be creative and think of 10 nice jobs that Mother would like to have done: clean your room, comb your hair, wash dishes, practice the piano.

STEP 4: Cut hands out with wrists included. Bend wrists to make a stand. Glue hands with fingers left loose and wrists bent to make a stand on the back of the house card.

STEP 5: Glue heart page to inside of card. Glue ONLY the 4 corners of heart paper. Do NOT glue down any of the hearts or your card will not unfold and pop up.

STEP 6: Open card; heart should pop forward when card is opened. Stand card up with doors open and wrists bent. Let dry. When card is completely dry, close card and present to Mom with a hug and a kiss.

Workstation 5: Witness to Faith

GETTING READY

Have pictures and step-by-step directions at workstation.

INSTRUCTION SIGN

Mom is a special friend who listens to your problems and shares your joys. Be an artist and create a book of "Remembrances for Mom."

STEP 1:   Fold construction paper in half lengthwise. Fold corners forward to form roof of house. See example and pattern. Match line A to line C from pattern to form roof overhang. Use scrap paper and add windows, doors, picket fences, garage doors, window boxes, or whatever else you like. Make a pretty house for the cover.

STEP 2:   Pick 6 different colors of paper. You may also use white paper if desired. Fold lengthwise. Trace pattern. Trim corners to fit inside cover. Stack all 12 pages together so that the colors alternate throughout the book.

STEP 3:   Read 1 Corinthians 13:4-8. Write one of the following lines from the Bible passage on each page.

Love is patient.
Love is kind.
Love is never jealous.
Love is never conceited.
Love is not proud.
Love is never ill-mannered.
Love is not selfish.
Love is never irritable.
Love does not keep a record of wrongdoings.
Love is happy with the truth.
Love never gives up.
Love is eternal.

STEP 4:   Starting with January, write each month of the year on a page in the booklet. Draw a picture or place a sticker on each page to correspond with the month. Cut "Note to Mom" to fit inside. Staple cover, "Note to Mom," and monthly pages together. Trim all edges. Give to Mom with a hug. Sign up to read 1 Corinthians 13:4-8 in service today.

A Note to Mom

A remembrance from your own childhood is one of the most special gifts you can ever share. Your child has made a Mother's Day Remembrance Booklet for you. Turn to May. Tell your child something you remember from your childhood that happened one day in May. It might be a special Mother's Day gift you made for your own mom. Write a short note on the page to remind the two of you of the incident. Take time each month to sit together and share another memory. By next Mother's Day you will have a keepsake of memories you both will treasure for years to come.

Workstation 7: Benediction

GETTING READY

Add yellow cotton balls to center of daisy for a special touch.

INSTRUCTION SIGN

Mom does many wonderful things for you each day. Take a few minutes to make her a pretty daisy and tell her thank you for the many kind ways she shows her love. Read 2 John 1:5-6 for help.

STEP 1: Trace petal and center patterns to make a daisy. Fold petals in half. On each petal, write one thing you enjoy doing most with Mom or something you are grateful that she does for you.

STEP 2: Glue tips of petals to back of daisy center.

STEP 3: Trace stem pattern. Roll stem on pencil and glue to back of daisy center. Use pattern and add leaves.

Give your daisy to Mom when she arrives. Sign up to read Bible verses.

The Worship Celebration

GETTING READY

The worship service is a service of action today. Each child has been given an assignment at each workstation. These assignments are ways to show love to Mom and family. The session will close with three brief Bible readings and prayer. Make sure readers sign up before service. Then, the service of action will begin as the children greet their moms with a hug and their gift. You may wish to check next week and see how many followed through on their sermon of action at home.

SIGN-UP SHEET FOR TODAY'S WORSHIP CELEBRATION

Call to Worship (read 1 John 3:11):
Affirmation/Offering (read 1 John 3:18):
Sermon/Prayer (lead the Lord's Prayer):
Witness (read 1 Corinthians 13:4-8):
Benediction (read 2 John 1:5-6):
All: Go and greet moms with hugs and gifts.

ITEMS TO GO HOME TODAY: CUP OF LOVE; DAFFODIL; BOOK OF REMEMBRANCES; POP-UP CARD; DAISY

Session 26
Giving to Others: Something Special for Father's Day

The Bible Lesson

Passages from Proverbs provide words of wisdom today.

What the Children Will Learn Today

Too often we think only of discipline or problems. If we learn to count our blessings each day instead of complaining, we often find life much happier.

Time Needed

5 minutes for story
29 minutes for workstations
1 minute for Bible reading in closing worship service

Supplies Needed (by Workstation)

1. Frozen-juice cans, cloth, paper, and craft supply basket
2. Construction paper supply basket
3. Scrap wood, paper, cloth, and craft supply basket
4. Tree patterns and construction paper supply basket
5. Paper fasteners, patterns, and construction paper supply basket
6. Car pattern and construction paper supply basket
7. Patterns and construction paper supply basket

Children's Meditation

STORY

Skiing on Chocolate Fudge Mountain

With skis in hand, we drank our last gulp of hot chocolate. We were off to ski. Ice-cream skiing was a tricky sort of sport. If you hesitated too long, the ice cream turned to slush.

There were no ski lifts, so if you were determined to ski an ice-cream mountain you had to inch and crawl your way to the top. As we heaved ourselves and our skis upward, we nose-dived right into a pile of whipping cream. I could have sat and licked whipping cream all day, but skiing was our mission.

Not many people ventured out this morning, so skiing down should be wonderful. Skiing twice in one day would be a rare treat.

As I reached to pull up onto the platform, my hand sank into sweet, sticky caramel. I licked the caramel from my glove and slid my tongue along the edge of my ski. Part of me wanted just to sit and sample the cookie-dough ice cream that surrounded me, but my quest was to ski the mountain. I could not risk a delay.

With a splat that sent strawberry ice cream flying through the air, I was off. Dad made a much more graceful start a few feet behind me.

I glided with ease. I pulled myself tightly into a tucked position. I would need speed to fly over the cherry vanilla humps in the dip below.

Smack! I was up and over the first cherry. I landed with a thud. I must remember to bend my knees. My second jump was better. I loved the freedom of flying through the air.

The mountain leveled out and became a little soft under my skis as I used my poles to maneuver around a praline crunch boulder in my path. The valley below was chocolate fudge with a whipping cream embankment built along the edge to catch you if you skied off the course. I hoped the chocolate fudge would not be too soft.

I gave myself a hard push with my poles as I entered the valley of chocolate. My skis were sinking in a little, but I had enough speed to continue. I slid to a stop and landed right in a mound of whipping cream.

The exuberance of success flowed through my body. Did I dare try again? Dad said no; once was enough for him. I knew the risks. The sun was hotter, the ice cream softer.

There was no margin for error. I climbed. I pulled. I gambled everything just for one more chance at the glory and thrill of flying down the mountain. If my calculations were wrong, I would pay the price.

At last, I reached the platform again. With a more dignified *whoosh* than the first time, I was off. I could feel the ice cream soft beneath my feet, but I pushed on. Around the strawberries, over the cherries, and *splat*—right into the chocolate fudge. It was like being on a water bed. I couldn't stand up; I rolled from side to side as others came down the mountain and joined me in a sea of chocolate.

I had chocolate in my hair, on my nose, and oozing down into my boots. There was no hope; I was stuck. I had pushed my luck too far. I had been greedy; I had wanted it all. I must now sit in defeat and wait till the melted chocolate floated me down to the lodge below.

I took off my glove, now covered with chocolate, and scooped up a heaping pile of chocolate fudge ice cream. Oh well! All was not lost; at least the ice cream was good.

It's true. I was covered in chocolate from head to toe. I would have to spend hours cleaning my skis. I would have a chocolate bathtub to clean tonight after I scrubbed the chocolate from my hair. Meanwhile, Dad sat at a banana split—shaped table on the patio at the lodge, licking his three-tiered ice-cream cone and laughing at me.

Had I learned my lesson? Probably not. I would be out again tomorrow morning when Chocolate Fudge Mountain would once again be frozen and perfect for skiing. Maybe I would be a little more sensible tomorrow and only ski down once, but then again, maybe not.

Workstations

Workstation 1: Call to Worship

GETTING READY

Use paper or cloth. Use pattern from Session 37, Workstation 1.

INSTRUCTION SIGN

Make Dad a pencil holder for his desk or office. Cut paper or cloth to fit around juice can. Draw a picture on your paper or make a card to go inside. Be creative.

Glue paper or cloth securely around juice can. You may even make a matching pencil holder for yourself.

Read Proverbs 21:21. Make Dad a gift certificate in the shape of a bookmark. Write or cut out letters for "L O V E." On the bookmark tell Dad something you enjoy doing with him. Then, add one job you plan to do around the house for Dad: take out the trash, wash the car, etc. Place your bookmark along with the Bible verse in your pencil container. You can also include a hug card that entitles Dad to a hug anytime he needs one. Sign up to read the Bible verse for today's service.

Workstation 2: Affirmation of Faith

GETTING READY

This is the first step in a series of workstations where children can make a Father's Day card. Each station increases with difficulty. The various levels of difficulty allow challenges for older children.

INSTRUCTION SIGN

Your dad does many special things for you. Take a few minutes to make a card to say "Thank you" to Dad. This card is a little challenging, but you can do it. Sometimes it is nice to do a hard task and succeed.

STEP 1: Fold 2 pieces of construction paper in half. One sheet should be green. The other sheet of paper will be the color of your house.

STEP 2: Trace and fold house paper as marked on pattern. Fold on the dotted lines. Color and decorate your house.

STEP 3: Workstations 5 and 6 have extra features that you can add to your Father's Day card to make it look even fancier. If you want to add moving parts to your card, cut slits as described below BEFORE you glue house in place. You CANNOT cut slits for car and job wheel after house has been glued to card. The car and job wheel are a little more difficult to make, so decide how willing you are to work hard before you continue.

STEP 4: Fold the right panel of the green sheet in half again and cut a slit in the right panel as marked on pattern. Now, fold the left panel and do the same. Do not cut through outside edges.

STEP 5: Fold tab on house as shown in example. Put glue on House TAB ONLY. Place house facedown with center "v cut" of tab EXACTLY on center fold of green piece of construction paper. This is a very important step; your card will not open correctly if you do not fold and glue house correctly. Glue EXACTLY as shown in example.

Read Proverbs 18:12, 15. Then go to Workstation 7 to finish cover of card or go to Workstation 4 to add trees.

Workstation 3: Offering or Carpenter Shop

GETTING READY

You may bring a Polaroid camera and take pictures of children or have the children draw pictures to glue on top.

INSTRUCTION SIGN

Dads do many special kindnesses for their families. Think of something special that your dad does for you. Make Dad a paperweight.

STEP 1: Select a piece of wood in the shape you want.

STEP 2: Cover wood with cloth or paper. Trace around wood. Then cut cloth or paper so that it completely covers wood. Cut strips to go around the sides. Work neatly and make your paperweight look nice. Glue paper or cloth in place.

STEP 3: Draw a picture or place a photograph on top of paperweight. On the bottom, write: "I Love You" and today's Bible verse. Read Proverbs 17:14.

Workstation 4: Sermon or Bible Study

INSTRUCTION SIGN

We are making a Father's Day card today. Workstations 4, 5, and 6 have special finishing touches. Start at Workstation 2. Then return here to add trees. Read Proverbs 4:14-19.

STEP 1:   Trace tree patterns. Make top green and trunk brown. Use scrap paper when possible. Add shrub if desired.

STEP 2:   Cut one 1" x 12" strip of scrap paper for each tree you make. Fold in half. Then fold in half again to make a cube. Glue to base and front of house.

STEP 3:   Glue tree to folded strips in front of house. Close card carefully to make sure card works correctly before glue dries. Your house and tree should pop up when you open the card. Reopen card; let tree dry completely before closing card.

Go to Workstation 5 if you are adding the job wheel to your card, Workstation 6 for car, or finish cover at Workstation 7.

Workstation 5: Witness to Faith

INSTRUCTION SIGN

After you have finished Workstations 2 and 4, start on the job wheel IF you cut the slits in the green paper before gluing the house in place. Read Proverbs 4:20-24 and especially 26 before starting to work. Place job wheel on the right-hand inside slit.

It is not possible to add job wheel if you did not cut slits at Workstation 2. Sometimes, we must plan ahead. Go to Workstations 1 and 3 when you have finished with your card.

STEP 1:   Cut circle using pattern. Write 2 nice things that your dad does for you around the edge of the circle. See placement of writing on pattern. Write in spaces as marked so that writing will show when wheel is turned. Then, on opposite sides, write 2 nice things or jobs you can do for Dad.

STEP 2:   Attach circle with small brass paper fastener to grass so that circle pokes up through slit about 1" and extends from right-hand bottom edge of card 1/4".

Write "You're Special Because . . ." on base of card below slit and complete the statement. Go to Workstation 6 for car or 7 for cover.

Workstation 6: Prayer and Sewing Center

INSTRUCTION SIGN

Just as with prayer, making your car move on your Father's Day card takes patience. Read Proverbs 4:10-17 before you start to work. Then, make a little car for the pop-up card. You must finish all steps at Workstation 2 and Workstation 7 before starting to work on the car. Follow directions carefully.

STEP 1: Trace car pattern, wheels, and pull tab. Fold on dotted line. Draw windows and headlights on car. Place car tab through left slit on card. Fold tab on dotted line. See pattern.

STEP 2: Cut pull handle using pattern. Glue car tab to pull handle so that it stands up straight. Glue ONLY folded tab as shown on pattern; otherwise, your car will not pull. Pull gently to make sure car moves before glue dries. Close card only after glue is dry.
Sign up to lead prayer for service today.

Workstation 7: Benediction

INSTRUCTION SIGN

STEP 1: Fold a piece of paper to make a card or decorate the outside cover of your card from Workstation 2. Read Proverbs 17:9, 24. Write: "Happy Father's Day." Then, write: "Thanks for . . ." List nice things that your dad does for you or draw a picture of something special that Dad does with you.

STEP 2: On the back of the card, write "I Love You." Give your card to Dad after our worship service today.

The Worship Celebration

SIGN-UP SHEET FOR TODAY'S WORSHIP CELEBRATION

Call to Worship (read Proverbs 21:21):
Prayer (lead the Lord's Prayer):
All: Go and greet dads with hugs and gifts.

ITEMS TO GO HOME TODAY: FATHER'S DAY CARD; PENCIL CONTAINER; LOVE PLAQUE; PAPERWEIGHT

APPENDIX

Frequently Used Recipes

Salt Dough

1 cup table salt
2 cups flour
1 cup water

Mix well. Knead by hand to make smooth. Do NOT add more water. Sprinkle flour on hands if dough is a little sticky.

Papier-Mâché

1 cup white school glue
2 cups water

Mix in washable tub or bowl. Stir slowly till mixed.
There are many recipes for papier-mâché that you may use. I use simple glue and water because it washes out of children's clothing easier than the traditional flour-and-water paste.

How to Use the Patterns

It's a proven fact that children learn best through action. Yet, if you peek into a Sunday school classroom on Sunday morning, you still see most children parked around a table listening to a lecture, completing worksheets, dot-to-dot activity pages, and, if they're lucky, an occasional craft project. It's time for a change.

Come, Follow Me! presents a wonderful new approach in Christian education that's packed with hands-on activities. Each session has been designed and tested with Sunday school teachers and children on Sunday mornings. All you need to do to take advantage of this program is to prepare yourself for a new way of thinking.

Children no longer sit around tables. Children stand up, move around the room, and go from learning center to learning center.

Teachers do not need to spend hours preparing lectures. There are no lectures.

The classroom can even be totally void of chairs. There's no need for them. No one will be sitting down.

Tables are helpful, though, especially tables that are the appropriate height for the ages of children in your class. Teens obviously need a taller table than five-year-olds, but, overall, it's easier for tall people to work at a lower table than for young children to stretch to reach a tall table. The children must be able to trace patterns, draw, write, and cut at the tables. Try to offer variety, something for everyone.

The key to successfully directing this hands-on program lies in how you organize supplies and use the patterns contained in this book. All you need to do is follow three easy steps: (1) check the "Supplies Needed" list before class to see if you need anything special, (2) photocopy the "Instruction Signs" each week, and (3) photocopy the patterns for each session. Remember that some holiday sessions use special supplies not contained in the supply closet, so check the list each week.

If you're a teacher who only teaches once a month, be sure you check the supply closet the week before you teach unless your church has a designated supply person who restocks the cabinet for you. Easy, ready-to-use patterns are useless if you don't have the necessary supplies. You must have the correct supplies in the quantity needed, the "Instruction Signs," and the patterns for each workstation in order for the program to work correctly.

There are fifty-three sessions, an entire year's worth of programming. Each session has a five-minute story, seven learning centers called workstations, and a ten-minute worship service that usually includes a puppet skit that can be used for the sermon.

The children work for twenty minutes at the workstations, reading the Bible, making a craft project that reinforces the Bible lesson, and preparing to lead a portion of that day's worship service.

Come, Follow Me! is designed to accommodate churches that have different people teaching each week. Photocopy the session you're leading the week before, take it home, look it over, then simply walk in and pass out the instructions and patterns to those who are helping at each workstation.

I have actually tested the program with teachers who never glanced at the book before class.

They simply walked in with the children after the children's story and taught the class successfully.

The essential ingredient is to read the "Instruction Sign" out loud to the children before you start, look up the Bible verse, and then work together on the craft project. The "Instruction Sign" is your teaching tool. The ready-to-use patterns enable you to teach the children about the Bible and to have fun at the same time.

The patterns and craft projects in this book can help you challenge and motivate your children to use their creative, inventive power. The church should be one place where we encourage children's imagination to soar.

Photocopy the patterns. Do not cut patterns from the book. Save the originals and use photocopies instead. Have the children cut copies, take special note to notice any instructions written beside the pattern.

Most patterns ask children to place one edge of the pattern on the fold. This may be a new concept for children. Placing patterns on the fold allows younger children to cut two equal halves, reduces tracing time, and enables more people to work at a workstation. If you have a large group or if you think a particular project might be overly popular with your class, photocopy several copies of the pattern so that more than one child can trace a pattern at a time.

Being patient, tracing patterns, striving for accuracy, following step-by-step instructions, working together in a group, cooperating, taking turns, and thinking about the needs of others are all benefits of working with learning centers, and these are life-long skills that everyone needs to learn. If we can teach these skills at church, we will have mastered the first step in helping children learn to become followers of Jesus.

If you are using the entire year-long program, then start with Session 1. If you are searching for craft projects to supplement your regular Sunday morning curriculum, then turn to the table of contents. Select a theme that fits with your planned lesson. Photocopy the session you have chosen, the whole session. Make sure you have the workstation "Instruction Signs" and the pattern for that particular session. Check supplies needed. Then you're ready to begin.

New Terms to Learn. There are a few basic concepts that are used throughout the book. "Place on fold" means to have children fold paper in half, matching side of pattern marked "place on fold" with fold on paper.

"Fold on dotted line; cut on solid line" is another expression frequently used throughout the book. Any time a pattern has a dotted line or series of dashes, this always means to fold. You only cut on solid lines.

Sometimes the "Instruction Sign" directions or the pattern will say to use scrap paper. Children are encouraged to keep a scrap paper basket and to use it whenever they only need a small piece, rather than cutting a tiny circle out of the center of a new piece of construction paper. Conserving and recycling are requirements. We must teach children at an early age not to waste resources, even something as simple as construction paper.

Keep Your Class Active. Make sure you use all seven workstations each week, unless you have a tiny class of five or six, in which case you may want to only set up a couple of workstations. Children need the freedom to choose between projects.

If you run out of time each week, analyze how you spend your time. Are you spending 10 minutes taking attendance? Do the children get right to work when they arrive? Each workstation is designed to keep the appropriate age level busy for twenty minutes. I intentionally do not plan goof-off time into the workstations. Free time turns into trouble. My class has an average of fifty-six children each week. Therefore, I keep everyone busy.

If any children have trouble, encourage them to start with an easier project next week. Workstation 7, the Benediction, is a good place to begin. This workstation has paper and glue projects that are simple but interesting. Help the children to work to a more challenging workstation. If you have extra youth helpers, assign a youth helper to give individual help to a child who has difficulty.

The ready-to-use-patterns and "Instruction Signs" make it easy for you to teach without hours and hours of preparation time. Cleanup is easy when you teach the children to be responsible for putting unused supplies back where they belong.

Save patterns. Don't throw patterns away even though they're just copies. Start a file.

Keep the pattern file in the classroom or storage closet used for supplies. If someone didn't finish or was absent during a long term project, they may simply go to the file, retrieve the pattern, and get right to work.

You're Ready to Begin. All you need now is a room or space for your class to meet, a group of energetic, fabulous children, an itty bit of patience, and bunches of love. *Come, Follow Me!* will do the rest.

Help, What Do We Do Next Year?

Don't panic! If you successfully completed the year, even if you used all fifty-three sessions, you still have plenty of material to work with. There are seven different workstations each week. It is highly unlikely that your children were able to do every project, unless you have an extremely large group. Repeat favorite projects. You may even repeat the entire program if you have substantial turnover in children attending each year.

I rerun favorite workstations, stories, or puppet skits. It's like reruns on TV, everyone has favorites.

Sometimes I even conduct an entire special request month, and call it "By Request Only." The children submit the names of favorite stories, puppet skits, and workstations that they would like to do again.

The children in my classes always beg to repeat the seasonal programs and projects. Children find comfort in repeating the traditions of Christmas and Easter.

I also have a group of children who insist on building the paper fold-up church from Chapter 6 every year. Sometimes it's the same children, sometimes not. Often younger children will decide that they are now ready to tackle the church. Or a child who only completed the outside structure of the church last year will decide to build the inside as well this year. Some of the more creative children have added Sunday school classroom wings onto the church, designed their own stained glass windows, and made tiny bricks to glue over the entire outside exterior of the church. It's wonderful to see what children can create when given an opportunity.

If your children had trouble finishing the church in the allotted eight weeks, this time around allow more time. As long as the children are enjoying the project, there's nothing wrong with spending more time building a church.

Another frequently requested repeat project is the paper biblical village. Some children want to make a fancier village than they made last time. This is an open ended project that encourages creativity and individuality so it's easy to repeat.

As you repeat favorite workstations, you may also supplement with new projects to offer variety. Not everyone wants to work on the same project.

While one child may work for three months on nothing but her masterpiece church complete with an attached Sunday school wing, designer windows, and brick exterior, another child may need the stimulation of a different project each week. Never have just one workstation for everyone. Keep seven workstations going even when doing reruns.

Use the Evaluation Questionnaire found in the Appendix. What are some of the children's favorite projects? Which projects did the children not get a chance to do? Are there projects that the children would like to repeat?

The Bible verses used each week throughout *Come, Follow Me!* are universal and never grow old. The children may choose to write their own puppet skits for the sermon or find a parable that teaches the same lesson and act out the parable.

Parables can be used for your children's story and sermon. Read or tell the parable during the children's meditation. Then for the sermon have the children practice how they would act out the parable, write a modern day version of the parable, or plan a puppet skit using the parable. Many of the children's favorite craft projects fit nicely with the teachings of the parables.

It's true that we do not have as much learning center Christian curriculum available as we need, but you can make do. One possible source of multiple age curriculum available is *One Room Sunday School*. It is graded for ages three through middle school and is available from Abingdon Press. The lessons can be easily adapted to the seven workstation format used in *Come, Follow Me!* There are activities and projects for younger children as well as challenging material for older ones. This is a quarterly publication, so it can be an ongoing source of new material for you.

Another source for children's worship curriculum is my previous book *No Experience Necessary!* (Meriwether, 1992). This, too, is a complete, year-long children's worship curriculum with seven learning centers or workstations each week. The highlight of *No Experience Necessary!* is building a wooden classroom-size children's church and having the children write their own sanctuary worship service.

Outreach Ministry. If your students are not interested in reruns and don't wish to repeat projects, you may want to develop a new program. Service projects may be your answer.

You may decide to organize your entire next year's program around outreach ministry projects. If so, remember that children need action. Select a project that is truly hands-on. Something that children can become involved in personally. Children's don't usually get excited about a canned food drive, but they love cooking Thanksgiving dinner for a needy family. Some of the organizations that deliver hot meals to shut-ins do not serve meals on weekends or holidays. Those who are dependent upon others for a hot meal would certainly appreciate having your group deliver a steaming hot dinner from your kitchen to their table.

The children in my class still talk about delivering Thanksgiving dinner straight from the oven to the table last year from a single mom with two small children. The mom had just been released from the hospital and was unable to stand, much less cook. As the children sat Thanksgiving dinner down on the table in front of a two and three year old, they realized how special their hard work had been.

Some items can be prepared ahead of time. Others will need to be done at the last minute. Your children's worship class may spend weeks or months planning such a project, assigning jobs to be done, planning the menu, or even going after church one Sunday to do the shopping.

The Appendix lists twenty service projects that have been tested and proven to work with children's worship programs. Add your own favorite projects and build a weekly curriculum based on outreach ministry.

Making Get-Well Cards. Many of the craft projects in *Come, Follow Me!* may be used as get-well cards for nursing homes and hospitals. The God's eye weaving, the huge paper bag fish, pop-up cards, and flowers are just a few suggestions. Each year, when we visit the nursing home, many of the residents rush to show us that they still have the God's eyes we made for them several years ago hanging on their well where they can look at them each day. God's eyes made on cinnamon sticks make a nice gift for seniors.

Pop-up cards are very popular with children and can actually be simple to make. They also make excellent gifts for sick children in the hospital. Remember not to place anything on a card going to a child that could be taken off and swallowed.

You can cut pictures from Christmas cards or any kind of greeting card, out-of-date curriculum, or even religious coloring books. If the paper is too thin to stand erect, have children glue a piece of construction paper behind it. Then make simple pop-up cards from the pictures.

Review the techniques taught in Session 26

for making a Father's Day card. You can make the same kind of tab that was used for the tree. With this one technique, you can make an entire picture pop up. Make the tab larger or wider depending upon the size of the picture.

You may also cut a picture into puzzle sections, stagger the tabs placed behind each section of the picture, and make a picture pop up in segments. Use the three simple techniques taught for making the Father's Day card in volume 1, and you'll be able to make dozens of pop-up cards. Children of all ages love pop-up cards.

A get-well card doesn't have to be in the shape of a folded card. Think of projects from both volumes that can be converted into a greeting card—fish, flowers, or even houses.

We undertook a gigantic project one year. We decided to make fifty of the large paper bag fish from Session 40 to pass out at the nursing home and hospital.

Instead of just decorating one side of the fish as described in Session 40. We completely covered both sides of the fish with scales.

Every workstation had a job. It was like an assembly line.

The Call to Worship workstation traced and cut out the paper bag fish. The Affirmation workstation stuffed each fish with scrap paper and stapled the edges shut. The Offering workstation traced and cut out mouths and tail fins for each fish. The Sermon workstation cut thousands of scales. Each of these pieces were passed along to the Witness workstation where tail fins and scales were glued into place. The Prayer workstation traced and cut out eyes and side fins. The Benediction workstation added the finishing touches by gluing the mouth, eyes, and side fins in place. Everyone helped, even the youngest child. It took us months to complete fifty fish, but the children were genuinely pleased when they saw the expressions of surprise and gratitude pleased when they saw the expressions of surprise and gratitude on the faces of the children at the hospital and the seniors at the nursing home. The residents at the nursing home

were just as proud of their fish as the children at the hospital, so it was truly an excellent project for all ages. We hung two fish from the ceiling in our classroom to always remind us of the year we made fifty paper bag fish.

Spend Several Months on the Same Theme. Your group may want to plan a big Christmas or Easter project. My class loved it the year I announced: "Christmas in September." We spent the entire fall getting ready for Christmas. We put on a church-wide Christmas Pageant, decorated a Christmas tree and sold it to help raise money for the local Children's Hospital, delivered Christmas dinner and presents to a needy family, and went Christmas caroling at the nursing home. It would have been impossible to coordinate all of these projects within the span of the four weeks of Advent. We started in September and the excitement grew each week as we got closer to Christmas.

Each week the children had assigned duties at the workstations—decorations to make for the Christmas tree, Christmas cards to make for the nursing home. During our worship time we studied the Bible story and practiced for the Christmas Pageant. My series called *The Christmas Tree* (Meriwether, 1998) includes a play kit and two books of patterns with forty-two different Christmas Christian ornaments for children and youth.

The ornaments are graded by age appropriateness the same as the projects in this book. The patterns are easy to follow, and the ornaments are inexpensive to make.

The children enjoy hanging their finished ornaments on the tree each week as work progresses. Many businesses are willing to purchase a fully decorated tree so that they do not have to bother with decorations. So children can use their decorating skills to earn money to help others. Be sure and contact local businesses to see what kind of tree they would like before you start decorating. Have the business select a theme—world peace, save the rainforest, an old fashioned Christmas . . . The possibilities are endless.

Puppets are a Wonderful Teaching Aid.
Children love puppets. A puppet show is a natural way to teach children about the Bible. The parables of Jesus provide an excellent variety of material that can either be used alone or in combination with other curriculum.

Children can often write their own puppet plays based on a parable, or they can simply act out the parable. Each workstation can be assigned a different job. Some workstations can be designated to make scenery while others make the puppets needed. The sermon workstation could be in charge of writing the skit.

The parable of the Good Samaritan, for example, needs at least seven puppets. These puppets could be made from pop bottles and paper plates as taught in previous sessions of this book. The paper plate becomes the head, the plastic pop bottle the body. The neck of the pop bottle becomes a handle for the puppeteer. An entire session can be built around making puppets to tell a parable as was done in Session 10.

You can also use the patterns and instructions in Session 45 and make string puppets. The Sunshine-share-a-lot puppet stage was designed for use with both hand puppets and string puppets. The double curtain gives you a perfect backdrop.

With just a paper plate and a popsicle stick, you can make a little girl with long curly hair and glasses, Dad with a black fuzzy beard, a tree, a beautiful rainbow, flowers, all kinds of animals, a sunshine with a big smiley face, or people from the Bible.

Paper plates provide a simple and inexpensive way to make puppets and even simple scenery for a puppet play. Puppets can be made with all sorts of materials: long paper curls, springy legs, tall hats, braided yarn hair, fake fur beards, painted faces, glitter, sequins, and even button eyes. Use tan and brown paper plates for skin color. Plain white plates can also be painted, colored with crayons, or covered with paper to give the color you want for the puppet's skin.

You can also make animal puppets or make believe characters of any color. If you do not have construction paper, use old shopping bags, cloth, or crayons to make the colors you want.

Cut paper slashes for special effects. When you cut slashes for eyelashes, bangs, grass, and flowers, remember cut down to about ¼" of the edge. Stop before you cut all the way across so that your slashes do not fall apart. You need that uncut edge to glue the eyelash in place.

Fake fur or fuzzy fabrics are fun to work with. You may use fake fur to create a kitty, puppy, or even people with fuzzy hair and beards.

White cotton balls or polyester stuffing make great hair for Grandma. Don't forget the granny glasses.

Cars, houses, or even a boat puppet can be built onto a pop bottle. Use the pop bottle as a base to build upon. Then create whatever you like.

You can also cut cars and boats from stiff paper, punch holes, and attach a long string at the front and at the end. Cars can be made to bump up and down on a bumpy road and boats to toss and pitch with the rolling waves.

Felt hand puppets are another easy alternative. Puppets can be made with only felt and fabric glue. You can make people or animals with felt. You may do simple sewing or absolutely no sewing. For a special effect, you may add buttons, pom poms, fake fur, yarn, feathers, hats, flowers, fancy fabrics, and even sequins.

Old socks can be used to make simple puppets that open their mouths and talk. A circular piece of cardboard is glued into place to form the mouth. Then, you can turn your sock puppet into any person or animal you wish.

Paper tubes from wrapping paper or paper towel rolls can be turned into fabulous inexpensive puppets. Make paper clothes, a round circle for a race, arms, and legs if desired, and, of course, don't forget to add hair.

Make city skyscrapers or a simple country cottage, biblical houses or the gates of Jerusalem from empty cereal boxes. You can create an entire city just with different size boxes. Attach a string and you can lower houses into place and even make them move in case of earthquakes or sudden storms.

Paper coffee filters for drip coffee machines make wonderful little bugs and insects that creep into your puppet plays. Attach a string to your critters and have them slide down suddenly from the top of the Sunshine-Share-a-lot puppet stage.

The addition of bubbles can add excitement to any puppet play. The children in my class use bubbles for skits they perform when visiting children in the hospital. One particular favorite is when a puppet tries to count and naturally gets confused.

With the basic supplies suggested and your imagination, you can make the cast for any puppet play or story. You might even decide to become traveling missionaries and take your puppet shows out into the world to tell others about God's love. You can spend an entire year devoted to puppetry if you want to.

KTBT News. If your class enjoys the KTBT news crew, encourage them to write their own skits and stories. Older youth might write stories and puppet skits for younger children.

You may even want to expand the KTBT news concept. Use time traveling reporters to investigate the Bible. Create a news room and produce a news program every week on what's happening in the world today. Send investigative reporters back-in-time to report on happenings from New Testament times as they happen.

The children might write, act out, and video tape their stories each week. Then they could send the video tape to anyone from the group who was sick or unable to come that week.

If your class likes to write and act out stories, have the children produce a news program, a video tape. They might spend several months preparing a script on "What does it mean to be a Christian?" They could write modern day stories from a child's point-of-view. At school! In the home! Around the neighborhood!

Build a Biblical Village. If you have your own classroom or a corner of fellowship hall that no one will object to having you convert into a biblical village, you can spend the year building a village. You have more than enough ideas and props to get you started. The children will love it.

Look back through Chapters 12, 14, and 15. You have complete instructions, everything needed. You may even want to make costumes and have the children act out each week's Bible story in the village.

Expand the basic plan given in Chapter 15. Add extra houses by simply covering more boxes. It's easy.

Use an old table, cover with cloth, and set up a marketplace. A piece of cloth can be suspended from the ceiling for an awning. Make extra clay jars for the well and clay pottery for the potter. Don't forget to have a carpenter's shop.

You'll definitely want to make extra sheep for the sheepfold. The children love the fluffy sheep.

You can have a fun-filled, spiritually enriching year learning about the Bible as you build a village and act out Bible stories. Follow the guidelines in Chapter 15. Set up seven workstations throughout the village.

If your church doesn't meet during the summer, as some churches do not, don't forget to use the material in Chapter 15. There are ten sessions tailor-made to fit perfectly into your biblical village. Use these sessions to get started, then develop your own ideas. This is also a good chapter to repeat since many children are away part of the summer. So even if you haven't used Chapter 15, you may want to repeat portions of it.

Develop new ideas and projects for your children. Plan long term and weekly projects. Some children need the comfort of taking home a completed project each week.

Many curriculum craft projects can be adapted to the learning center concept. Write a list of step-by-step directions for children to follow. Make patterns.

Remember to check your local library. Many

children's crafts can be modified to fit a religious theme.

Be creative; don't despair. The end of the year does not need to bring an end to your children's worship program. Quite the contrary, it's only the beginning.

Twenty Possible Service Projects That Have Been Tested and Used with Children

1. Adopt a family for Christmas or for the year. You can provide meals if family members are sick or elderly. Decorate and donate a Christmas tree. Plan birthday parties for children. Offer to do the grocery shopping. Our group played a musical Christmas concert for a family who couldn't get out to enjoy the music and festivities of the year. The possibilities are endless.

2. Decorate Christmas trees to sell and raise money. Check with businesses. Secure a potential buyer before you decide to decorate.

3. Cook meals for shut-ins or others who rely on organizations to deliver hot meals during the week. Many of these people are without a hot meal on weekends and holidays. You might want to adopt a specific family and make sure they receive a hot meal every weekend and especially for holidays.

4. You may also volunteer to help deliver food for Meals-on-Wheels during the summer. Children are allowed to accompany an adult and visit with those who receive the meals. Your class can make cards to send with the meals.

5. Host a church-wide dinner to raise money for the homeless and hungry. Invite everyone to help. Children can help cook, make table decorations, or even plan and provide a program for the dinner. Families, the women's society, or possibly even an adult Sunday school class might volunteer to help. Some grocery stores will donate turkey or ham for a good cause.

6. Christmas caroling at a nursing home or hospital works well with children, particularly if you live in a part of the country where the weather is cold and wet at Christmas time.

7. Adopt a mission school or church in a financially challenged area. Have the children write letters to the children at the school. Prepare school supply kits or health kits for each child. If possible, encourage your children to becom e pen pals. Try to write letters, send holiday cards, and pictures back and forth between your group and the mission school or church. If you live within driving distance, you might plan an end-of-the-year picnic to bring both groups together.

8. Adopt a grandparent or shut-in from your church. Bake cookies. Send cards, Visit when possible. Plan a birthday party.

9. Clown ministry is a wonderful outreach to use with children. They are less inhibited as their clown personality. Visit hospitals, nursing homes, and use puppets. Puppets allow the children to teach stories of sharing and caring for others.

10. Don't forget the ever-popular bake sale. Children can bake cookies at home to bring and sell after church or bake during the children's worship time. Our group bakes homemade bread and sells it after church to raise money. Use the bread recipe listed for Thanksgiving. It's very popular.

11. Children love to raise money for farm animals or for specific villages in need. You can incorporate learning about the animals or country you are sending your donation to as part of your workstation activities. Many relief organizations will send you free information if you ask. Check with your minister for suggestions. Heifer Project International is one example. If you have a small group, you can buy portions or shares in an animal as well. Call Heifer Project, Int. at 1-800-422-0474.

12. Habitat for Humanity is another world wide organization that fits nicely into the learning center study format of this book. You can build houses out of paper, soap boxes, cereal boxes, or even milk cartons. Then raise money to buy nails, windows, doors, or just to help build a house. The nice thing about Habitat is that you may specify your donation to go toward a house being built in your area. Then, if desired, the children may bake cookies and deliver cookies to the volunteers building the house that the children helped to raise money for. Call 1-800-HABITAT.

13. Plan a game party for a nursing home. You'd be surprised how much residents enjoy playing children's board games and working big-piece children's puzzles. Our first game party was scheduled to last for an hour. It went for two straight hours because the residents didn't want it to end. Children can read game cards for residents who can't see well enough to read game pieces.

14. Decorate Easter eggs. You can see the decorated eggs to members of your church to raise money for a good cause. There are plenty of suggestions in the Lenten section for making all kinds of eggs. You might also choose to deliver decorated eggs to children in the hospital or even plan a decorating party for the residents of a nursing home.

15. If you have students who take music lessons on the piano, violin, or suitable instruments, go to a nursing home or even a homeless shelter. Have children play songs they've learned during the dinner hour. Children who do not play instruments may pass out cards. Residents enjoy the music and appreciate the children taking the time to make them feel special.

16. Homeless shelters are always in need of help. Children might bring warm mittens, hats, or scarves to fill a basket. The children can also make small cards to attach to each item. Telling others you care is a wonderful way to learn to express God's love. When the basket is full, the mittens can be sent to the homeless shelter for distribution.

17. Our group planned a unique sort of project with one of our local homeless shelters. It's a small shelter that serves as home to those who need a chance to start over. My class filled grocery bags of nonperishable food for what we called "Feed a Family." The idea was to provide a balanced day's diet for each family's first day back out on their own in a new apartment or house. The children planned menus: breakfast, lunch, and dinner. They then went shopping with their parents and filled a grocery bag full of food to feed a family for a day. If you wish to involve your entire church in this project, announce the project in your church newsletter or bulletin. Then have the children take a wagon around during Sunday school to collect donated food. Afterwards, the children can sort and bag food according to the menus they've made. Staple the menu to each bag. Tuck a "Have a Nice Day" card inside.

18. Cooking Thanksgiving dinner is probably the most popular service project the children in my group have ever done. Everyone knows that we always cook the Sunday before Thanksgiving every year. I often have youth who have graduated from the program, show up, and volunteer to help. Many families and seniors in the church know about our project and often drop off bags of groceries.

19. Each year, the Salvation Army hosts a Christmas toy store. They often need volunteers to help dress or decorate stuffed animals and dolls. Your children can put ribbons on teddy bears or sew simple dresses for dolls. Check with your local Salvation Army. See what they need. They often provide the bears and the dolls.

20. Plant a "Sharing Tree." If your church has space, get permission to plant an evergreen tree. The children can then make pine cone bird feeders to hang on the tree in winter and early spring. If appropriate, decorate the tree with tiny clear lights at Christmas time to remind children to be gentle with animals and to care for all of God's creation. You might also plant flowers around the tree and encourage the children to care for their garden. Bulbs work nicely or start seeds inside and then move them outdoors when weather permits. Wonderful lessons can be learned from growing a flower garden.

Evaluation Questionnaire

What was your favorite craft project(s)? Would you enjoy doing it again?

What story would you enjoy hearing again?

Did you have a favorite puppet play? Did you get a chance to be in the skit? Would you like to?

Did you have a favorite Bible verse? Do you remember it?

Were there any projects that you didn't get a chance to work on that you would like to do?

What did you like best about the program?

What would you change about the program?

What did you learn this year in children's worship?

Do you plan to attend children's worship again next year?

Do you like having seven different workstations to choose from each week? What was your favorite workstation? Why?

Would you enjoy working on service projects—helping those in need? If so, tell two or three projects you would like to see our group do.

Do you like making puppets? Would you like to learn more about puppetry? Would you be interested in writing and presenting puppet plays to children at the hospital or residents at the nursing home?

Would you be willing to write a puppet play? A story? If so, what topic would you like to write on? What Bible verse would you use?

Would you be interested in having our class write its own worship service to present in the sanctuary? Would you be willing to help? What would you like to do?

Questions

Question 1. How do you handle ongoing projects with new children?

Answer. The church in Chapter 4 is an example of a project that children may get interested in starting after others are partially finished. Not a problem. Children can start on the church at any time. The church can be completed in stages. I have seen children who only make the outside of the church. Others will make the entire church, floor, pews, banners, balcony, and all. Some children like details. Other children only have the patience for the basic frame. Those who did not decide to start on the church till the fourth week can still complete the outside frame of the church and be very proud of their work.

Two third grade boys in my church's group started at the exact same time on a church. Each boy worked hard during every session. One boy finished every step, pews, banners, siding on the outside, and everything. The other boy worked just as hard but was only able to finish the basic church and windows. Yet, both boys went home beaming with pride.

Having a project that can be completed at several different levels allows children of different ability levels to work together in harmony. If you try to have all children work together at the same pace, some will be left behind while others are bored.

Make envelopes or packets for children to store their projects. Keep instructions for each week posted. This will allow children to work successfully at their own pace, even if they start late.

Question 2. If the Sunday school classes uses the same learning centers that we use in children's worship, won't the children be bored and uninterested by the time they come to the children's worship program?

Answer. No, because you have seven different learning centers every week. There is always something new and different for the children to work on. If the 4th grade Sunday school class worked at Workstation 2, the Affirmation during Sunday school and then many of those same children come the next hour to your children's worship program, just encourage them to work at a different station. You have more than enough material to keep you going for hours. Each workstation is timed to take 20 minutes, providing over 2 hours worth of material every week.

Question 3. We have lots of guests each week and also children who come regularly but on an every other week basis because of parent custody and visitation situations. What should we do when there are ongoing projects that take several weeks?

Answer. If you know that the children are just visiting Grandma and won't be back next week, encourage them to work at a station that can be completed in 20 minutes. The Benediction, for example, changes every week and needs only 20 minutes to complete. Older children who are just visiting may enjoy sewing on the prayer banner or working in the carpenter shop or helping with the sermon for the day.

If you have children who attend regularly but on an every-other-week basis, make envelopes or packets to hold their projects till they return. They will appreciate having their projects waiting for them.

If you know a child is just visiting, always send their project home with them even if it is not finished.

Question 4. Why are the patterns placed on a fold? Isn't that harder for young children?

Answer. No, actually working with paper on the fold is easier once you teach the children to trace and cut their projects on the fold. Even young children who do not always cut straight will be able to assemble their projects if they cut on the fold because both sides will turn out identical. Cutting on the fold also requires less time. If you are cutting two sides at the same time, it takes half the time to complete the project.

Question 5. Some of the projects at the Benediction workstation look too hard to 4- and 5-year olds. What if the children can't do the project?

Answer. Each workstation has been timed and tested with children and can be completed in twenty minutes by the age group listed. When a harder project is offered at the Benediction workstation to challenge the children, there is always a simple version offered as well. As adults, we often look at a project and tell children, "This project is too hard for you. You'll never be able to do this project." In truth, the children could do the project if we would take the time to help them. The child would also acquire a great deal of pride and motivation from doing a project that seems a little bit harder. Too often we think that 4 and 5 year olds can't do anything but color or glue pictures that we have cut out. Children do not learn unless we take the time to teach them.

Some children acquire skills faster than others. If you have a child that has trouble each week, assign a youth helper to work specifically with that child. The child will appreciate having a buddy.

Question 6. Some of the projects look too hard. I can't even figure the project out, so how will the children figure out what to do?

Answer. Adults often have more trouble with the craft projects than children do. Children are willing to try something new or to give it a try before they decide it's impossible. Adults often walk in, look at the picture, and say, "O dear! that looks hard. I couldn't even do that."

I saw an adult helper one day go around and look at each project without reading the directions or even trying to make the project. Within two seconds, she told the children which projects were too hard for them and which ones they were allowed to try.

One of the primary lessons taught in *Come, Follow Me!* is not to give up before you try. The words "I can't" do not exist.

We are raising our children in a world of ready access, computers, video games, microwave snacks, and a school system based on worksheets. We have grown to expect everything to be easy and not require any effort. Yet, real life is not easy and young people must often grow up and go out and work in a world where they have to read the directions and figure out how to solve a problem or make something work.

Some of the projects in this book are very easy and some are a definite challenge, but each and every project is workable by children.

I work with two totally different groups of mixed age level children each week. One group consists of approximately three to eight children. The other group has over fifty children in attendance most Sundays.

I test each project. I also have other teachers test projects.

As you go through the year, watch the sense of accomplishment grow. Children will often depart for home and leave behind the simple workbook cut and glue project from Sunday school but rarely ever forget to take home a project they have spent twenty minutes constructing with their own two hands in children's worship. Our society needs to redevelop a sense of pride in our work. Help the children start today.

Question 7. What do I do with all of these tiny pattern pieces?

Answer. Since I use the program year after year, I save all pattern pieces in an expandable file. I place the patterns for each project in a separate envelope and place them in a pattern file arranged by session. When I need a particular pattern, I can just turn to the file and easily find what I need.

Question 8. We don't have enough time. There's too much to do at each workstation for twenty minutes. Can children really finish each project listed in twenty minutes?

Answer. Yes, children can and do finish in just twenty minutes, but not all children work at the same speed. Each workstation is designed to be fast-paced and keep children very busy for twenty minutes. To finish, the children will have to work and not waste time. When chldren have too much free time on their hands, trouble and mischief set in; therefore, I do pack each session with lots to do and intentionally design each workstation with the maximum amount of work possible. I find when children are busy, discipline is not a problem. If a child continuously works veryslowly, the child can start on easier projects and gradually work up to harder projects.

Question 9. Should I repeat special projects for those who missed it?

Answer. Ongoing projects are a good way to encourage attendance each week. For example,

on World Communion Sunday, I always have the children make bread to take home. The next Sunday, the children can't wait to tell me how delicious their bread was or how high it rose. New children or those who were not in attendance for the bread making session feel a little sad at first that they didn't get to make bread too, but I always cheerfully remind them that we make bread several different times throughout the year, so they will get a chance later on. Smiles immediately return and usually their attendance improves.

Keep the excitement going so that children do not want to miss. As one child told his parents, "We have to come each Sunday; otherwise, you never know what you'll miss."

Churches should be an exciting place for children to come. Children should look forward to coming to God's house for worship more than staying home watching TV or playing outside on Sunday morning. Your goal is to make each week's program so exciting that the children just can't wait to see what will happen next.

Question 10. I think children would be overwhelmed by so much moving around. As a teacher, I would feel more comfortable if children only had one activity to choose from. Do you think children really learn from this program?

Answer. I frequently check to make sure what the children in my program learned from the week before. I will ask periodically, "What was the Bible lesson last week?" Since the lessons are presented with child-oriented examples, the children can easily remember the main idea of the lesson.

One Sunday, I asked who remembered what last week's sermon and Bible lesson was about, and a little five year old boy raised his hand. If you had asked me before he answered, I would have said that he had no idea what last week's lesson was about because he didn't seem to be paying attention last week. Yet, he said, "the lesson was about saying your're sorry when you hurt someone's feelings and being kind to others if you want them to be kind to you." The lesson was from Luke 6:37-38.

We must remember that children do not learn the same way adults do. What might look like a well organized orderly program to an adult might look boring and totally uninteresting to a child.

Keep the lesson short and simple each week. Do not try to cover the entire Bible in only thirty minutes. Just take one small bit that Jesus taught and build an entire lesson around that one central idea. In this way, it is easier for children to remember the lesson and how it applies to their life today.

Each week's lesson is taught in nine different ways. The story, the workstations, and the puppet play sermon are all based on the same theme and same central Bible verse. The key is to get children and adults to read the workstation signs and related Bible verses.

ABOUT THE AUTHOR

Elaine Clanton Harpine, Ph.D., is a program design specialist and group training consultant specializing in conducting and evaluating youth and children's group programs. A Methodist minister's daughter, Dr. Clanton Harpine has spent the last twenty-seven years working in both volunteer and staff positions in The United Methodist Church.

She earned her doctorate in Educational Psychology and Counseling from the University of Illinois, where her research focused on leadership development in The United Methodist Church. She has worked as a Director of Christian Education and as a Youth Coordinator.

Dr. Clanton Harpine's published writings include: *The Christmas Tree: How to Make Christian Ornaments for your Christmas Tree, Pattern Book,* Volume I and II (1998); *The Christmas Tree: A Tree-trimming Workshop and Program Using Christ-centered Ornaments* (1994); *No Expeience Necessary!: A "Learn by Doing" Guide for Creating Children's Worship* (1992) (selected as one of the top five worship curriculums in the nationwide survey, 1995); *Youth-Led Meetings: 10 Step-by-Step Meeting Plans Designed for Teenagers to Lead Themselves* (1989); and "A Creative Retreat: Popularity Pursuit," reprinted in *More Group Retreats* (1987), edited by Cindy Hansen. Other programs published in *Directions in Faith* (Graded Press, 1986–87) deal with peer pressure, coping with failure, witnessing, alcohol abuse, parental pressure, suicide, and leading your friends to Christ.

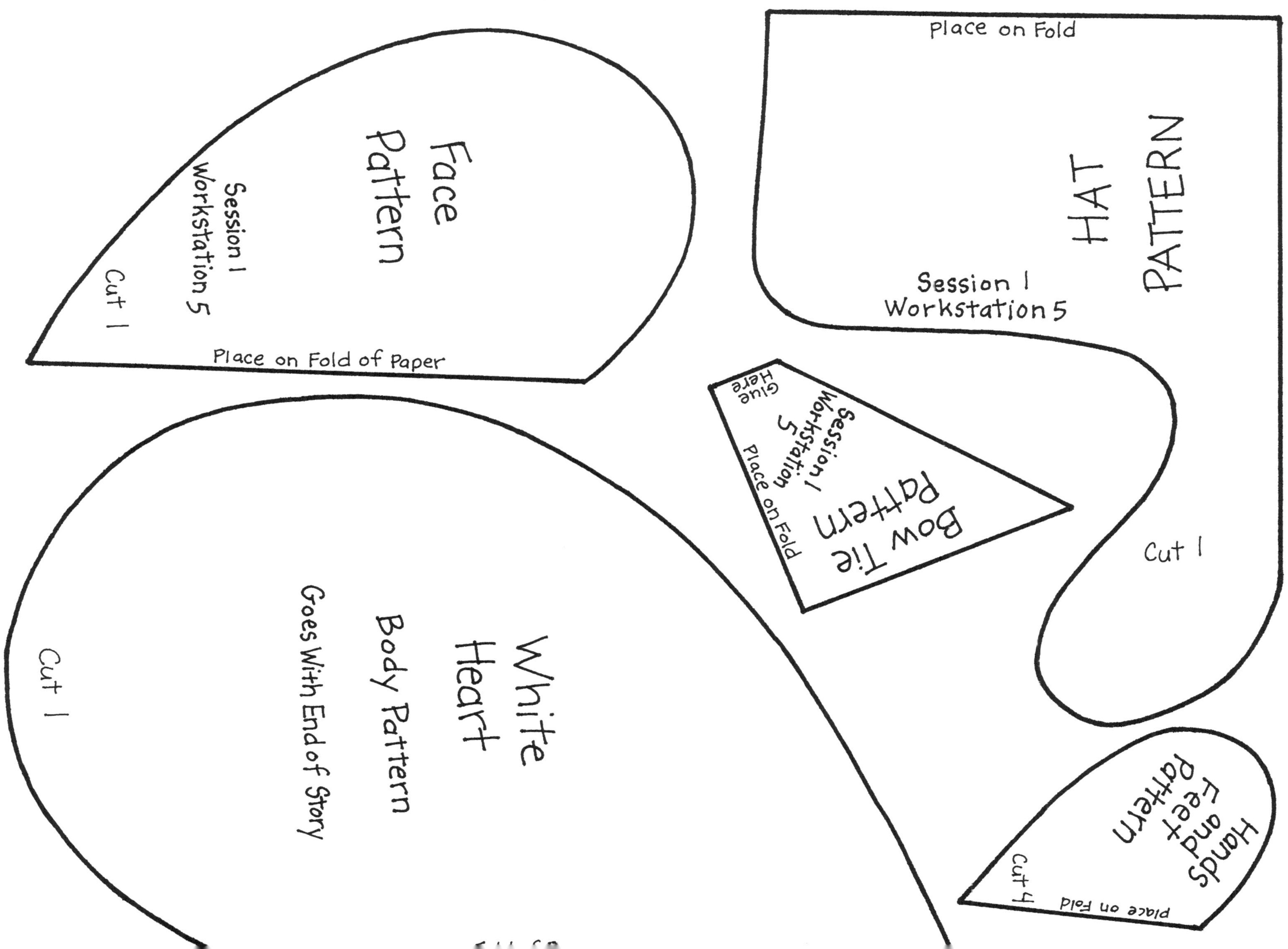

Place on Fold
HAT PATTERN
Session 1
Workstation 5
Cut 1
Face Pattern
Session 1
Workstation 5
Cut 1
Place on Fold of Paper
Glue Here
Bow Tie Pattern
Session 1
Workstation 5
Place on Fold
White Heart
Body Pattern
Goes With End of Story
Cut 1
Hands and Feet Pattern
Cut 4
Place on Fold

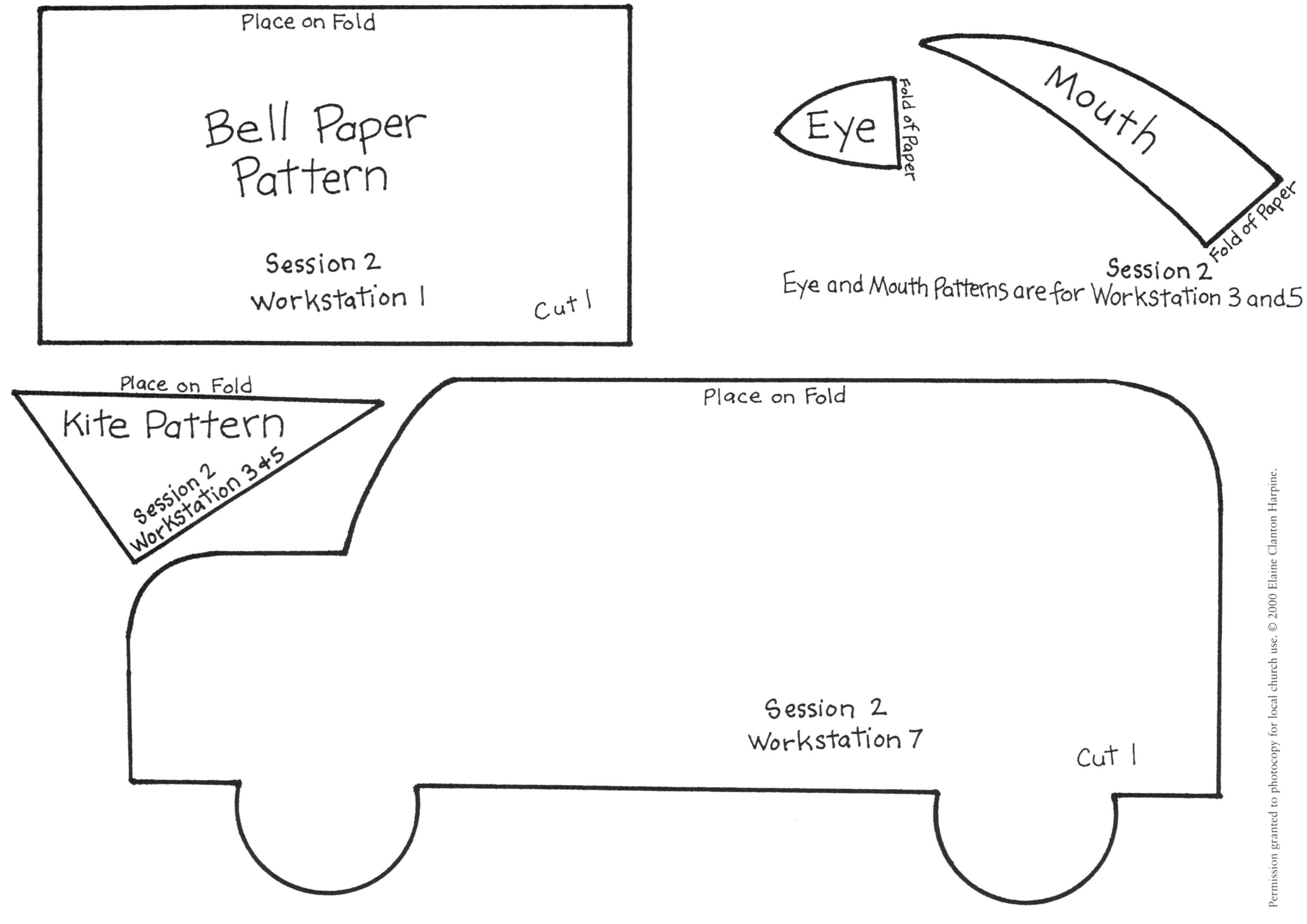

Place on Fold
Bell Paper
Pattern
Session 2
Workstation 1
Cut 1
Eye
Fold of Paper
Mouth
Fold of Paper
Session 2
Eye and Mouth Patterns are for Workstation 3 and 5
Place on Fold
Kite Pattern
Session 2
Workstation 3+5
Place on Fold
Session 2
Workstation 7
Cut 1

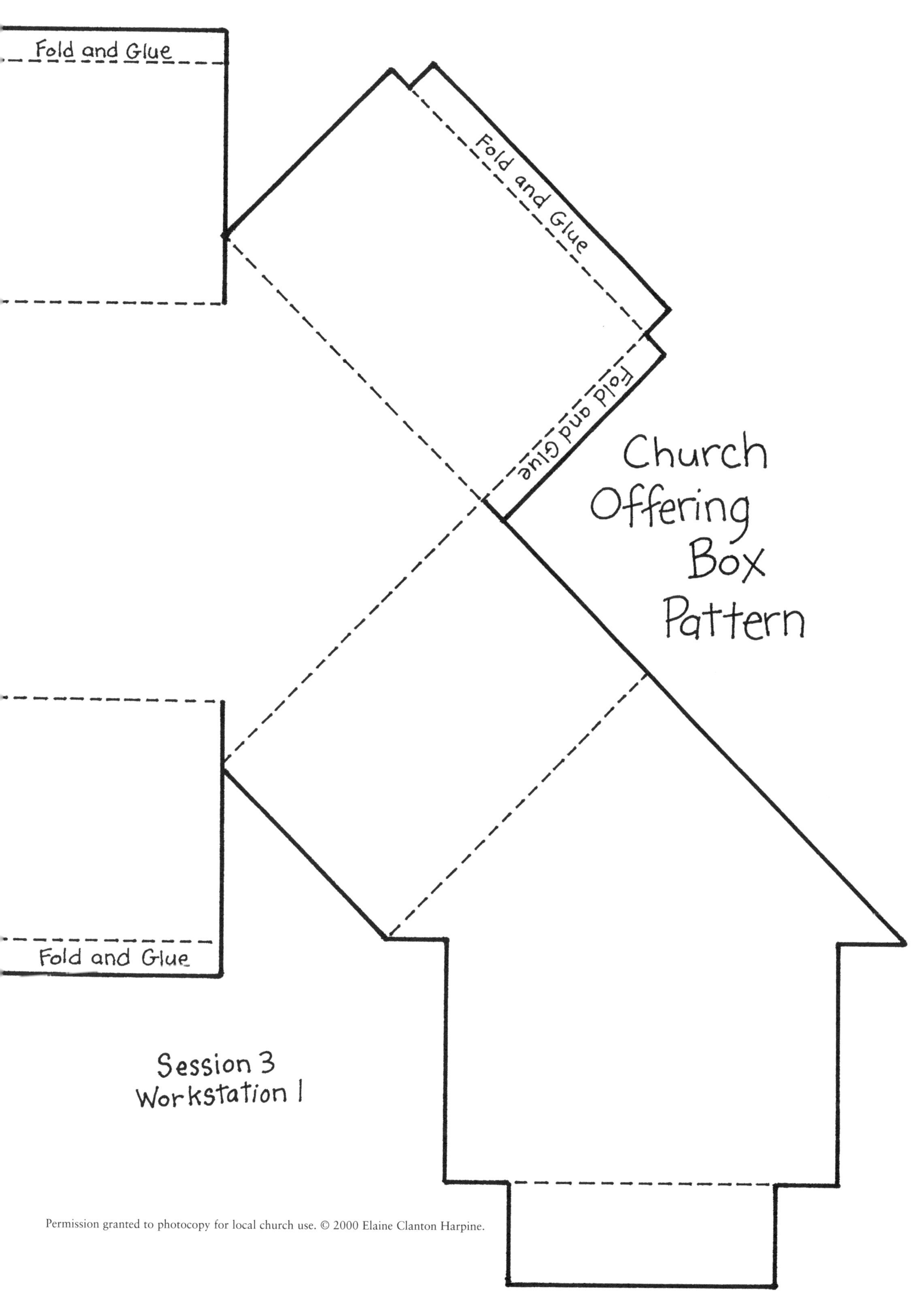

Fold and Glue
Fold and Glue
Fold and Glue
Fold and Glue
Church
Offering
Box
Pattern
Session 3
Workstation 1

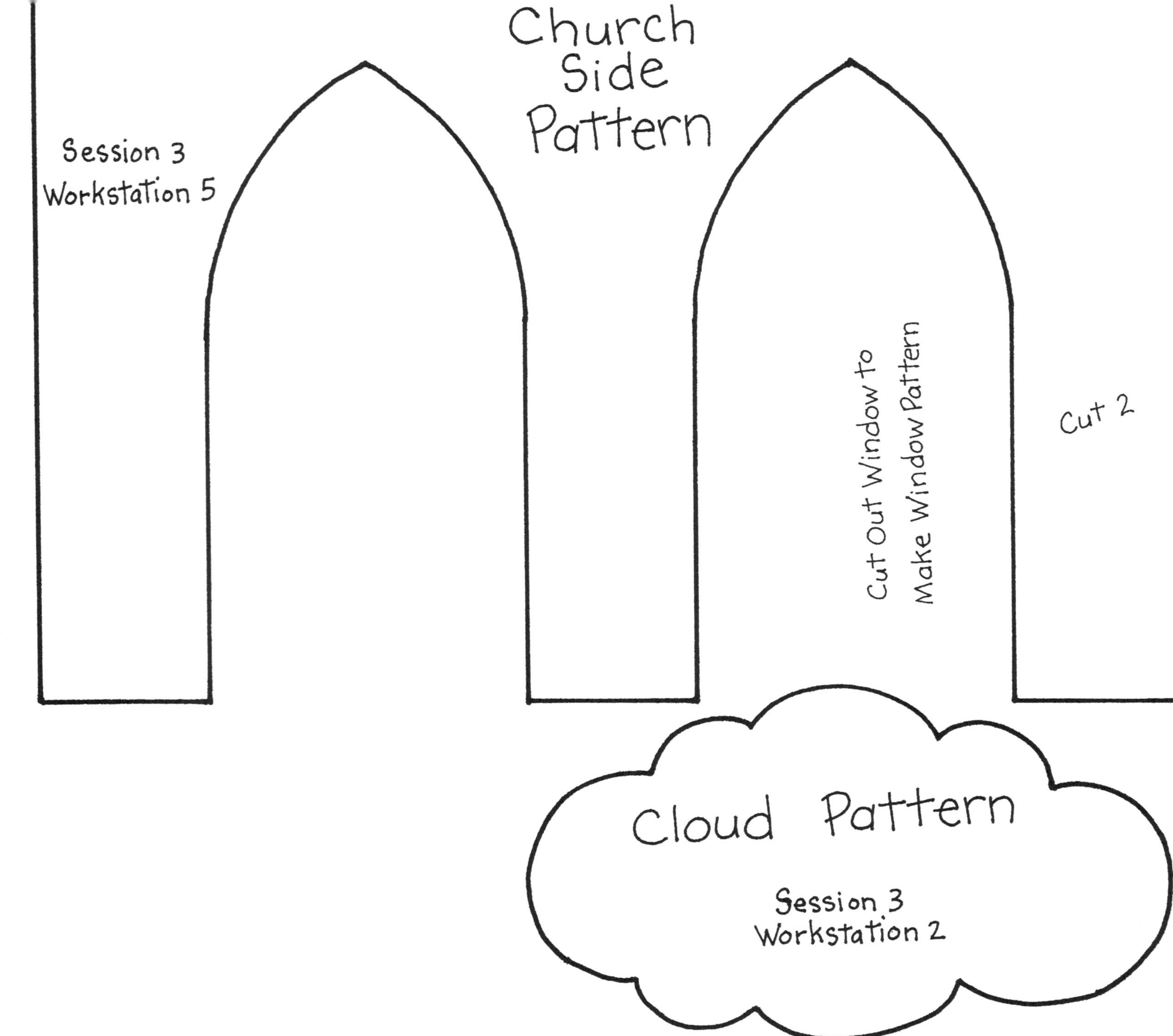

Church Side Pattern
Session 3
Workstation 5
Cut Out Window to Make Window Pattern
Cut 2
Cloud Pattern
Session 3
Workstation 2

Church
Front and Back

Session 3
Workstation 5

Cut 2

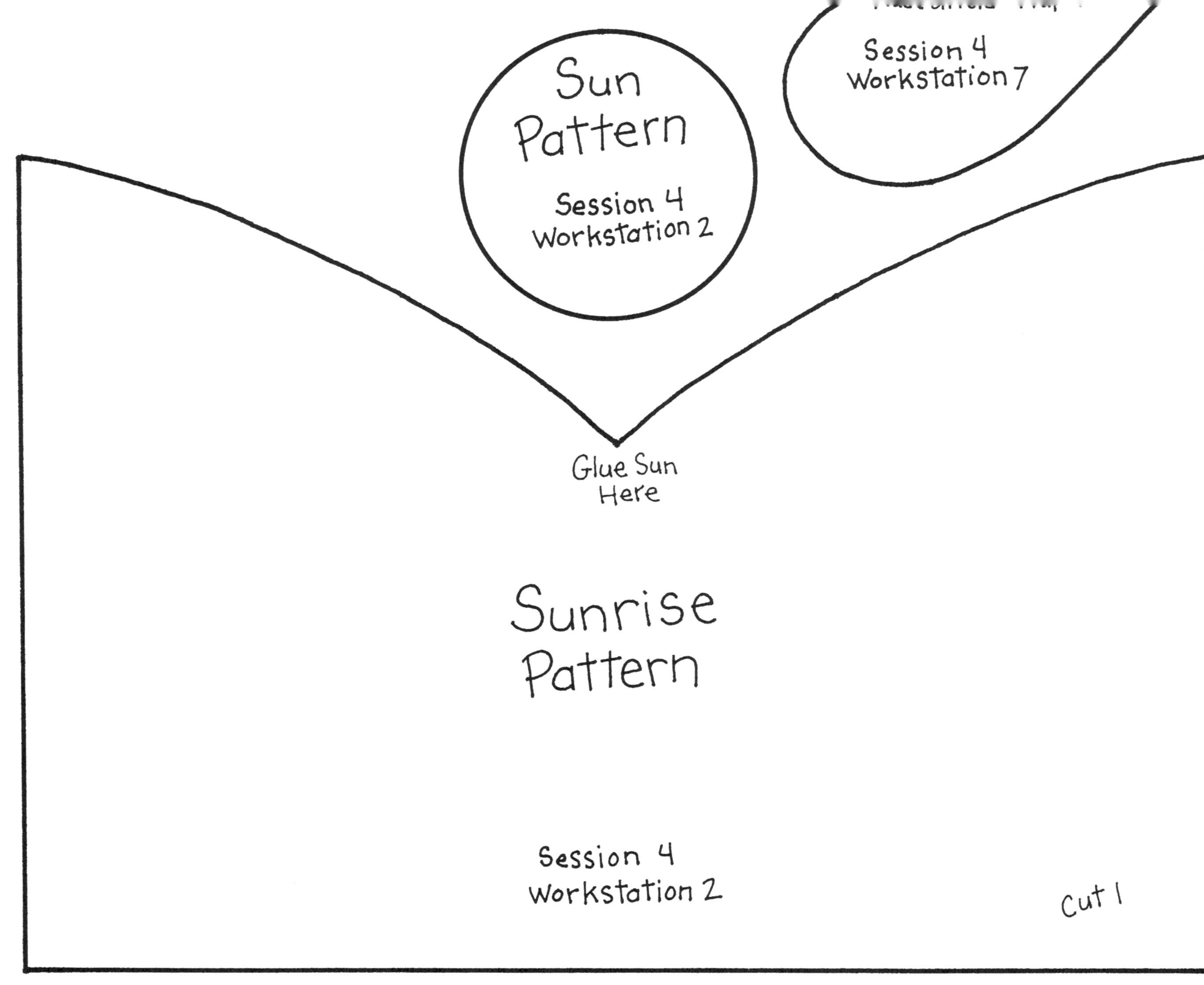

Sun
Pattern

Session 4
Workstation 2

Session 4
Workstation 7

Glue Sun
Here

Sunrise
Pattern

Session 4
Workstation 2

Cut 1

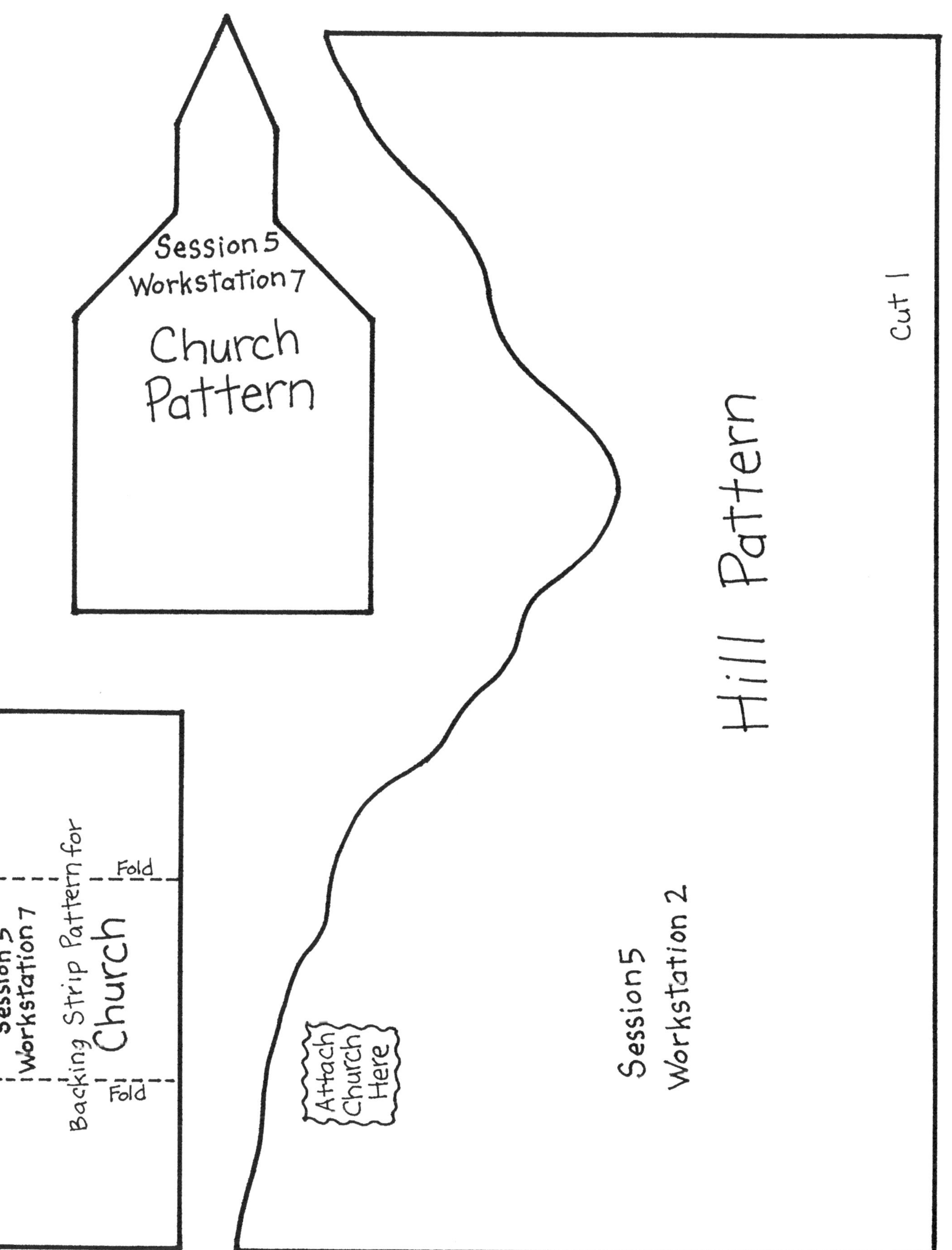
Session 5
Workstation 7
Church
Pattern
Session 5
Workstation 7
Backing Strip Pattern for Church
Fold
Fold
Hill Pattern
Cut 1
Session 5
Workstation 2
Attach Church Here

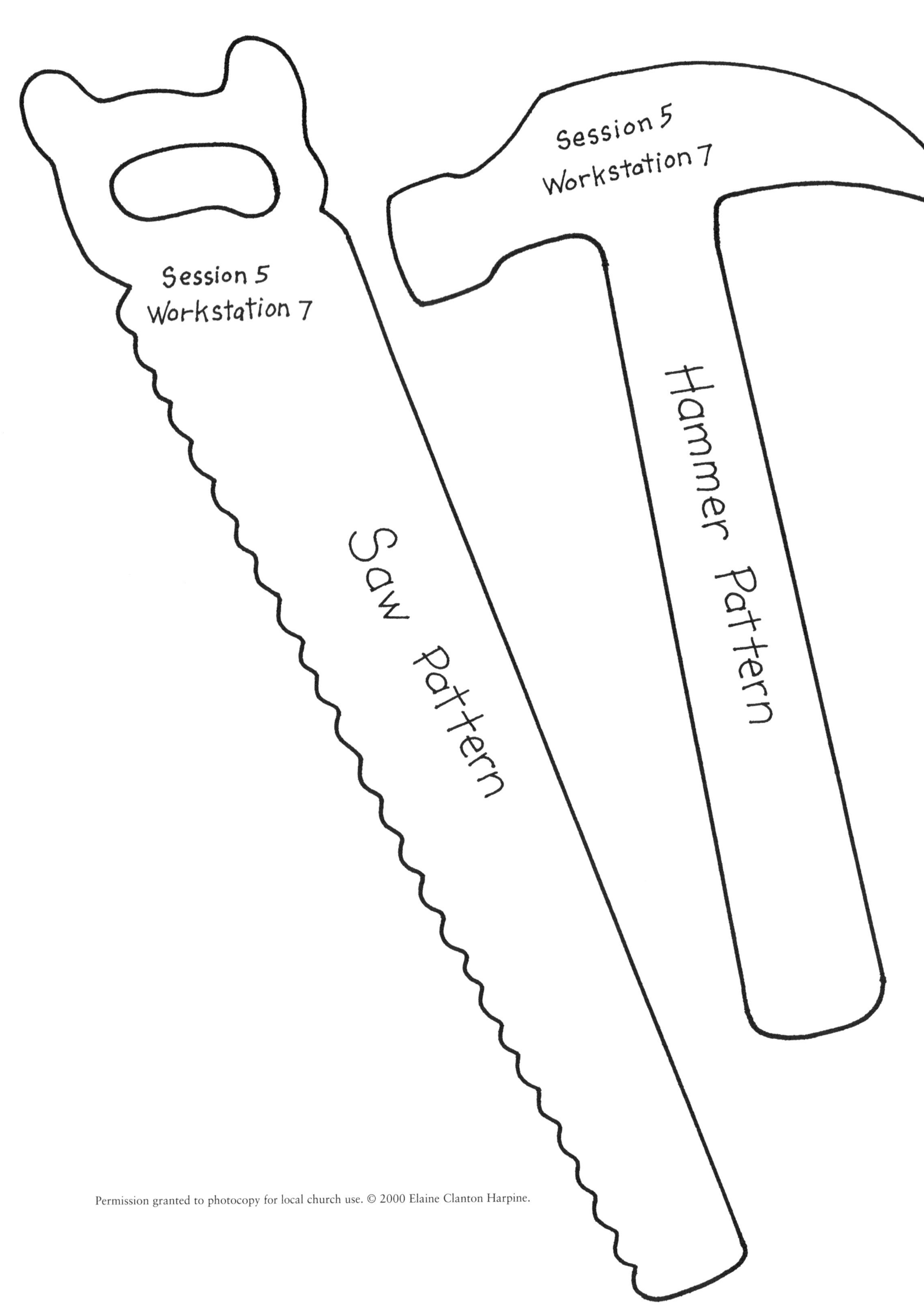

Session 5
Workstation 7
Session 5
Workstation 7
Saw Pattern
Hammer Pattern

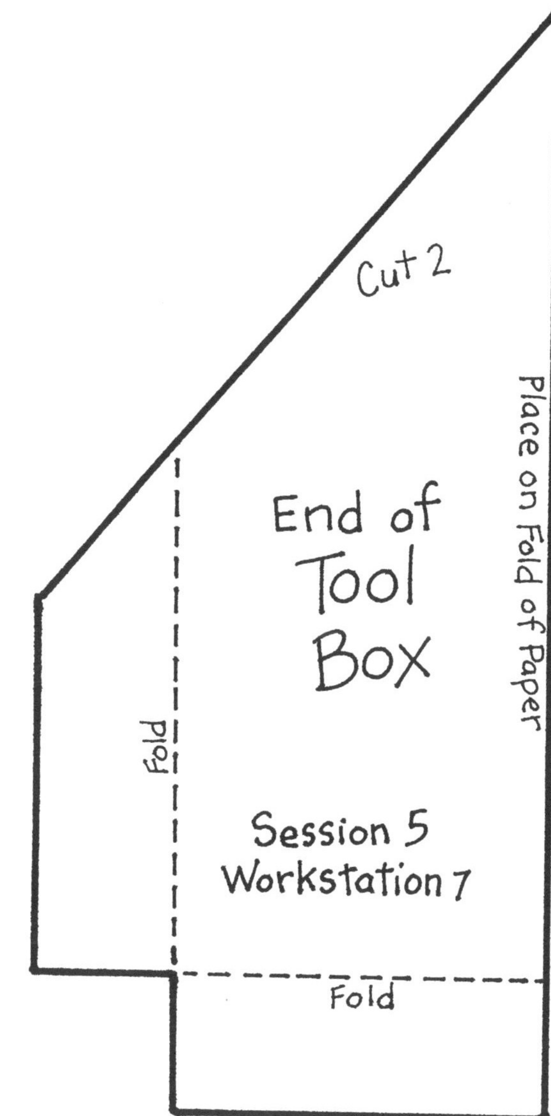

Cut 1
Fold on Dotted Line
Toolbox Pattern
Session 5
Workstation 7
Cut 2
Place on Fold of Paper
End of
Tool
Box
Session 5
Workstation 7
Fold
Fold

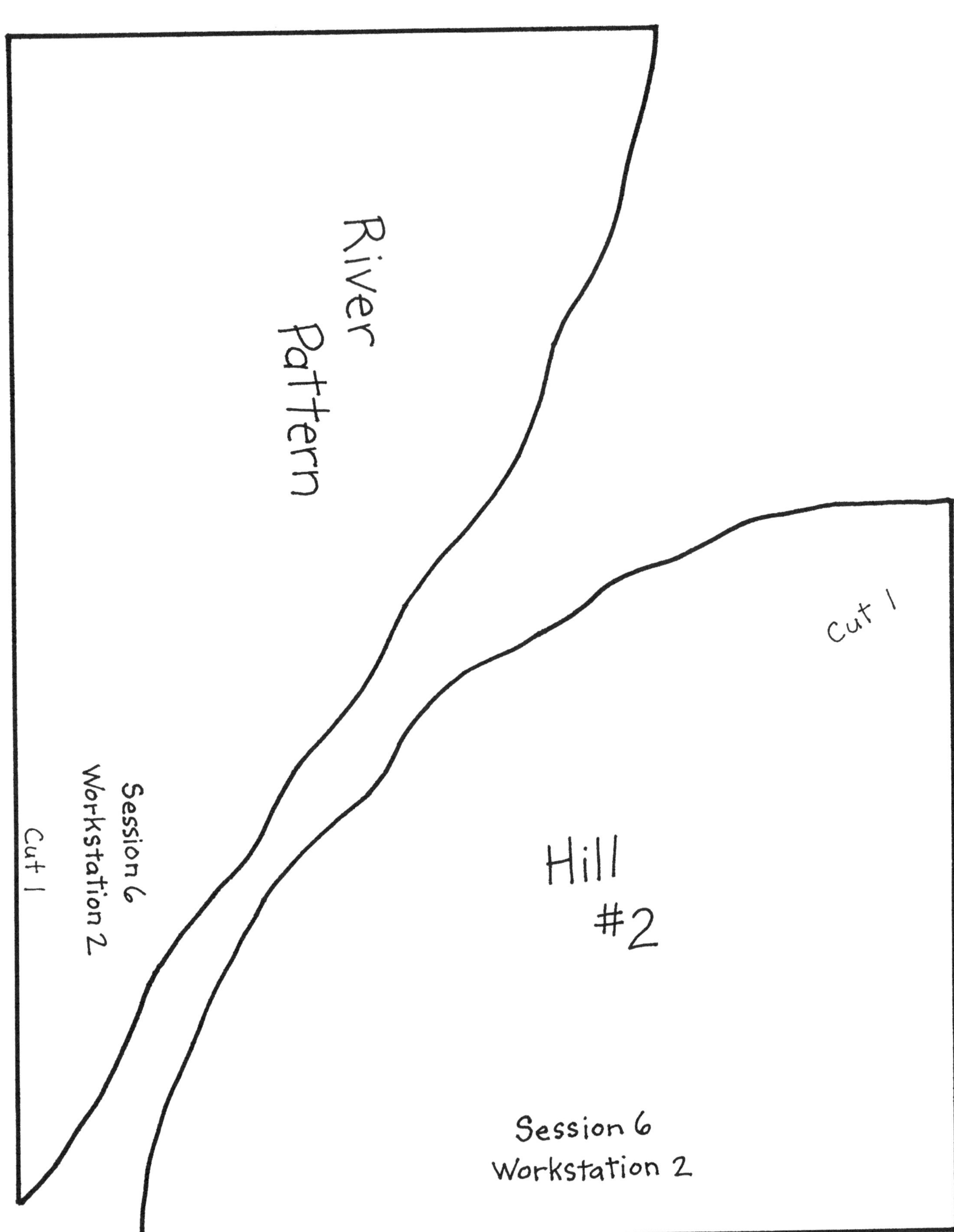

River
Pattern
Session 6
Workstation 2
Cut 1
Cut 1
Hill
#2
Session 6
Workstation 2

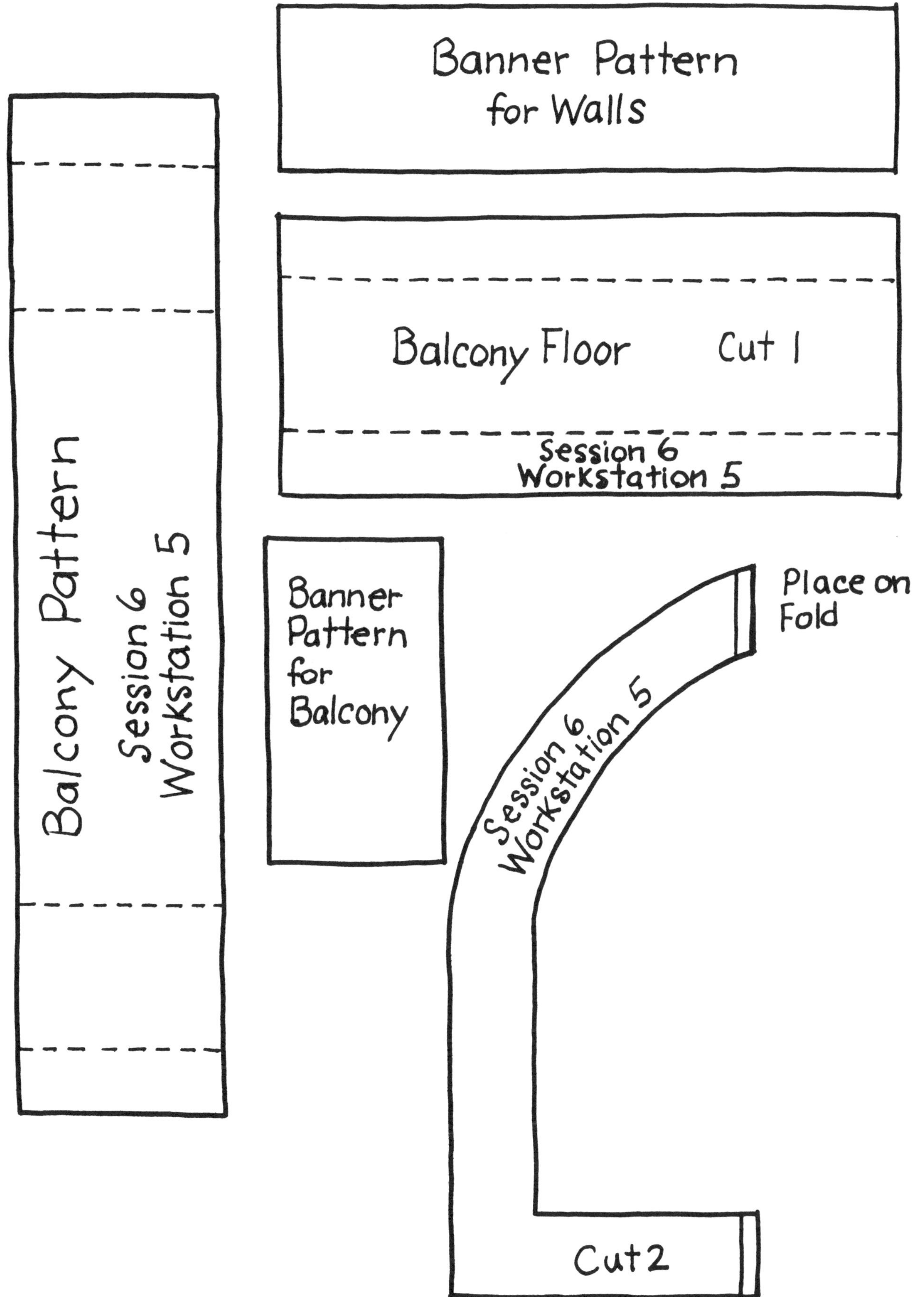

Banner Pattern
for Walls
Balcony Floor   Cut 1
Session 6
Workstation 5
Balcony Pattern
Session 6
Workstation 5
Banner
Pattern
for
Balcony
Place on
Fold
Session 6
Workstation 5
Cut 2

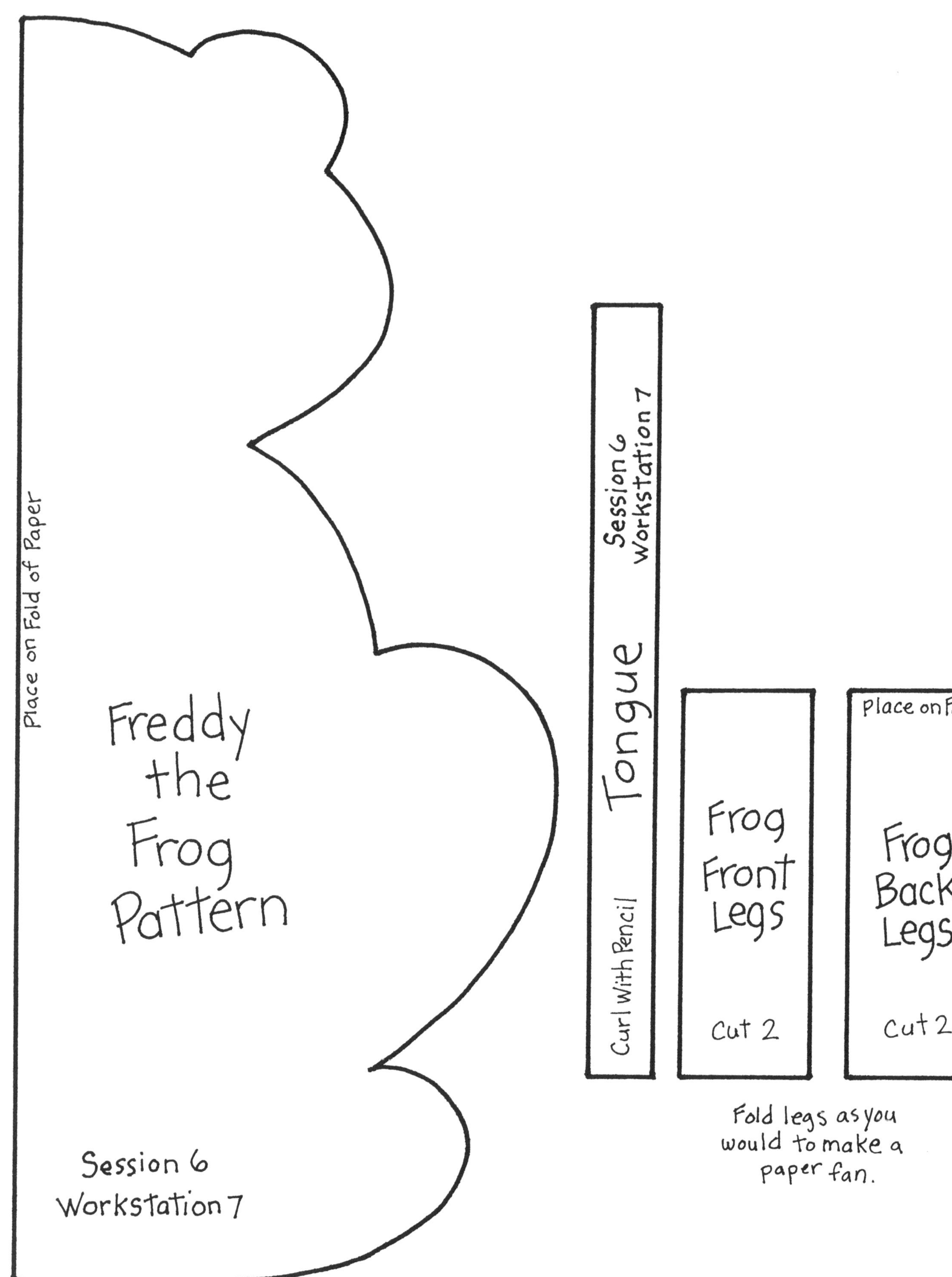

Place on Fold of Paper
Freddy
the
Frog
Pattern
Session 6
Workstation 7
Tongue
Session 6
Workstation 7
Curl With Pencil
Frog
Front
Legs
Cut 2
Place on Fo
Frog
Back
Legs
Cut 2
Fold legs as you
would to make a
paper fan.

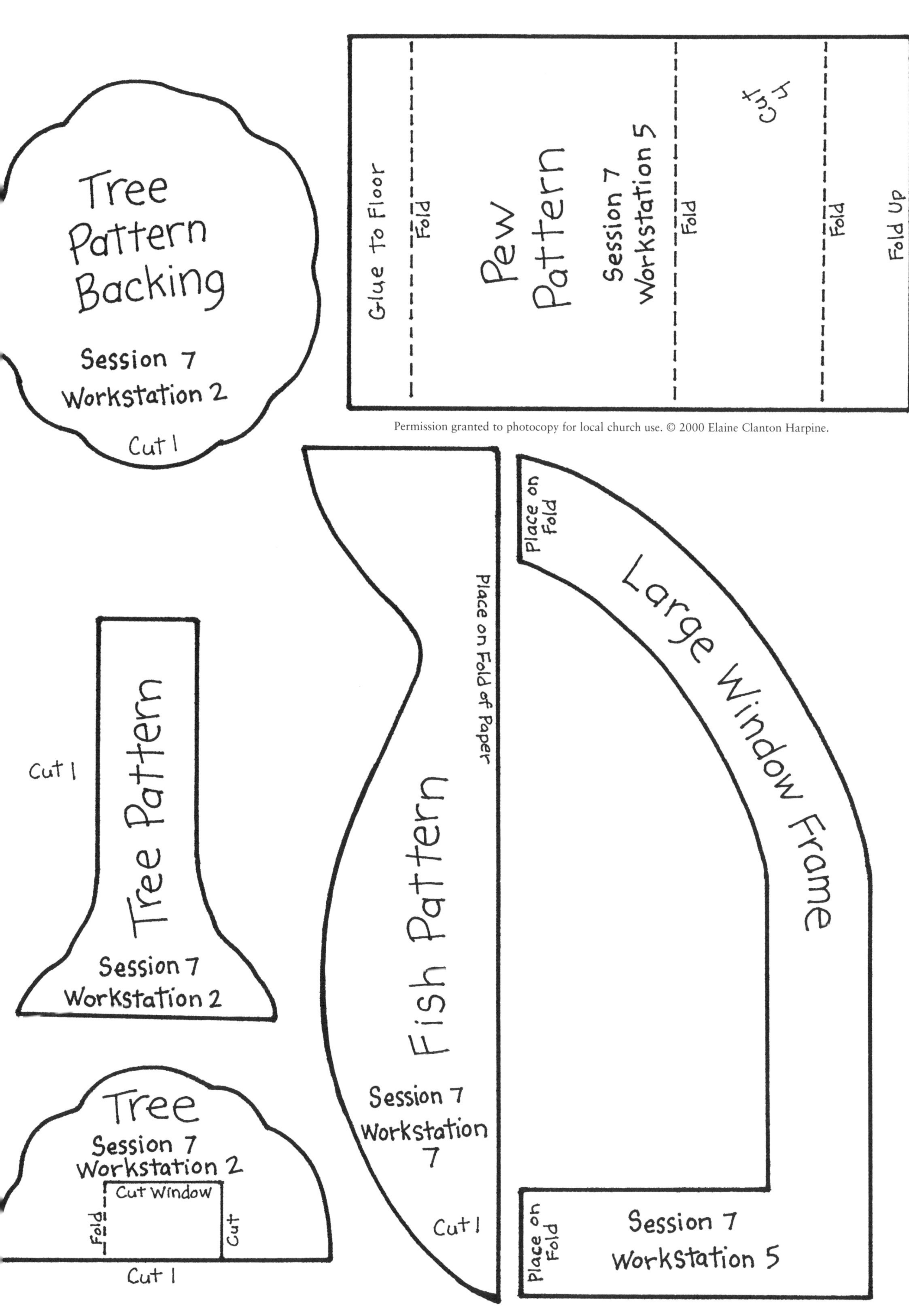

Tree Pattern Backing
Session 7
Workstation 2
Cut 1
Glue to Floor
Fold
Pew Pattern
Session 7
Workstation 5
Cut
Fold
Fold
Fold Up
Permission granted to photocopy for local church use. © 2000 Elaine Clanton Harpine.
Tree Pattern
Cut 1
Session 7
Workstation 2
Place on Fold of Paper
Place on Fold
Large Window Frame
Fish Pattern
Session 7
Workstation 7
Cut 1
Place on Fold
Session 7
Workstation 5
Tree
Session 7
Workstation 2
Fold
Cut Window
Cut
Cut 1

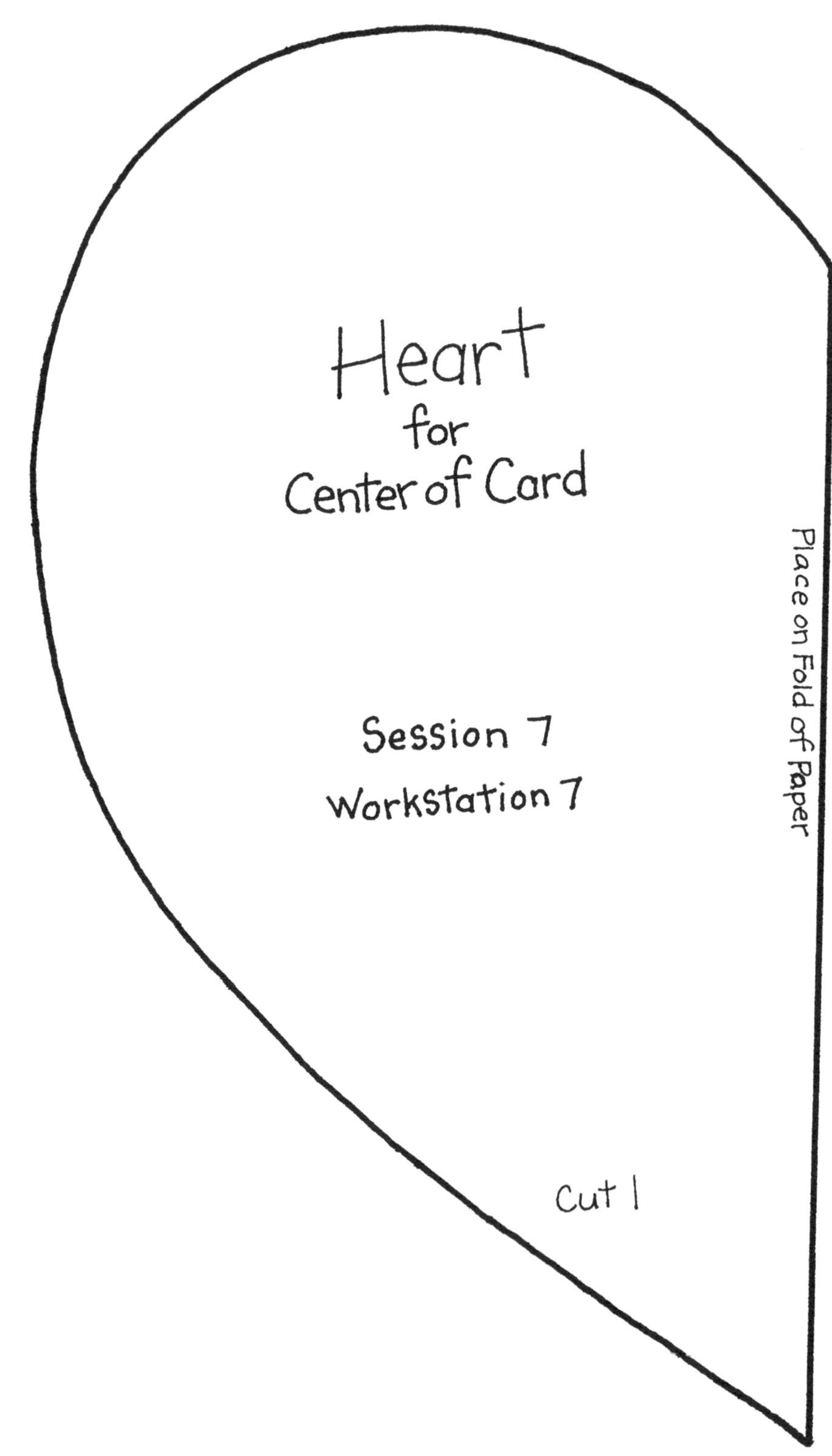

Heart
for
Center of Card

Session 7

Workstation 7

Place on Fold of Paper

Cut 1

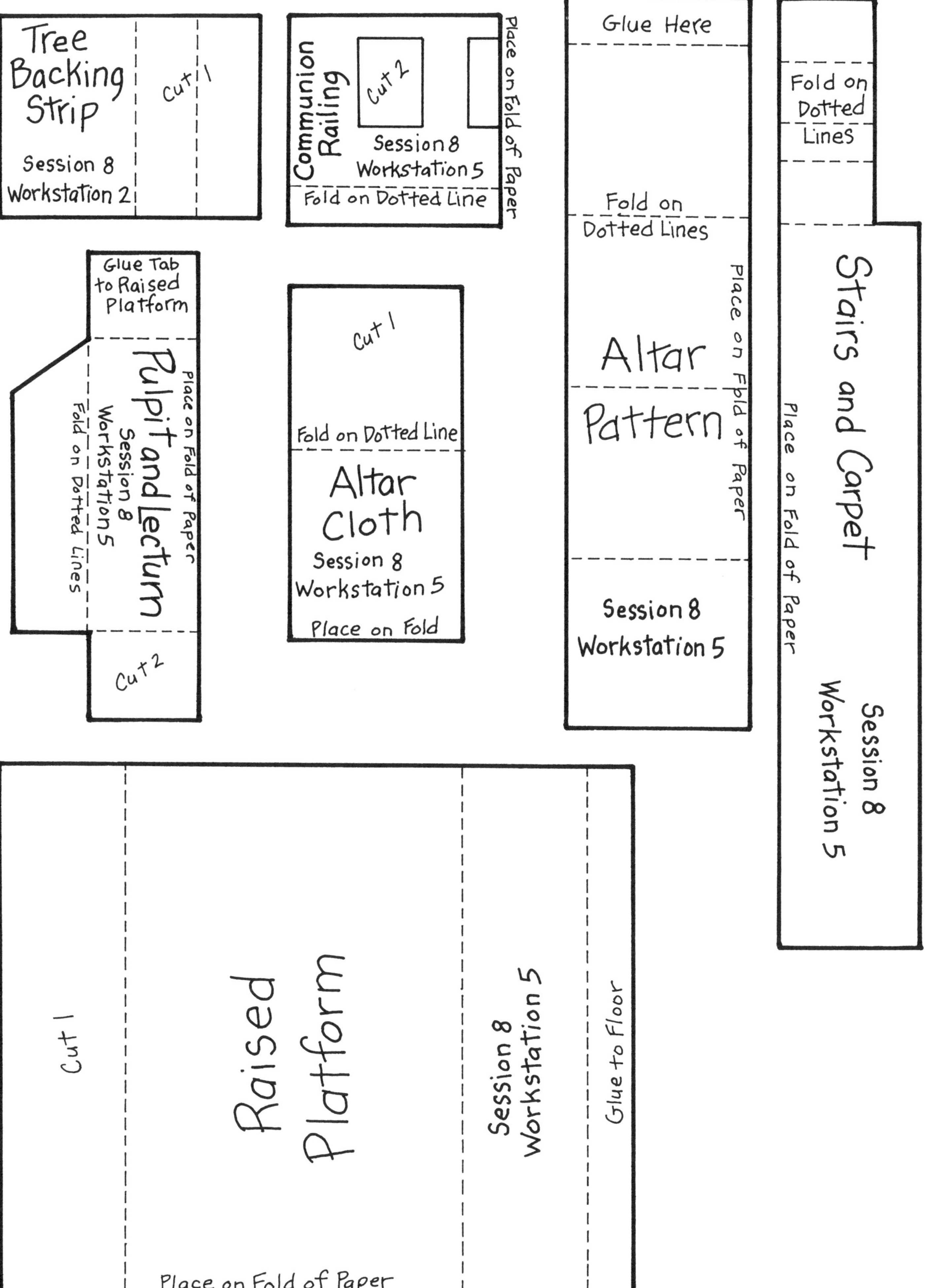

Tree Backing Strip
Cut 1
Session 8
Workstation 2
Communion Railing
Cut 2
Session 8
Workstation 5
Fold on Dotted Line
Place on Fold of Paper
Glue Here
Fold on Dotted Lines
Altar Pattern
Place on Fold of Paper
Session 8
Workstation 5
Fold on Dotted Lines
Stairs and Carpet
Place on Fold of Paper
Session 8
Workstation 5
Glue Tab to Raised Platform
Pulpit and Lectern
Session 8
Workstation 5
Place on Fold of Paper
Fold on Dotted Lines
Cut 2
Cut 1
Fold on Dotted Line
Altar Cloth
Session 8
Workstation 5
Place on Fold
Cut 1
Raised Platform
Session 8
Workstation 5
Glue to Floor
Place on Fold of Paper

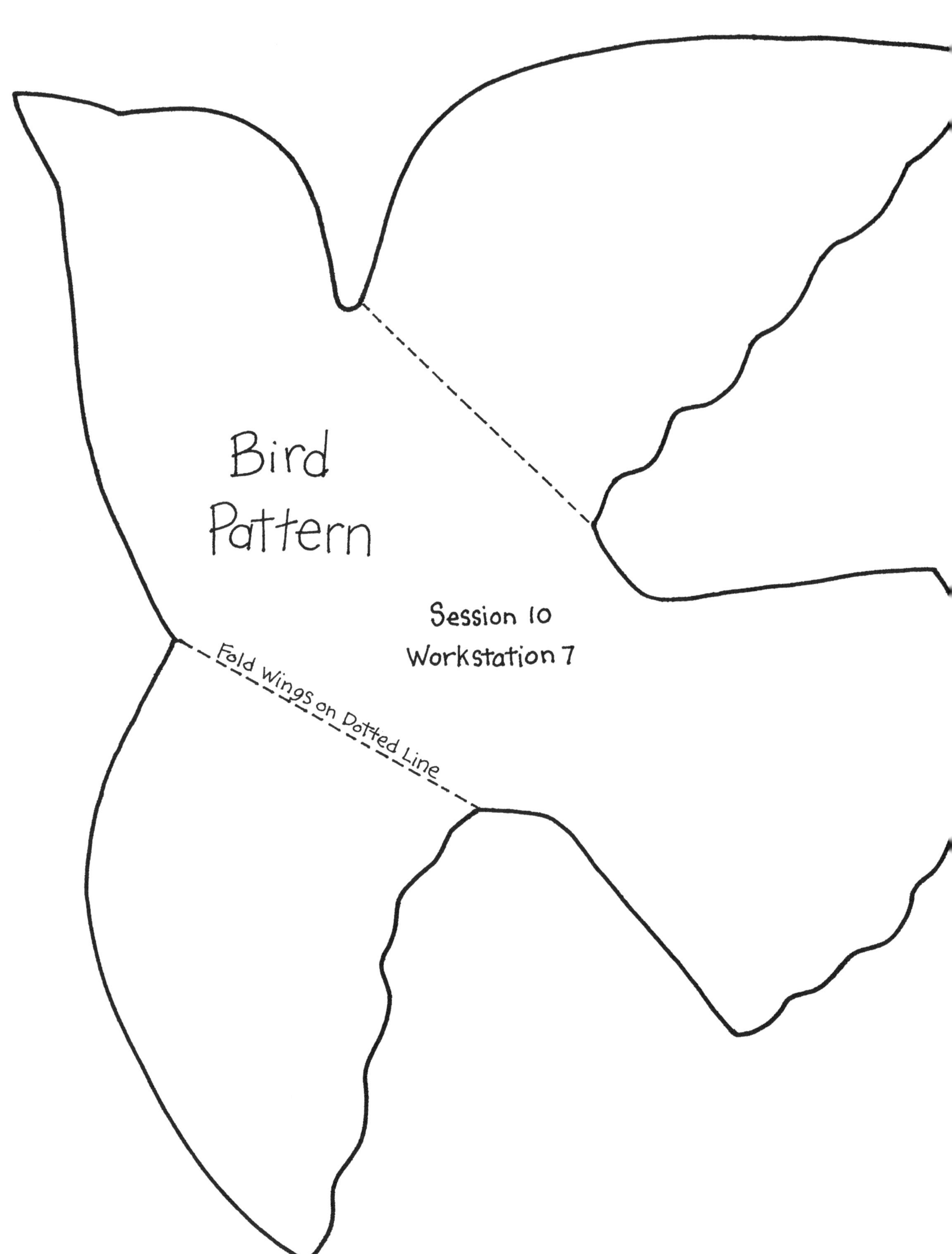

Bird
Pattern
Session 10
Workstation 7
Fold Wings on Dotted Line

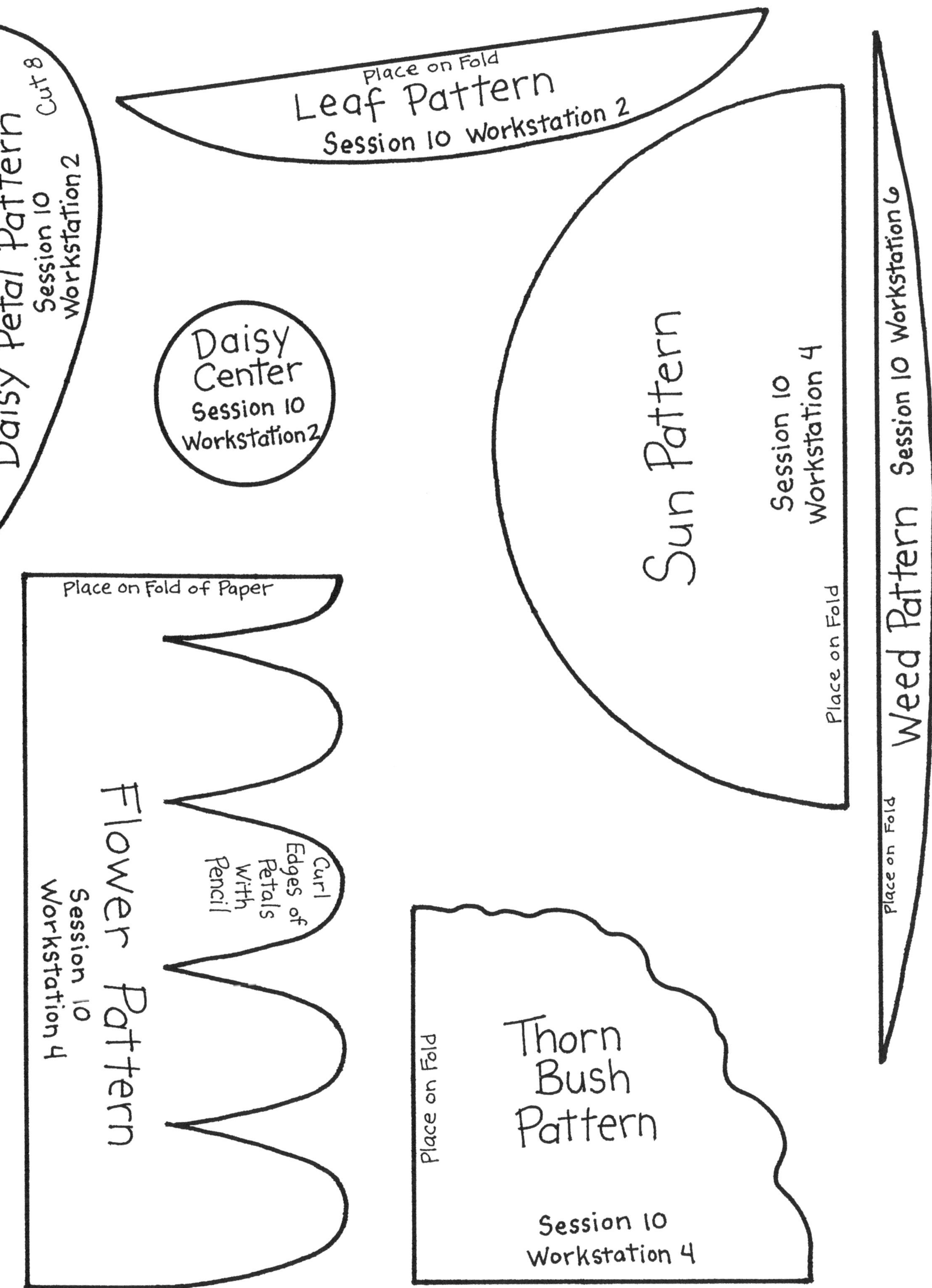

Place on Fold
Leaf Pattern
Session 10 Workstation 2
Daisy Petal Pattern
Session 10
Workstation 2
Cut 8
Daisy
Center
Session 10
Workstation 2
Sun Pattern
Session 10
Workstation 4
Place on Fold
Weed Pattern Session 10 Workstation 6
Place on Fold
Place on Fold of Paper
Curl
Edges of
Petals
With
Pencil
Flower Pattern
Session 10
Workstation 4
Place on Fold
Thorn
Bush
Pattern
Session 10
Workstation 4

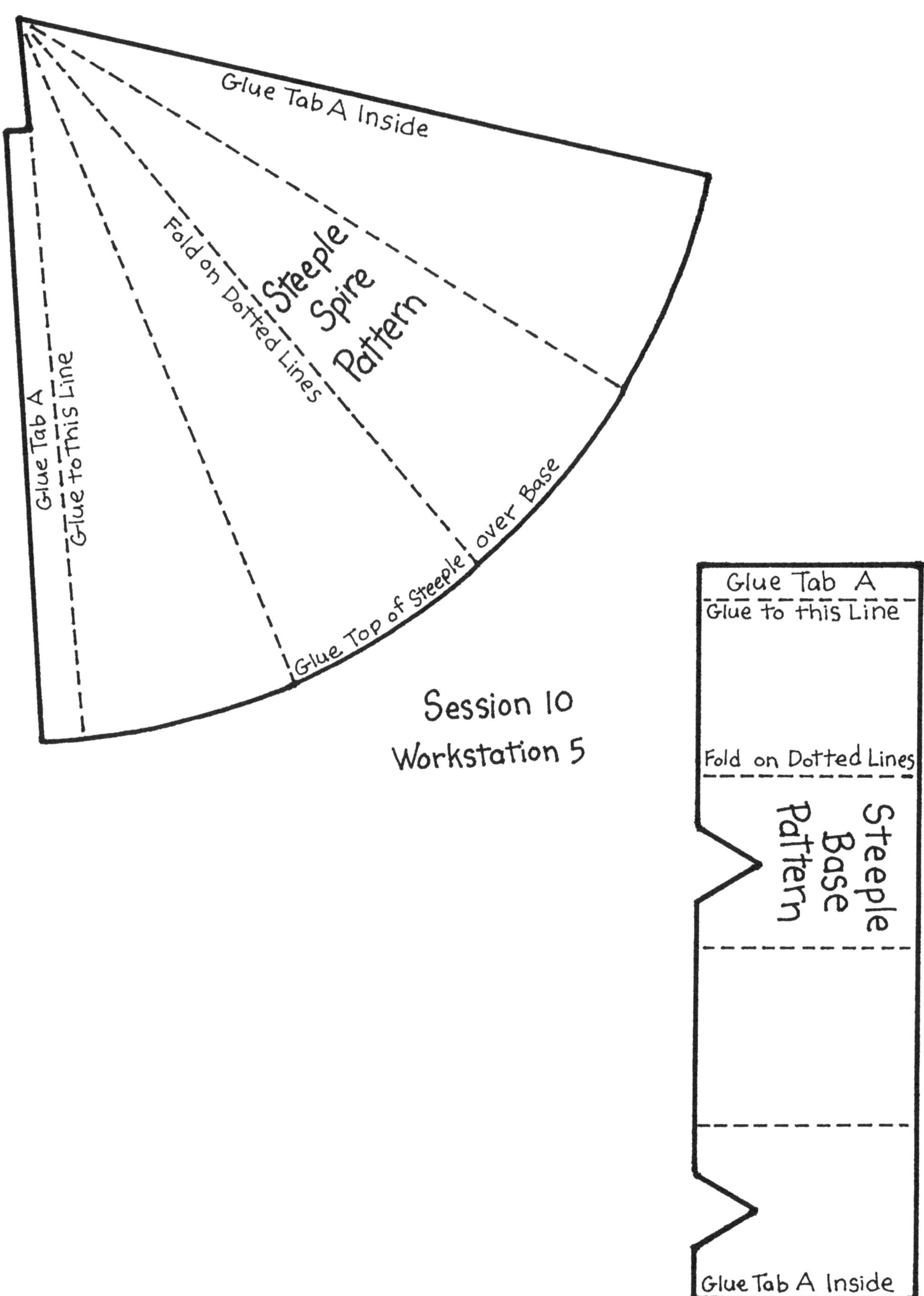

Glue Tab A Inside
Fold on Dotted Lines
Steeple Spire Pattern
Glue Tab A
Glue to this Line
Glue Top of Steeple over Base
Session 10
Workstation 5
Glue Tab A
Glue to this Line
Fold on Dotted Lines
Steeple Base Pattern
Glue Tab A Inside

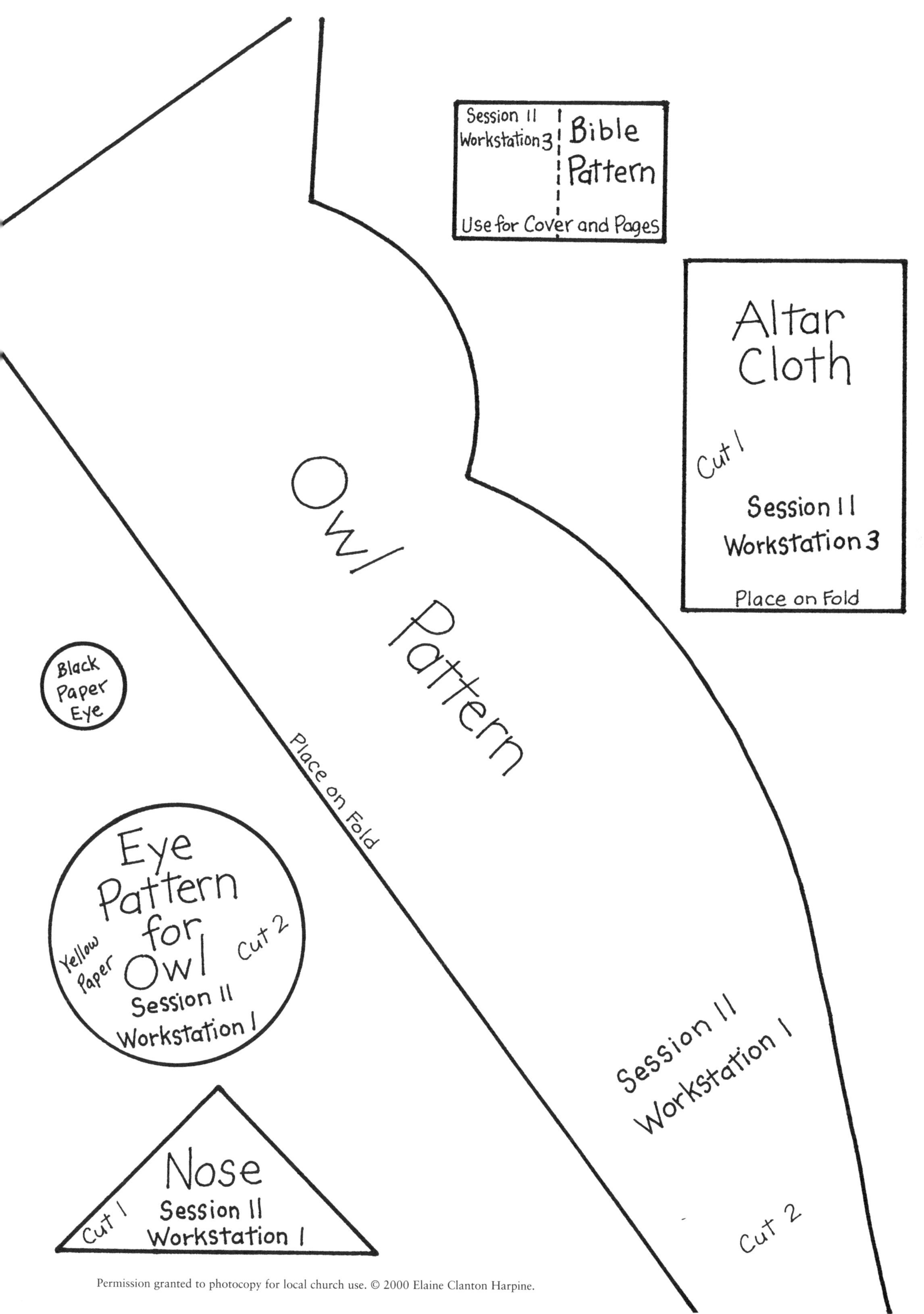

Session 11
Workstation 3
Bible
Pattern
Use for Cover and Pages

Altar
Cloth
Cut 1
Session 11
Workstation 3
Place on Fold

Owl Pattern
Place on Fold

Black
Paper
Eye

Eye
Pattern
for
Owl
Yellow Paper
Cut 2
Session 11
Workstation 1

Session 11
Workstation 1

Nose
Cut 1
Session 11
Workstation 1

Cut 2

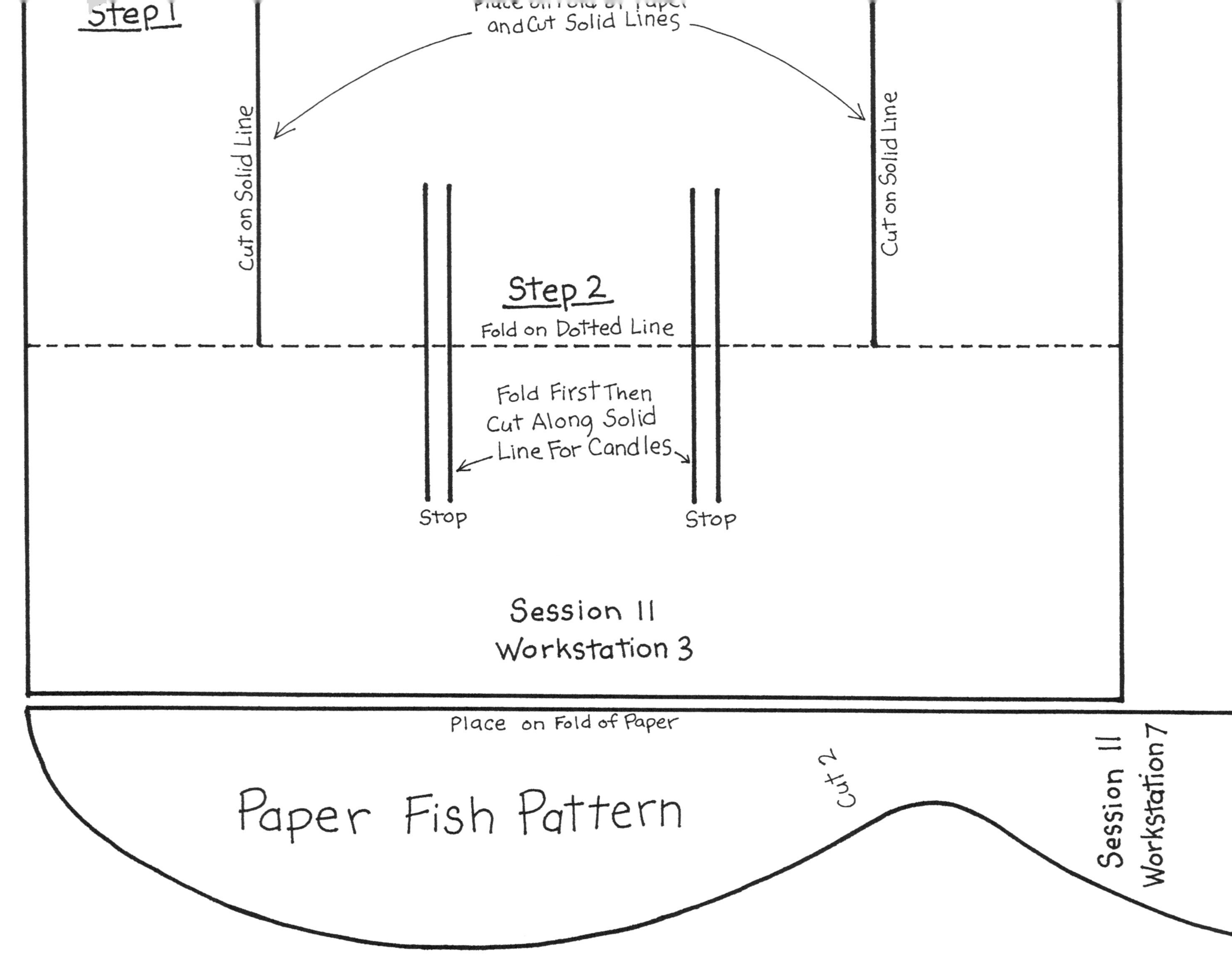

Step 1
Place on Fold of Paper
and Cut Solid Lines
Cut on Solid Line
Cut on Solid Line
Step 2
Fold on Dotted Line
Fold First Then
Cut Along Solid
Line For Candles
Stop
Stop
Session 11
Workstation 3
Place on Fold of Paper
Paper Fish Pattern
Cut 2
Session 11
Workstation 7

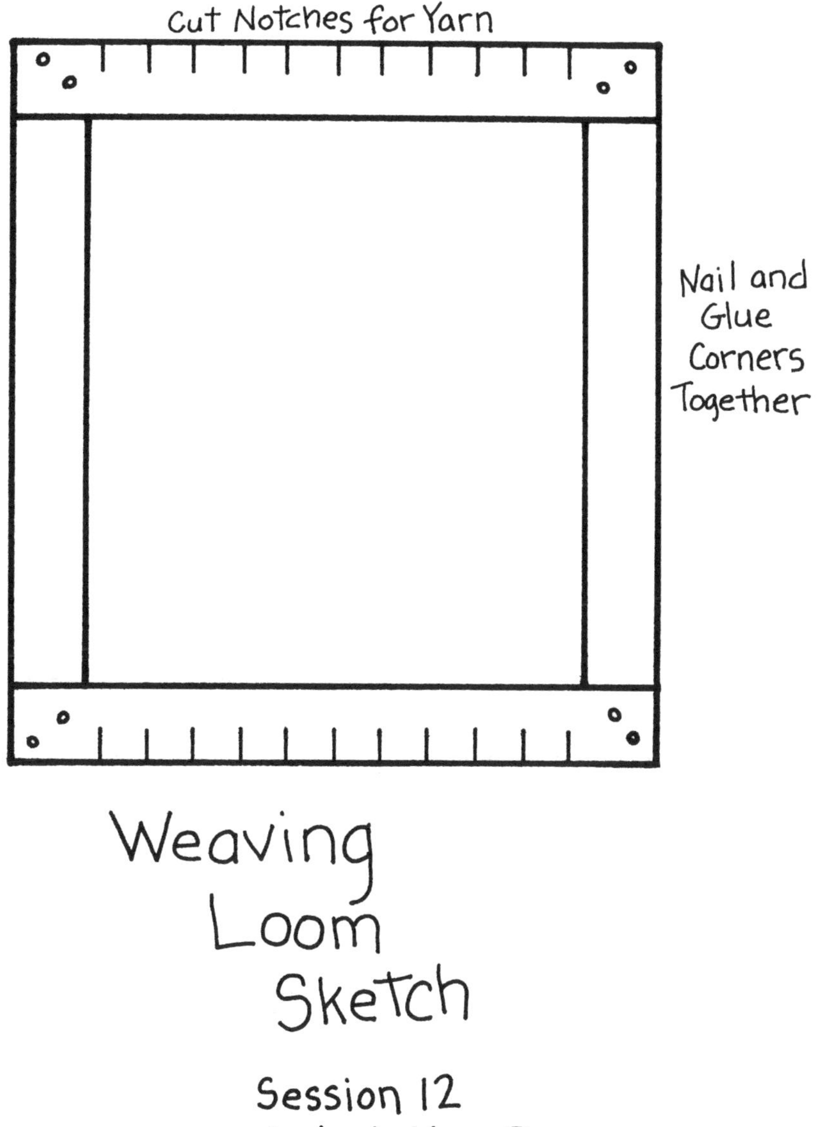

Cut Notches for Yarn
Nail and
Glue
Corners
Together
Weaving
Loom
Sketch
Session 12
Workstation 3

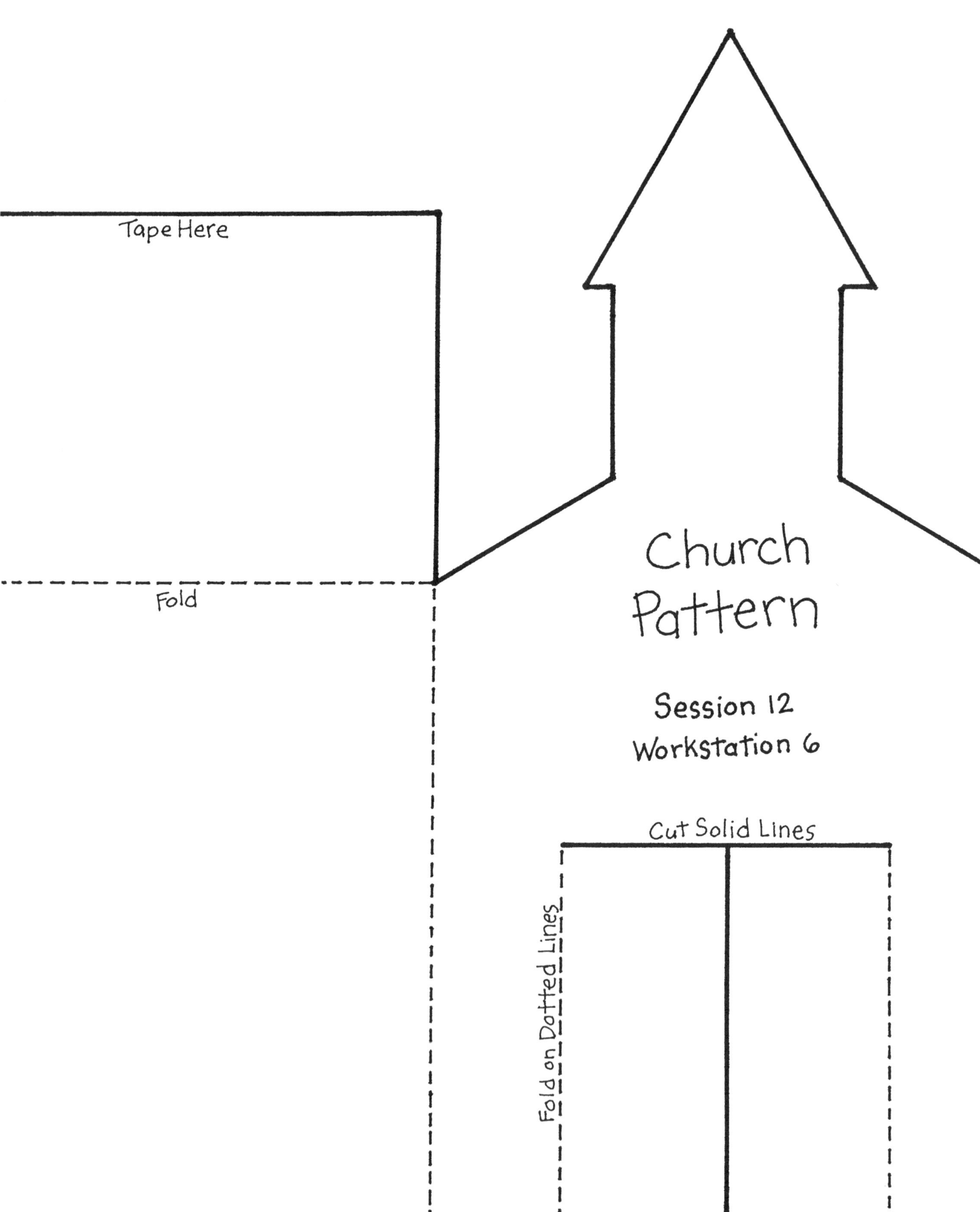

Tape Here
Fold
Church
Pattern
Session 12
Workstation 6
Cut Solid Lines
Fold on Dotted Lines

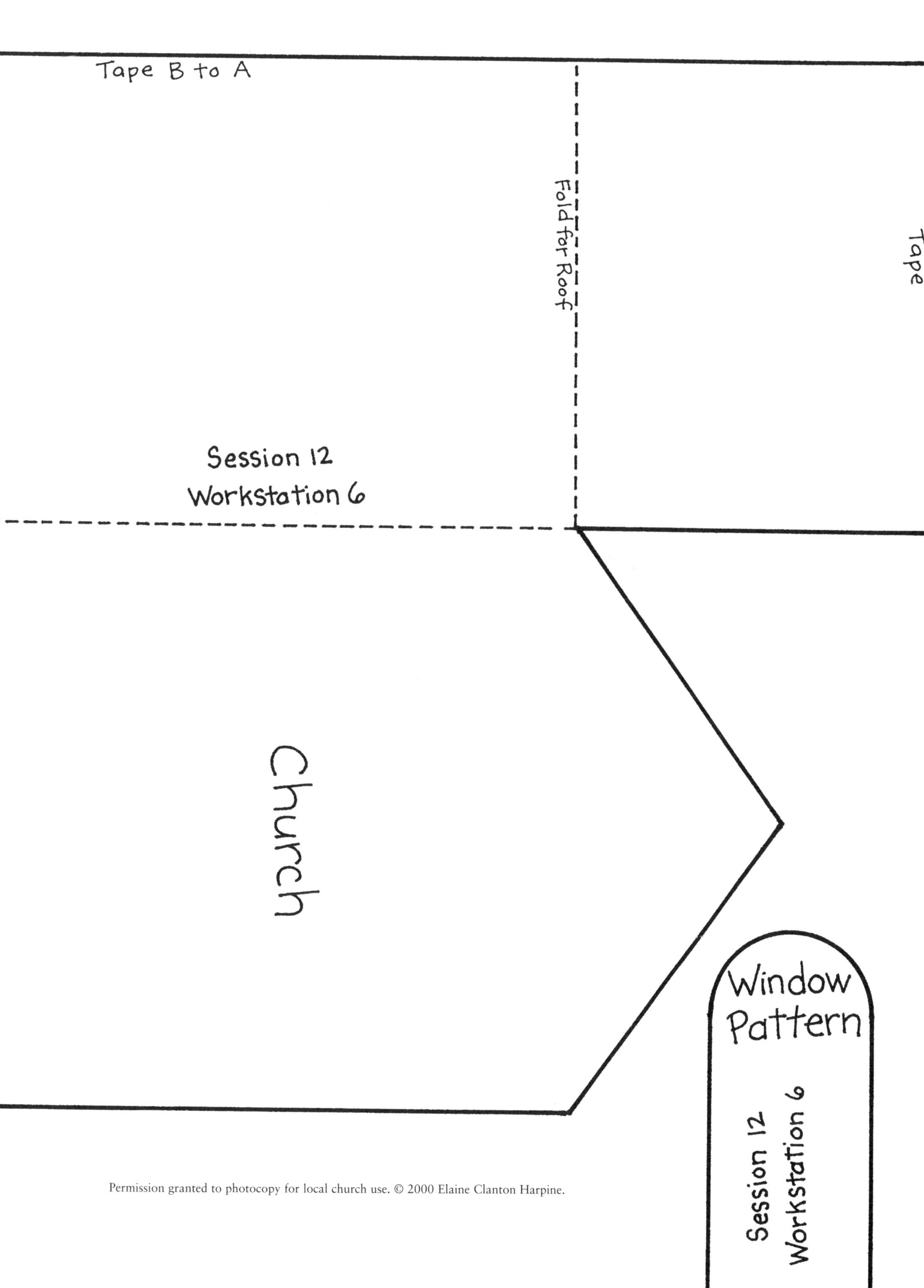

Permission granted to photocopy for local church use. © 2000 Elaine Clanton Harpine.

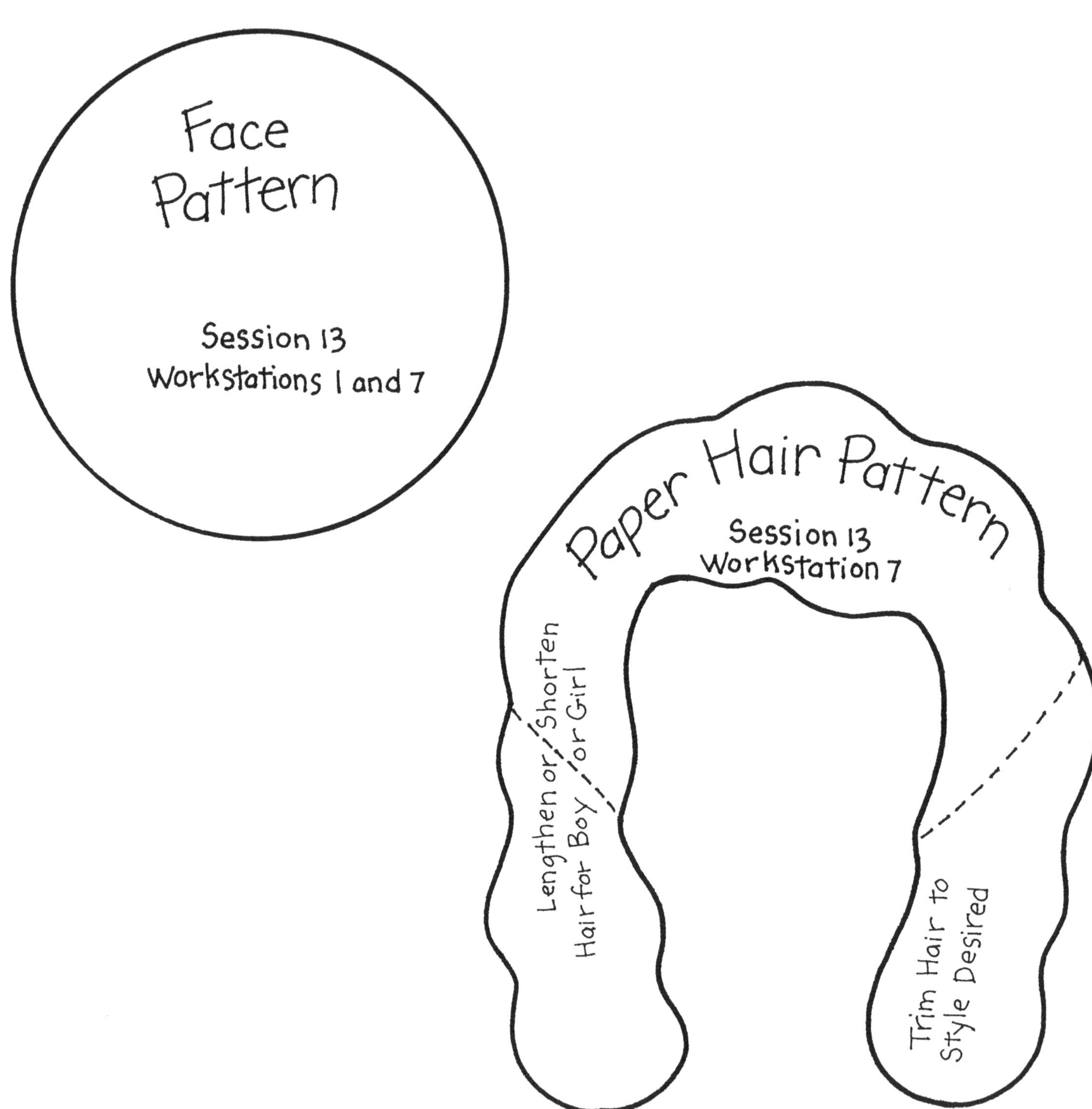

Face
Pattern

Session 13
Workstations 1 and 7

Paper Hair Pattern
Session 13
Workstation 7

Lengthen or Shorten
Hair for Boy or Girl

Trim Hair to
Style Desired

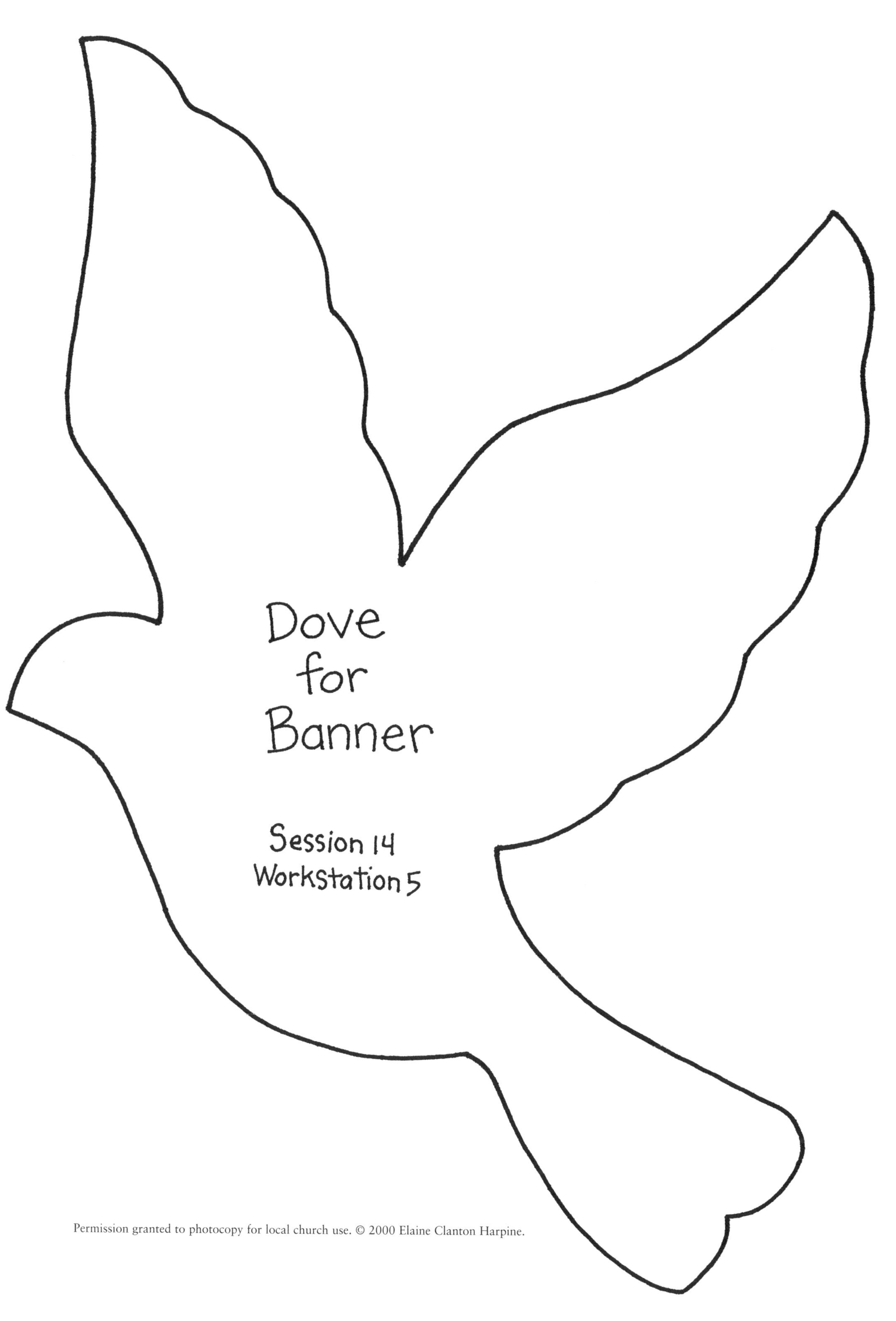
Dove
for
Banner

Session 14
Workstation 5

Dove

Session 14
Workstation 7

Egg Carton
Weaving Loom
Pattern

Session 14
Workstation 6

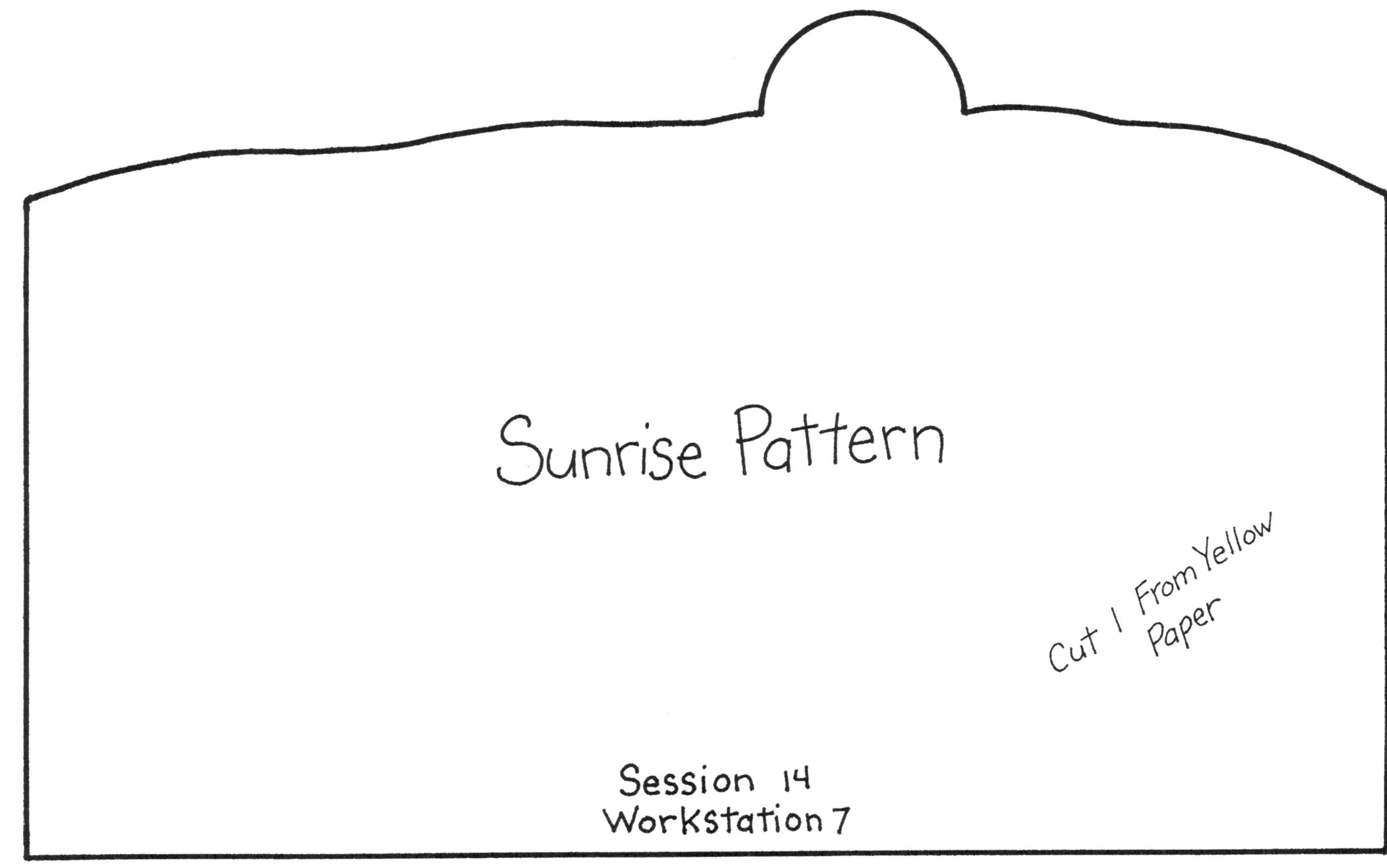

Sunrise Pattern
Cut 1 From Yellow Paper
Session 14
Workstation 7

Sunrise
Pattern
Place on Fold
Cut 1 From
Pink Paper
Session 14
Workstation 7

Place on Fold
Grass and Trees
Pattern
Cut 1 From
Green Paper
Session 14
Workstation 7

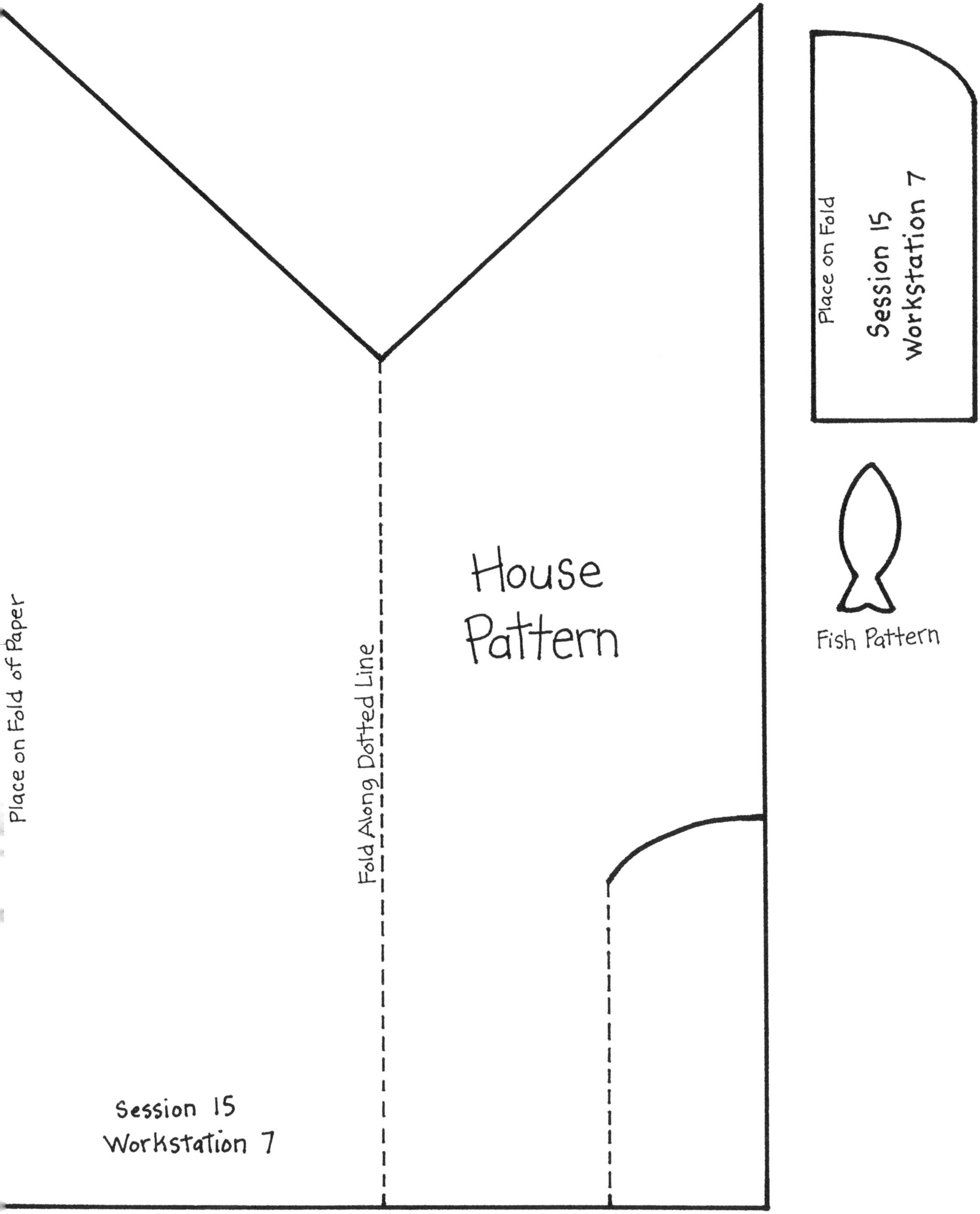

House
Pattern

Fish Pattern

Place on Fold of Paper

Fold Along Dotted Line

Session 15
Workstation 7

Place on Fold

Session 15
Workstation 7

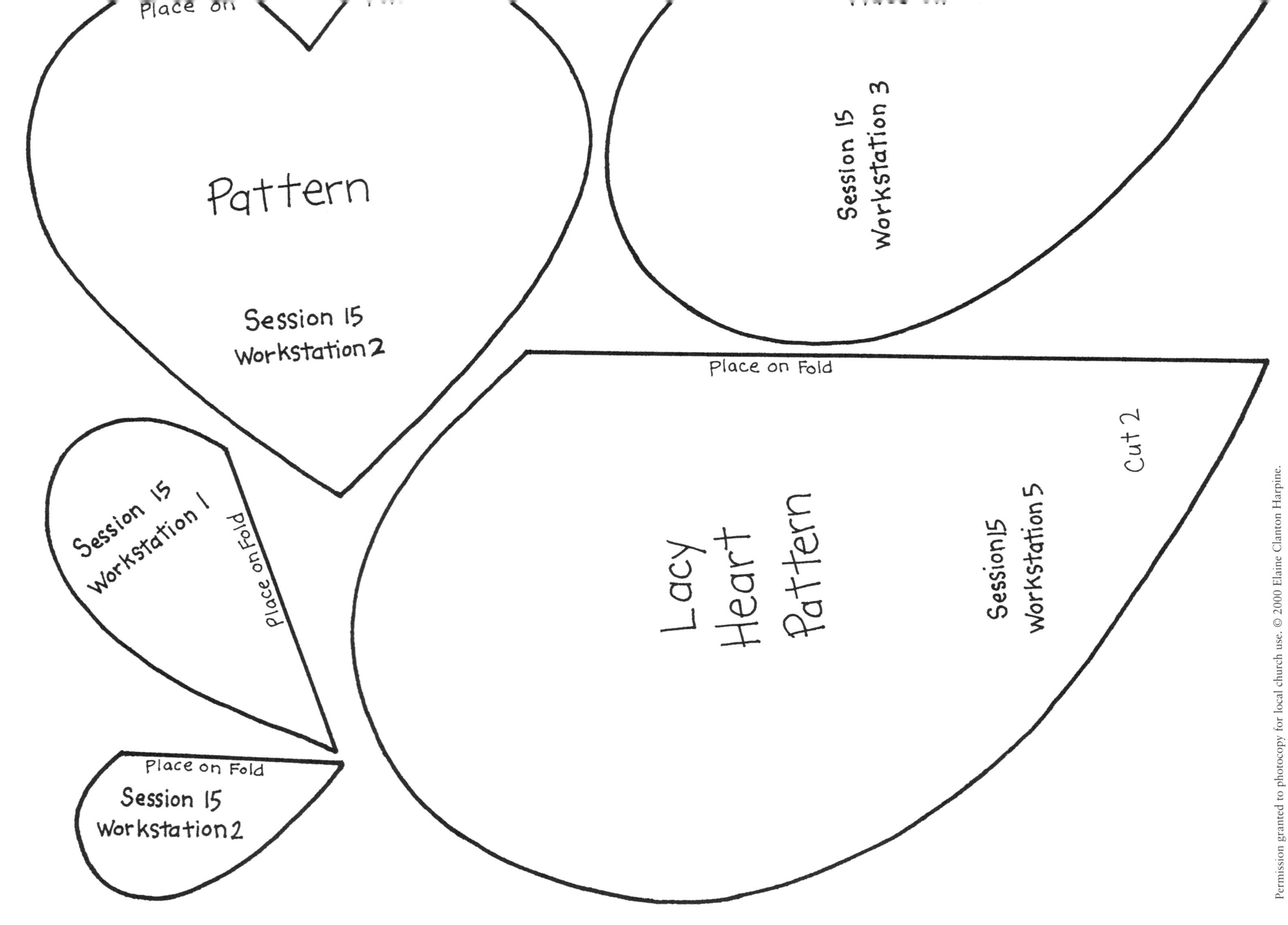

Place on
Pattern
Session 15
Workstation 2
Session 15
Workstation 3
Place on Fold
Session 15
Workstation 1
Place on Fold
Place on Fold
Session 15
Workstation 2
Lacy
Heart
Pattern
Session 15
Workstation 5
Cut 2

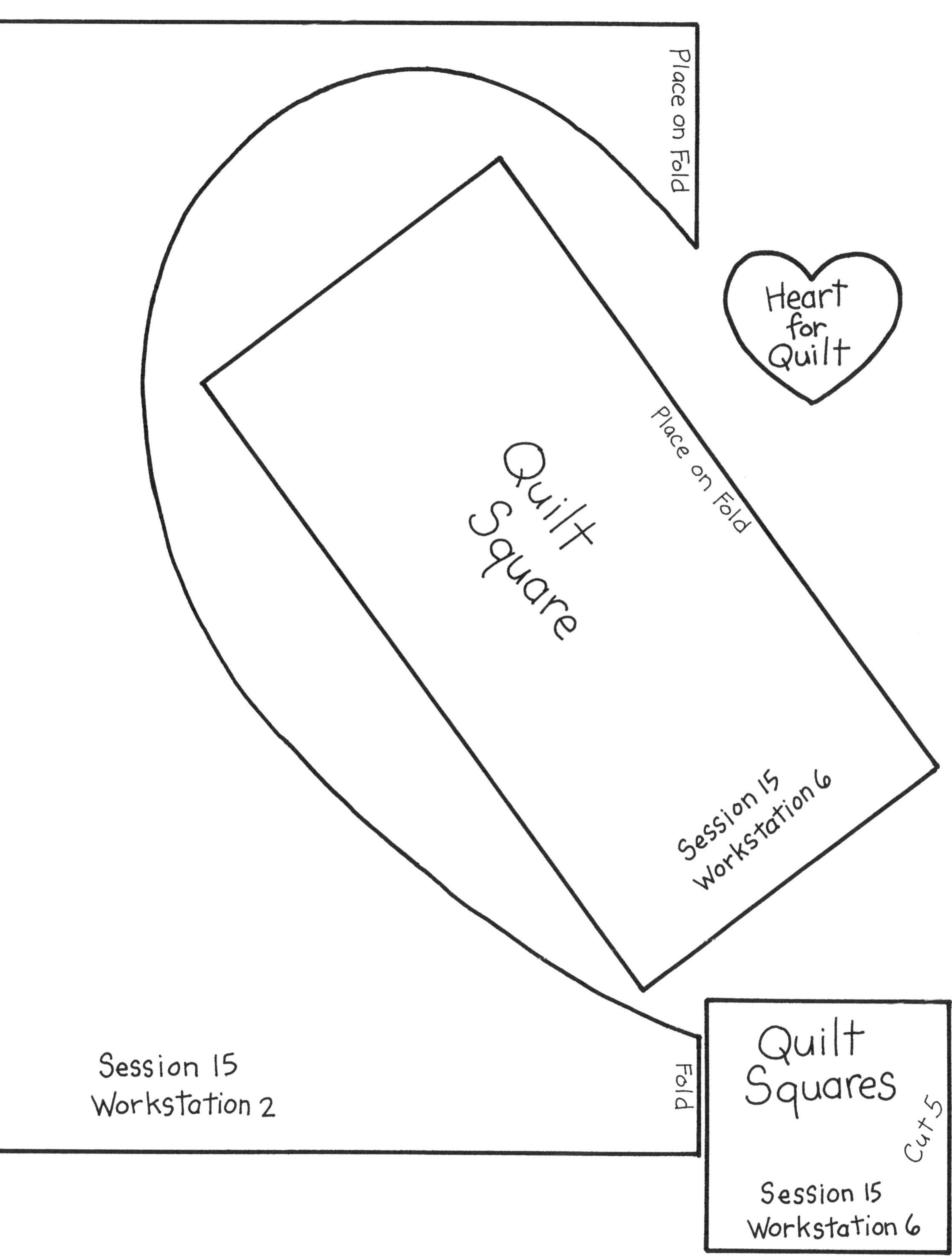

Place on Fold
Heart
for
Quilt
Quilt
Square
Place on Fold
Session 15
Workstation 6
Session 15
Workstation 2
Fold
Quilt
Squares
Cut 5
Session 15
Workstation 6

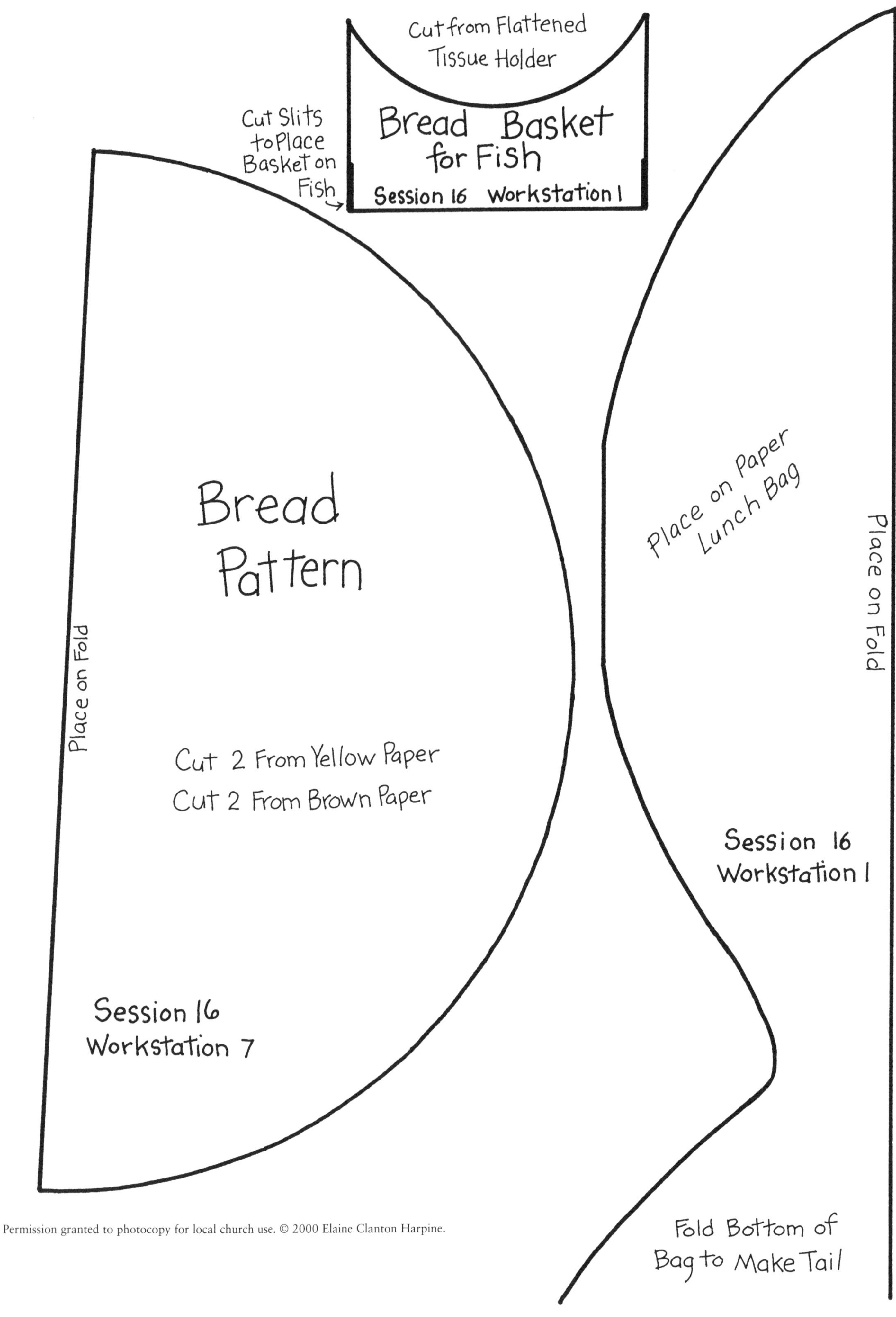

Cut from Flattened
Tissue Holder
Bread Basket
for Fish
Session 16   Workstation 1
Cut Slits
to Place
Basket on
Fish
Bread
Pattern
Place on Fold
Cut 2 From Yellow Paper
Cut 2 From Brown Paper
Session 16
Workstation 7
Place on Paper
Lunch Bag
Place on Fold
Session 16
Workstation 1
Fold Bottom of
Bag to Make Tail

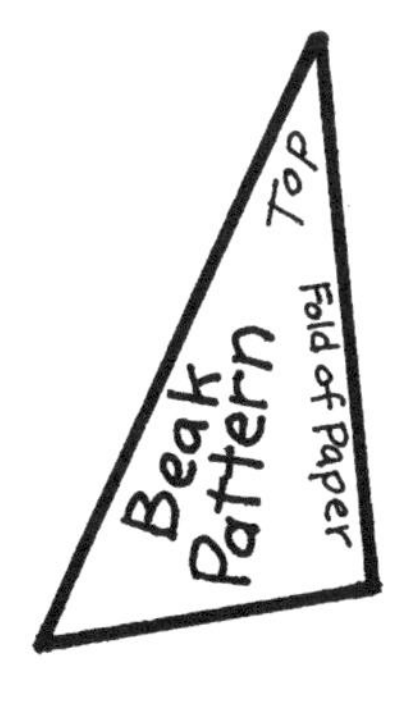

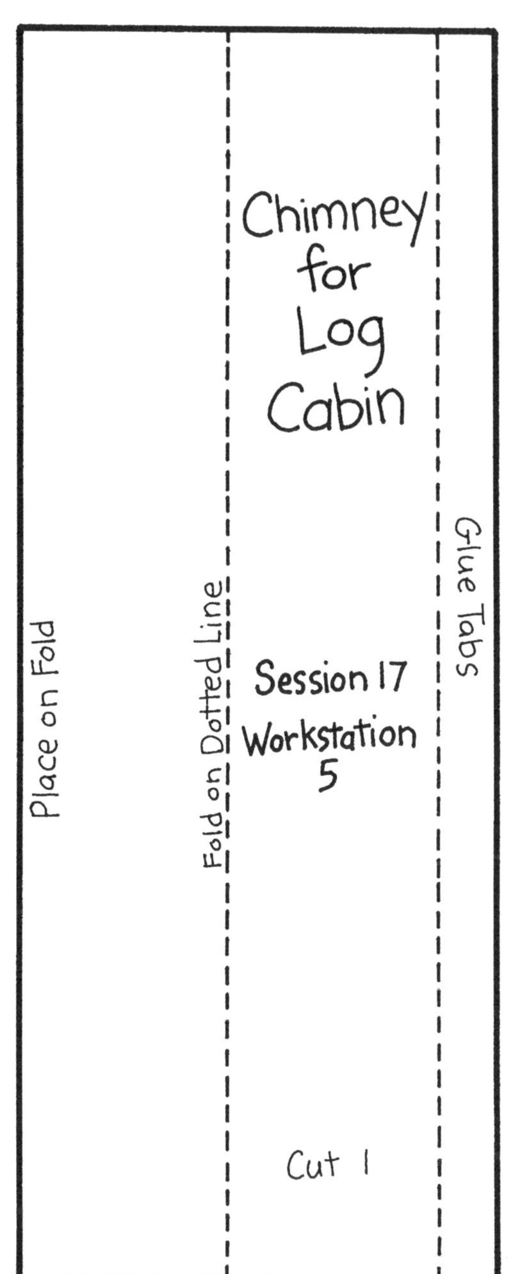

Top

Totem Pole Pattern

Session 17
Workstation 5

Cut 1

Chimney for Log Cabin

Session 17
Workstation
5

Place on Fold

Fold on Dotted Line

Glue Tabs

Cut 1

Totem Pole Wing Pattern

Session 17
Workstation 5

Place on Fold

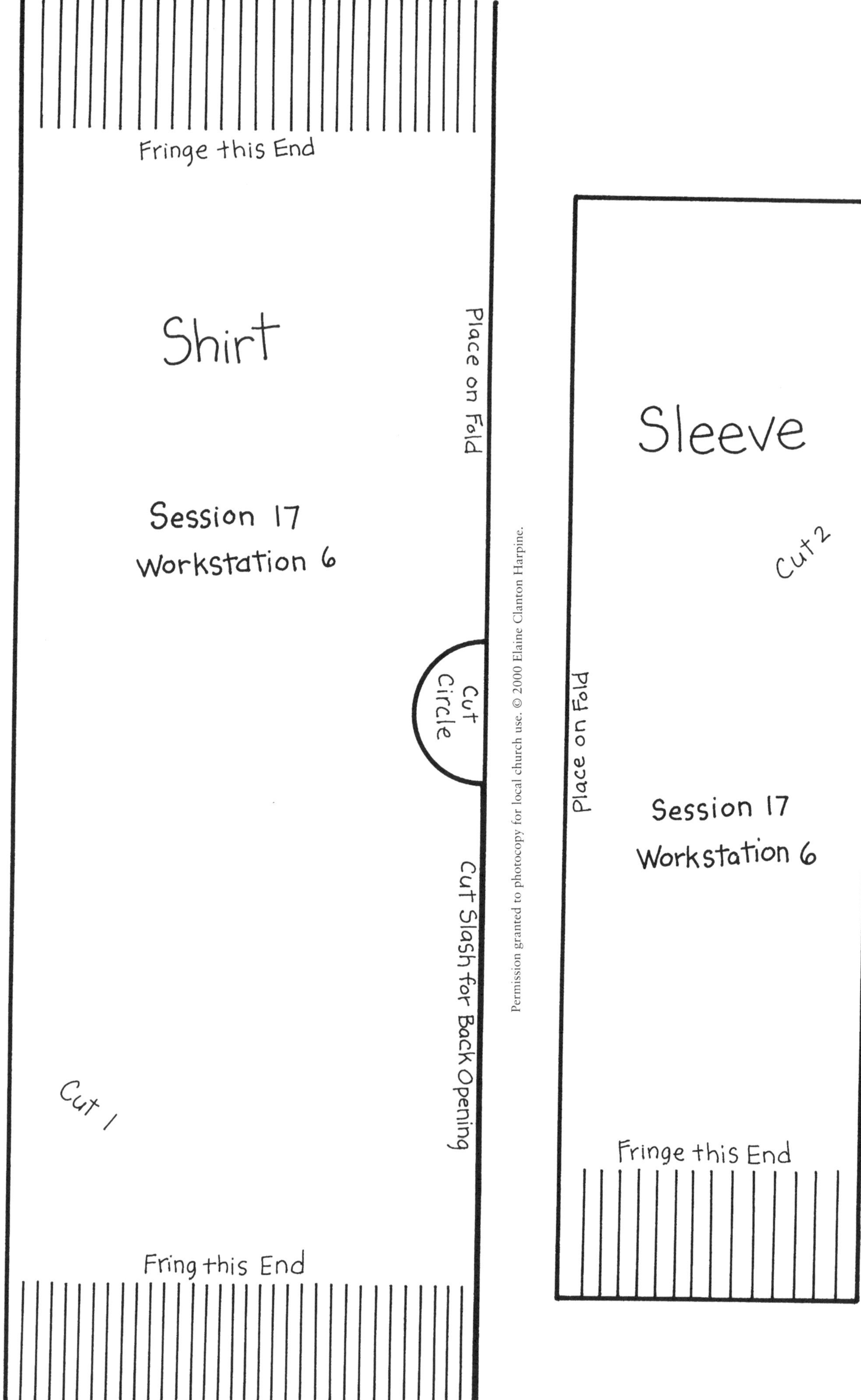

Fringe this End
Shirt
Session 17
Workstation 6
Cut 1
Place on Fold
Cut Circle
Cut Slash for Back Opening
Fring this End
Sleeve
Cut 2
Place on Fold
Session 17
Workstation 6
Fringe this End
Permission granted to photocopy for local church use. © 2000 Elaine Clanton Harpine.

Apron Pattern

Session 17

Workstation 6

Fringe this End

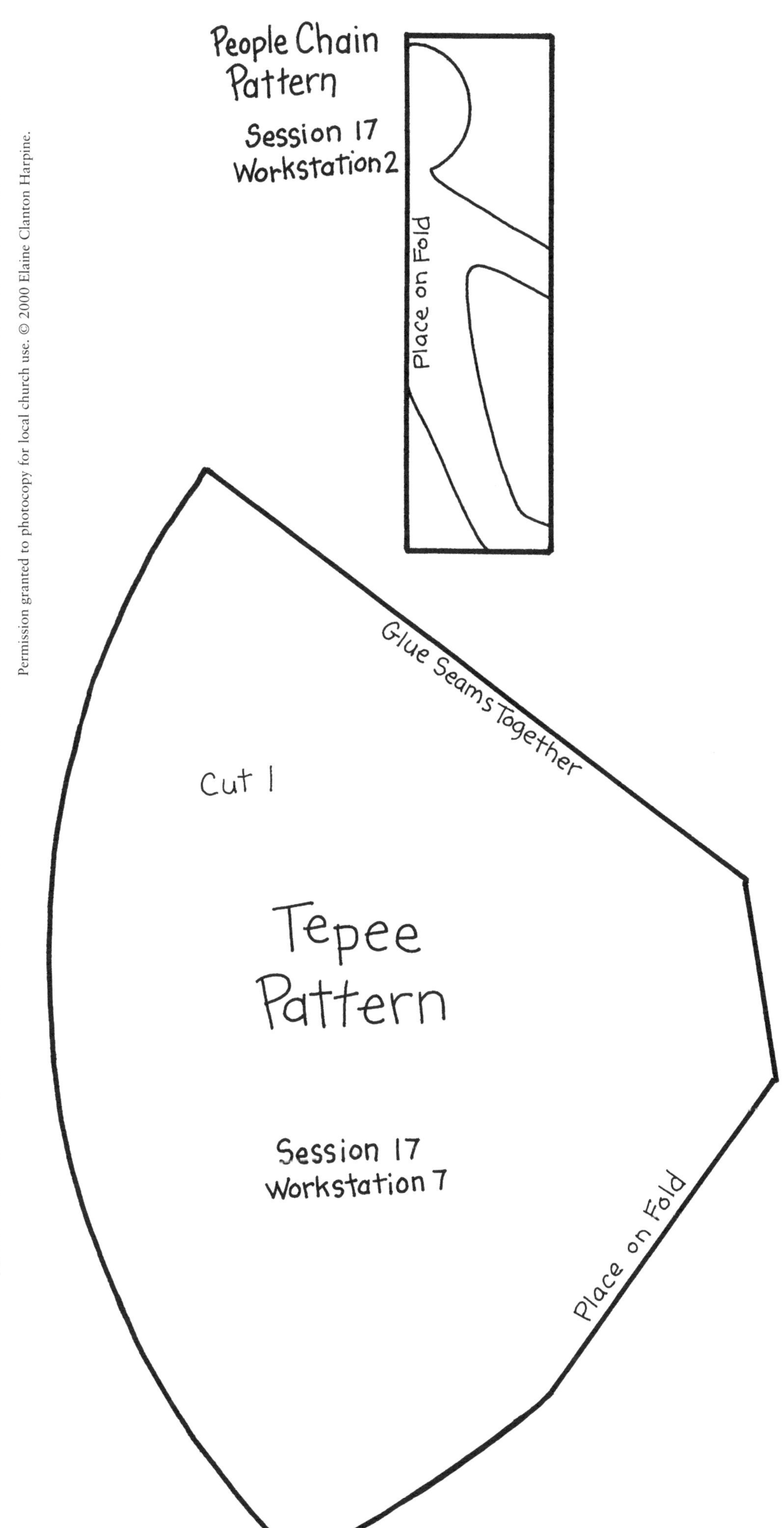

Place on Fold
Glue at Neck
Indian Blanket
Session 18
Workstation 5

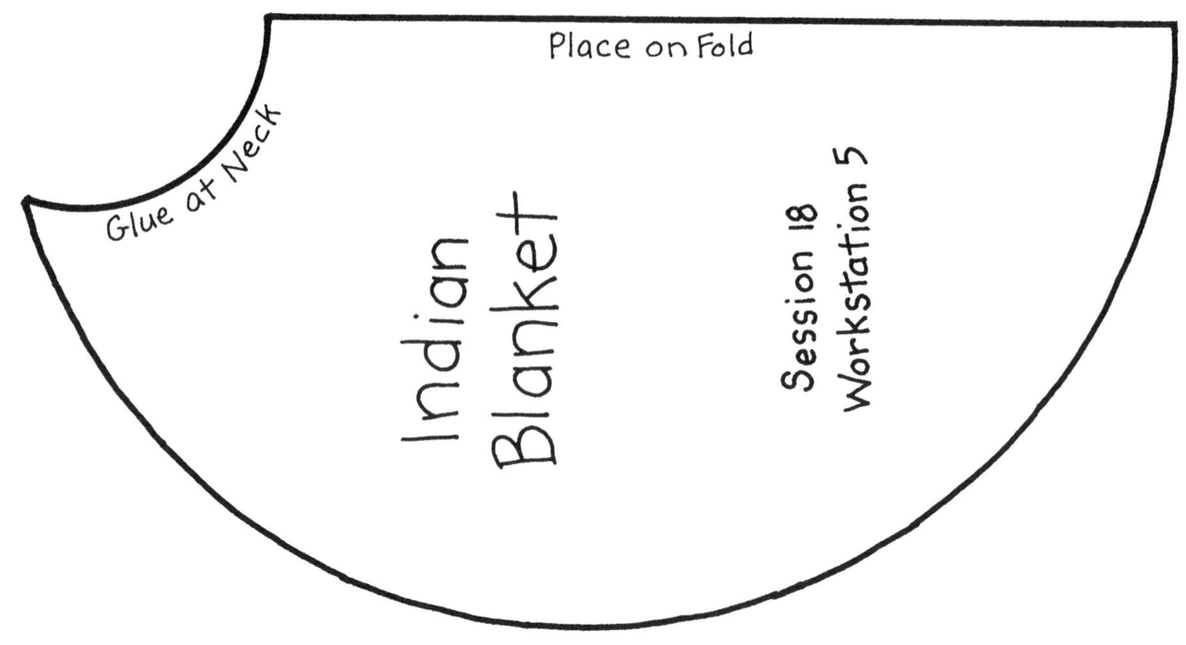

Place on Fold of Paper
Hem
Dress Pattern
Session 18
Workstation 5
Top of Dress

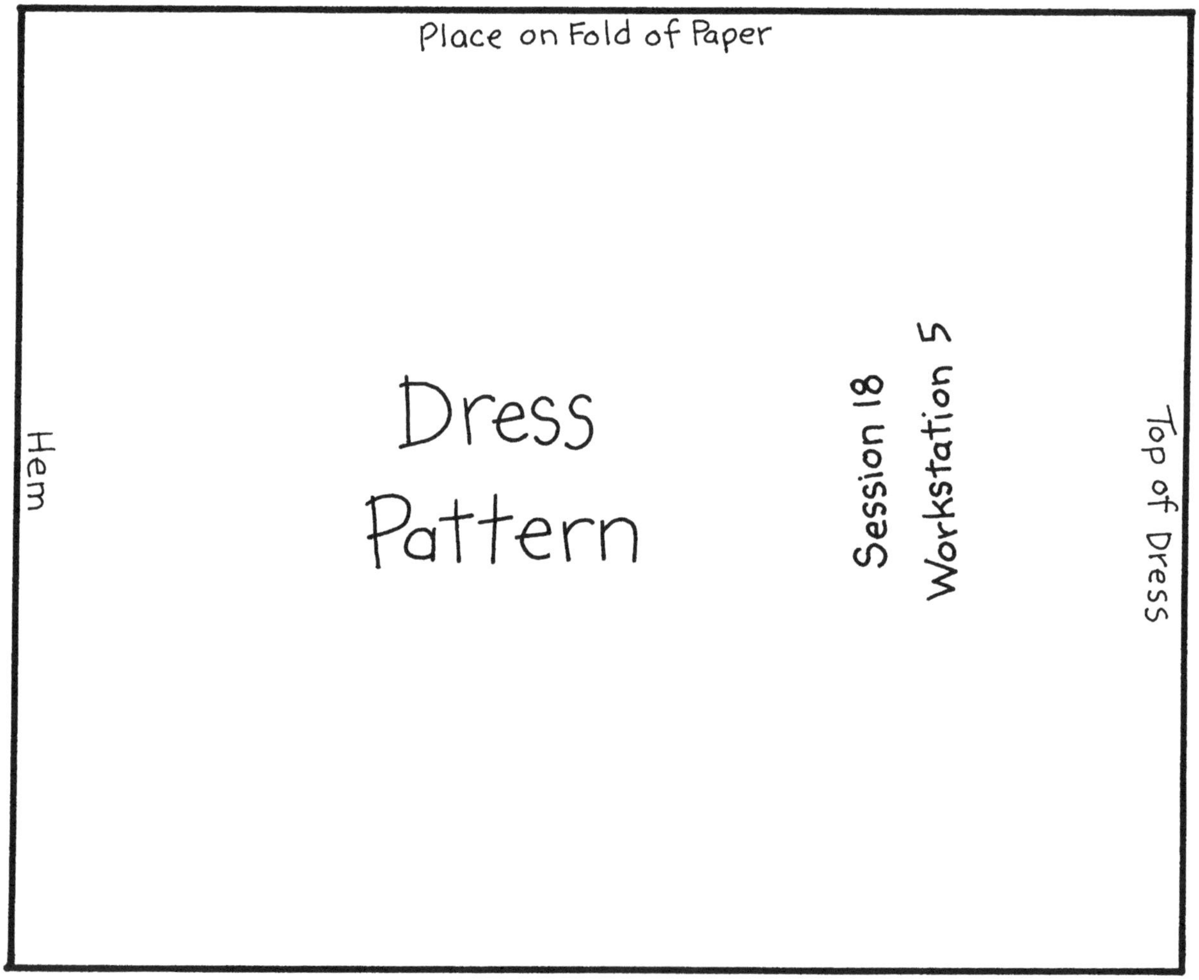

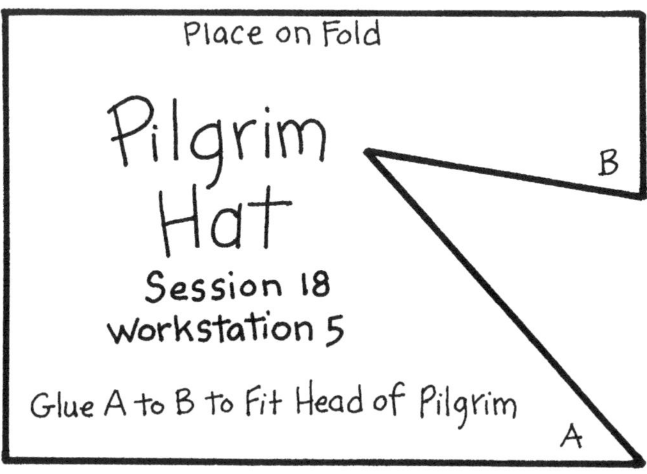

Place on Fold
Pilgrim Hat
Session 18
Workstation 5
Glue A to B to Fit Head of Pilgrim
B
A

Place on Fold
Cut Center Back Seam Open
Neck
Pilgrim and Indian Collar
Session 18   Workstation 5

Glue Seams Together
Sleeve Pattern
Place on Fold
Session 18
Workstation 5

Place on Fold of Paper
Table Pattern
Glue Table Leg at Fold
Session 18
Workstation 7

Fold Up
Glue to Table
Cut 2
From
Stiff Paper
or
Double
Thickness
Place on Fold
Session 18
Workstation 7
Fold Back
Glue to Card

Pilgrim Apron
Place on Fold
Session 18
Workstation 5

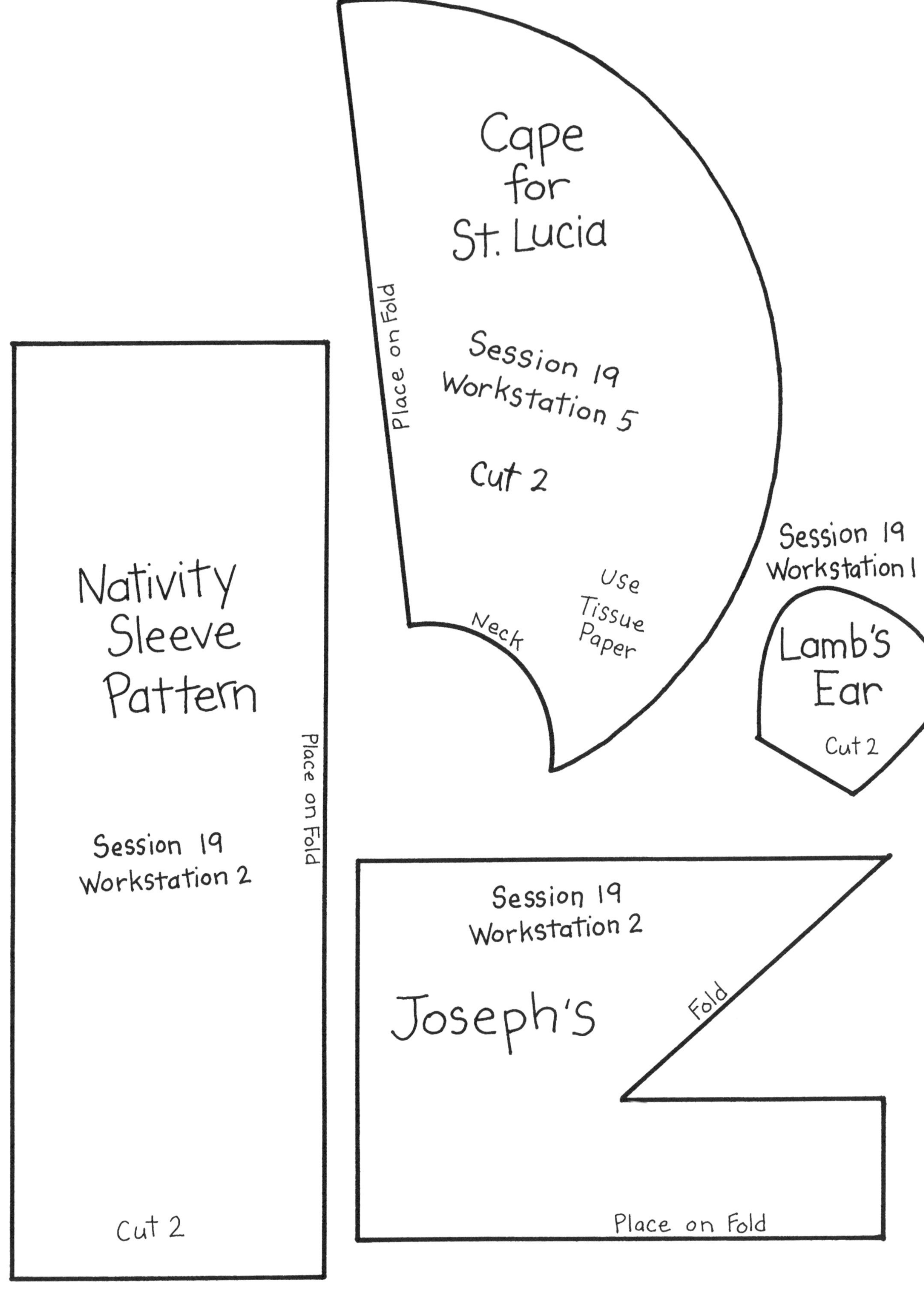
Cape
for
St. Lucia
Place on Fold
Session 19
Workstation 5
Cut 2
Neck
Use
Tissue
Paper
Session 19
Workstation 1
Lamb's
Ear
Cut 2
Nativity
Sleeve
Pattern
Place on Fold
Session 19
Workstation 2
Cut 2
Session 19
Workstation 2
Joseph's
Fold
Place on Fold

Tunic Pattern

Session 19
Workstation 2

Glue Seams Together

Cut 1

Cloak Pattern

Session 19
Workstation 2

Session 19
Workstation 5

St. Lucia
Sleeve

Place on Fold

Cut 2

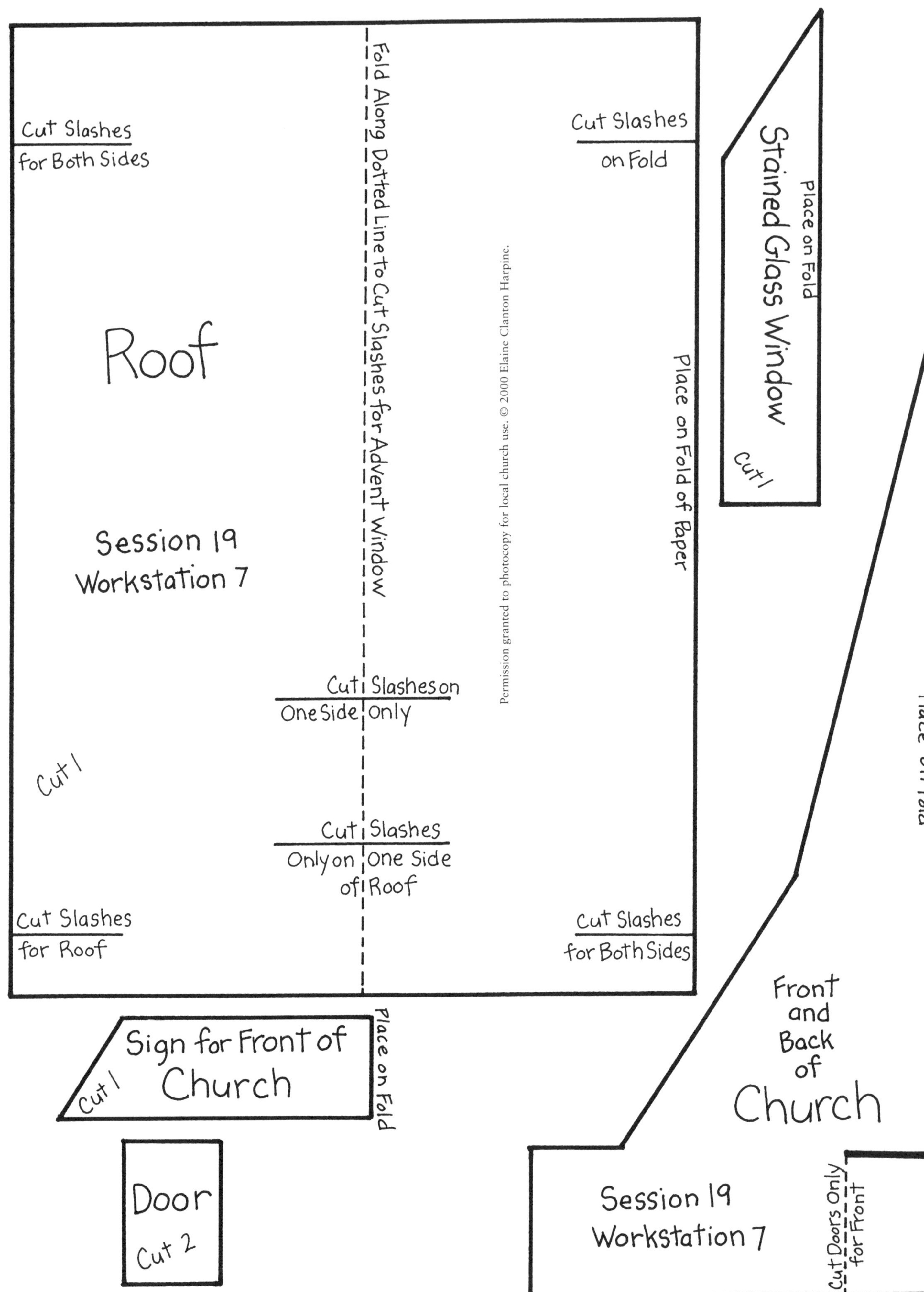
Cut Slashes
for Both Sides
Fold Along Dotted Line to Cut Slashes for Advent Window
Cut Slashes
on Fold
Place on Fold
Stained Glass Window
Place on Fold of Paper
Cut 1
Roof
Session 19
Workstation 7
Cut 1
Permission granted to photocopy for local church use. © 2000 Elaine Clanton Harpine.
Cut Slashes on
One Side Only
Place on Fold
Cut Slashes
Only on One Side
of Roof
Cut Slashes
for Roof
Cut Slashes
for Both Sides
Front
and
Back
of
Church
Sign for Front of
Church
Place on Fold
Cut 1
Door
Cut 2
Session 19
Workstation 7
Cut Doors Only
for Front

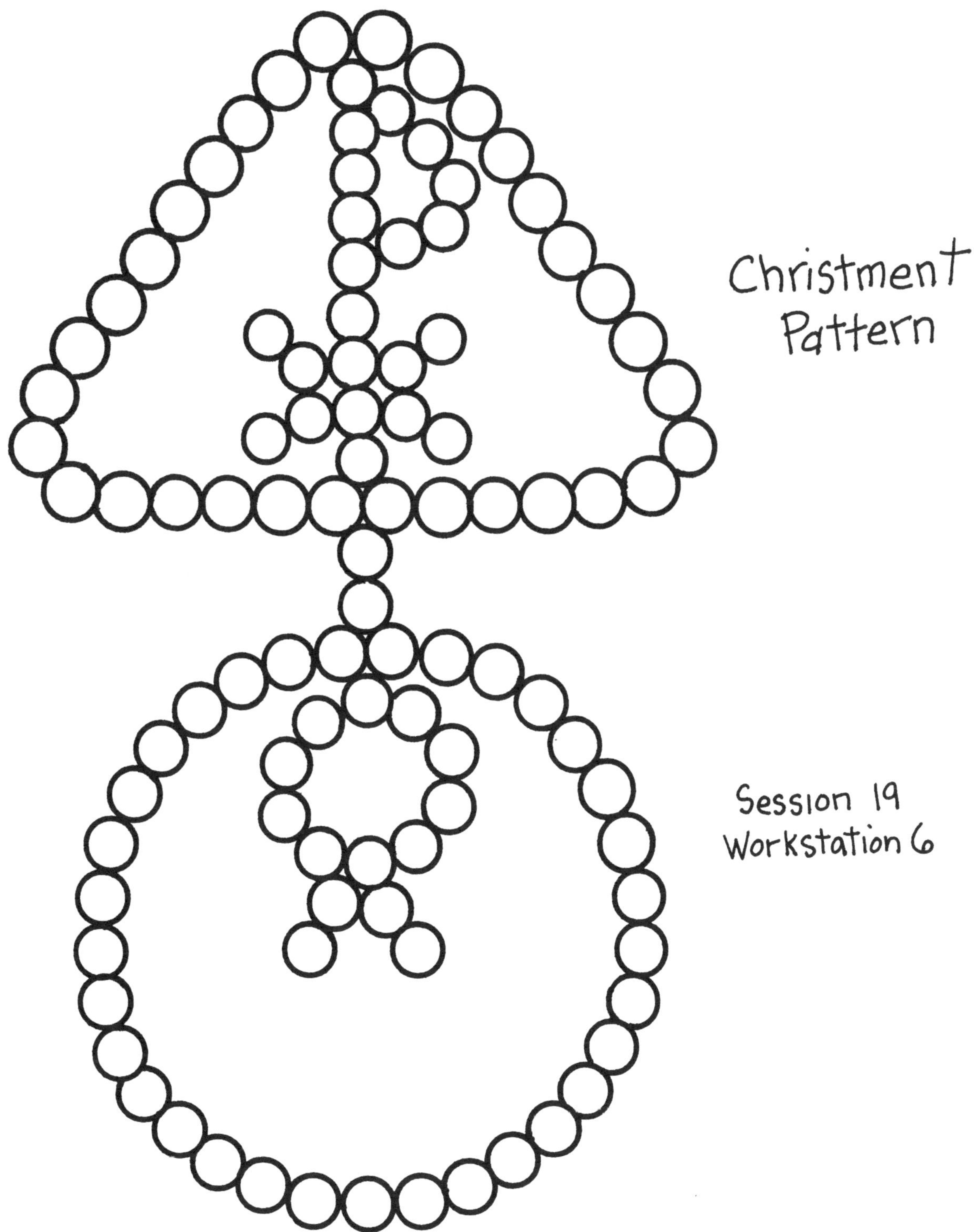

Christment
Pattern

Session 19
Workstation 6

CHURCH ADVENT WINDOW
HANDOUT

Cut into weekly strips and tape or glue together to make one long
strip to thread through window on church.

1st Week in Advent	Clean Your Room.	Try to Finish A Project.	Talk About A Problem.	Help A Friend.	Don't Lose Your Temper.	Help Someone In Need.	Try! Try! Try! Again!
2nd Week in Advent	God Loves You.	You're Special.	Be Kind.	Be Happy.	Give A Compliment	Tell Someone You're Sorry.	Smile.
3rd Week in Advent	Jesus Cares About You.	Don't Give Up.	Help Mom.	Help Dad.	Help Your Neighbor.	Tell Someone You love Them.	Prayer Helps.
4th Week in Advent	Finish Each Line: God . . .	Jesus . . .	I Need . . .	I Can Give . . .	I Believe . . .	I Want To . . .	Christmas Is . . .

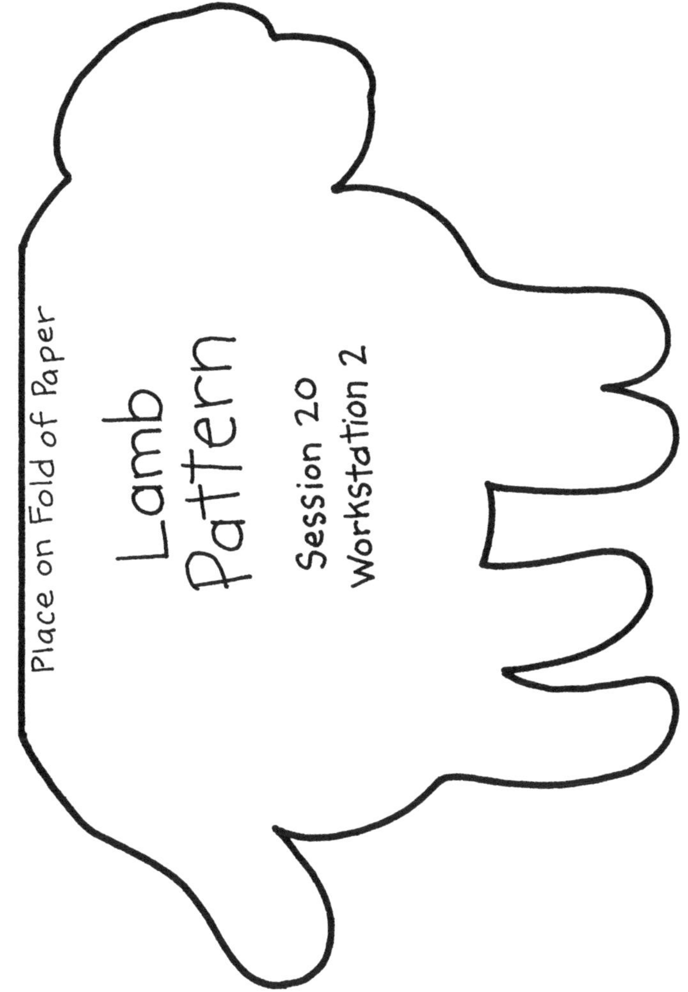

Place on Fold

Fold on Dotted Line
Lamb Brace
Session 20
Workstation 2

Fold and Glue Inside
Lamb

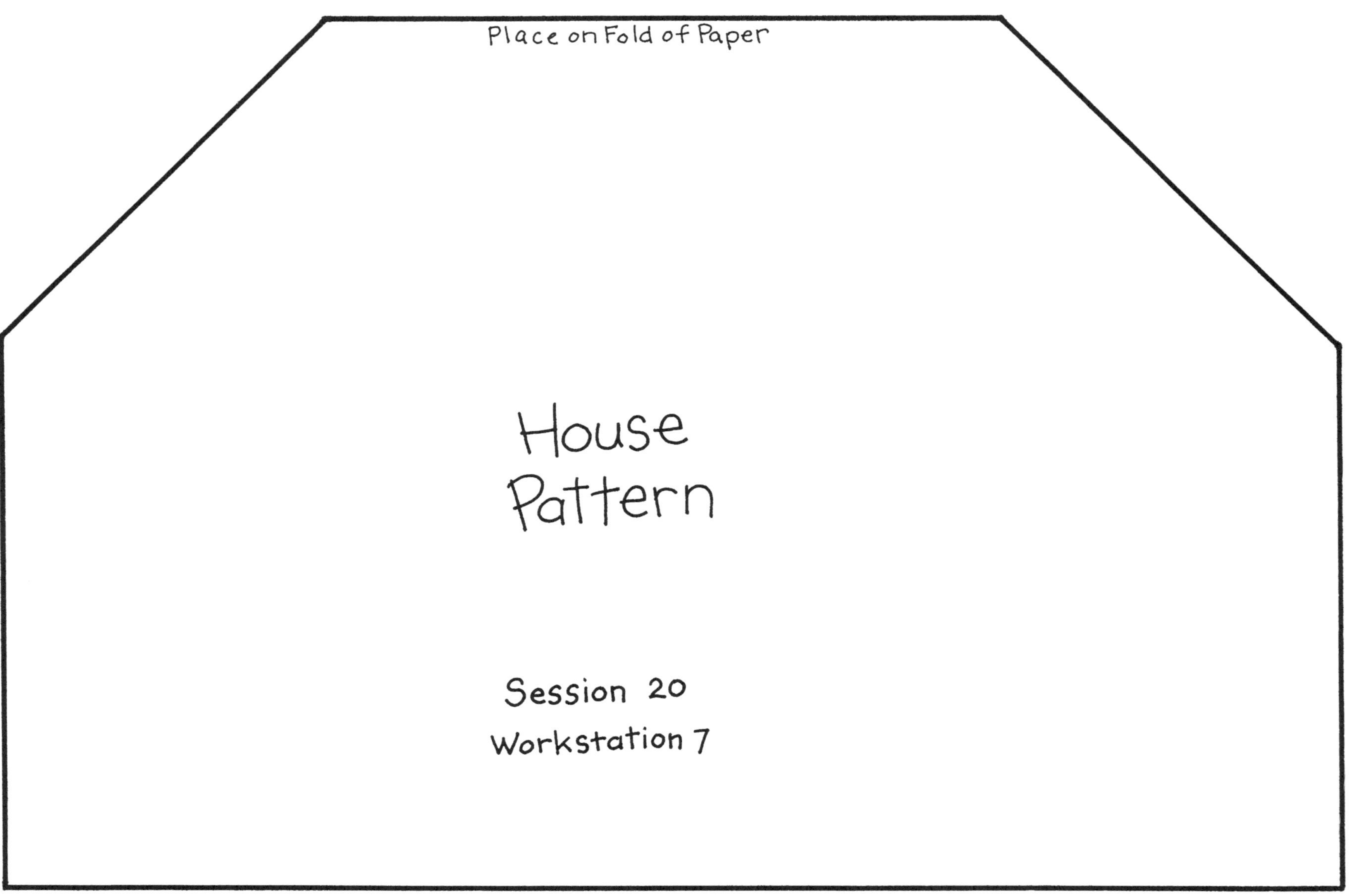

Place on Fold of Paper
House
Pattern
Session 20
Workstation 7

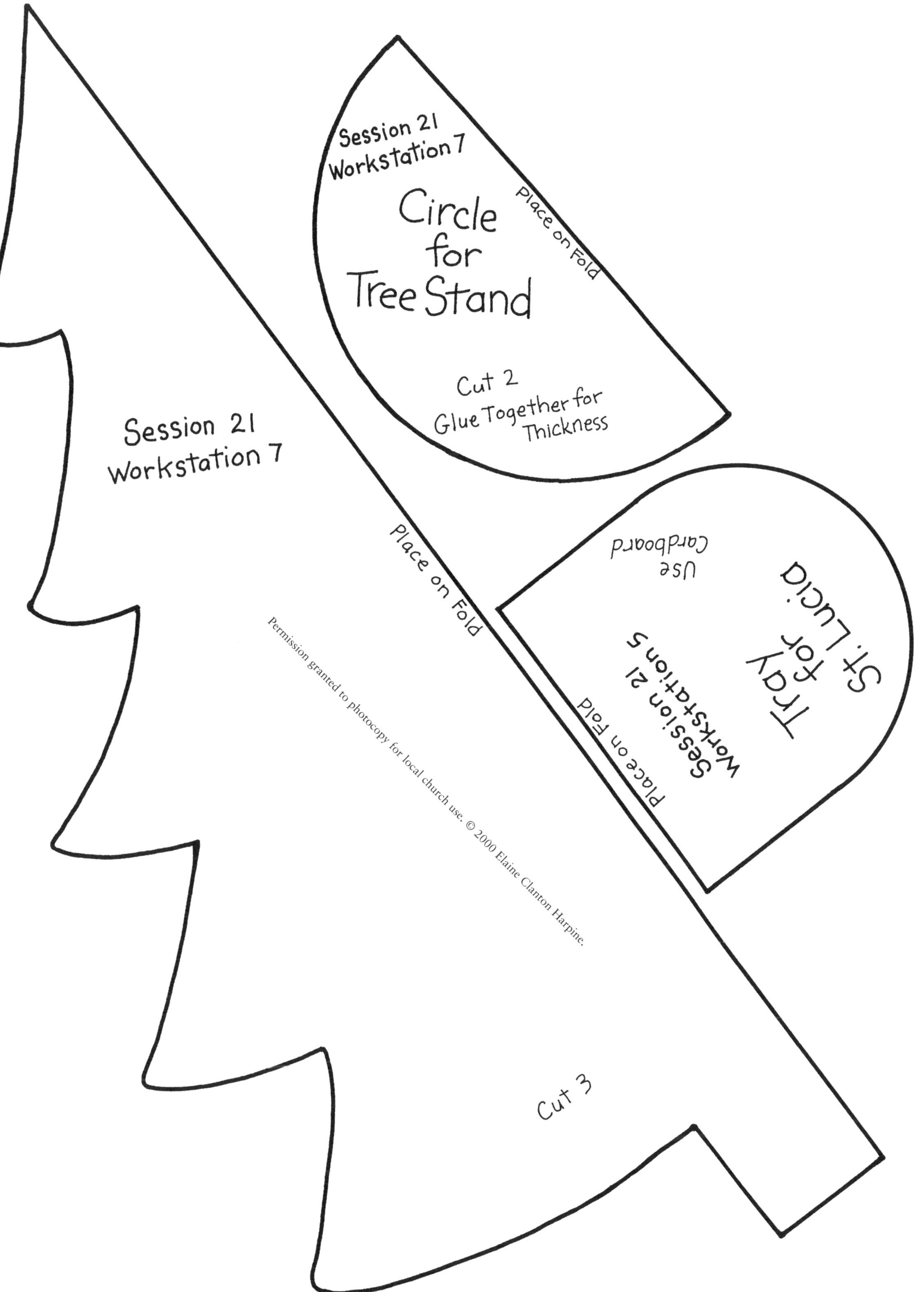

Session 21
Workstation 7
Circle for Tree Stand
Place on Fold
Cut 2
Glue Together for Thickness
Session 21
Workstation 7
Place on Fold
Use Cardboard
Tray for St. Lucia
Session 21
Workstation 5
Place on Fold
Cut 3
Permission granted to photocopy for local church use. © 2000 Elaine Clanton Harpine.

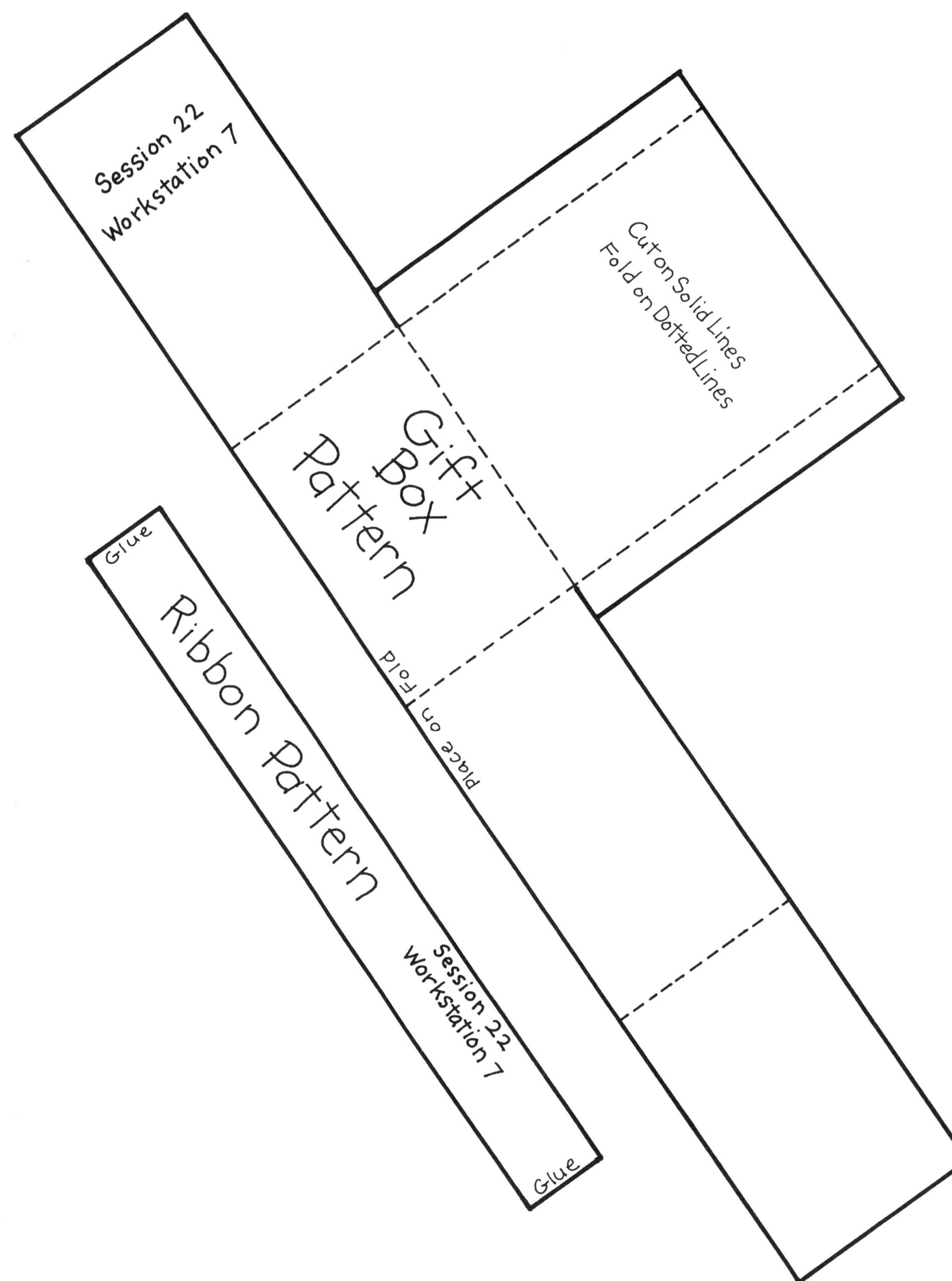

Session 22
Workstation 7

Cut on Solid Lines
Fold on Dotted Lines

Gift
Box
Pattern

Place on Fold

Glue

Ribbon Pattern

Session 22
Workstation 7

Glue

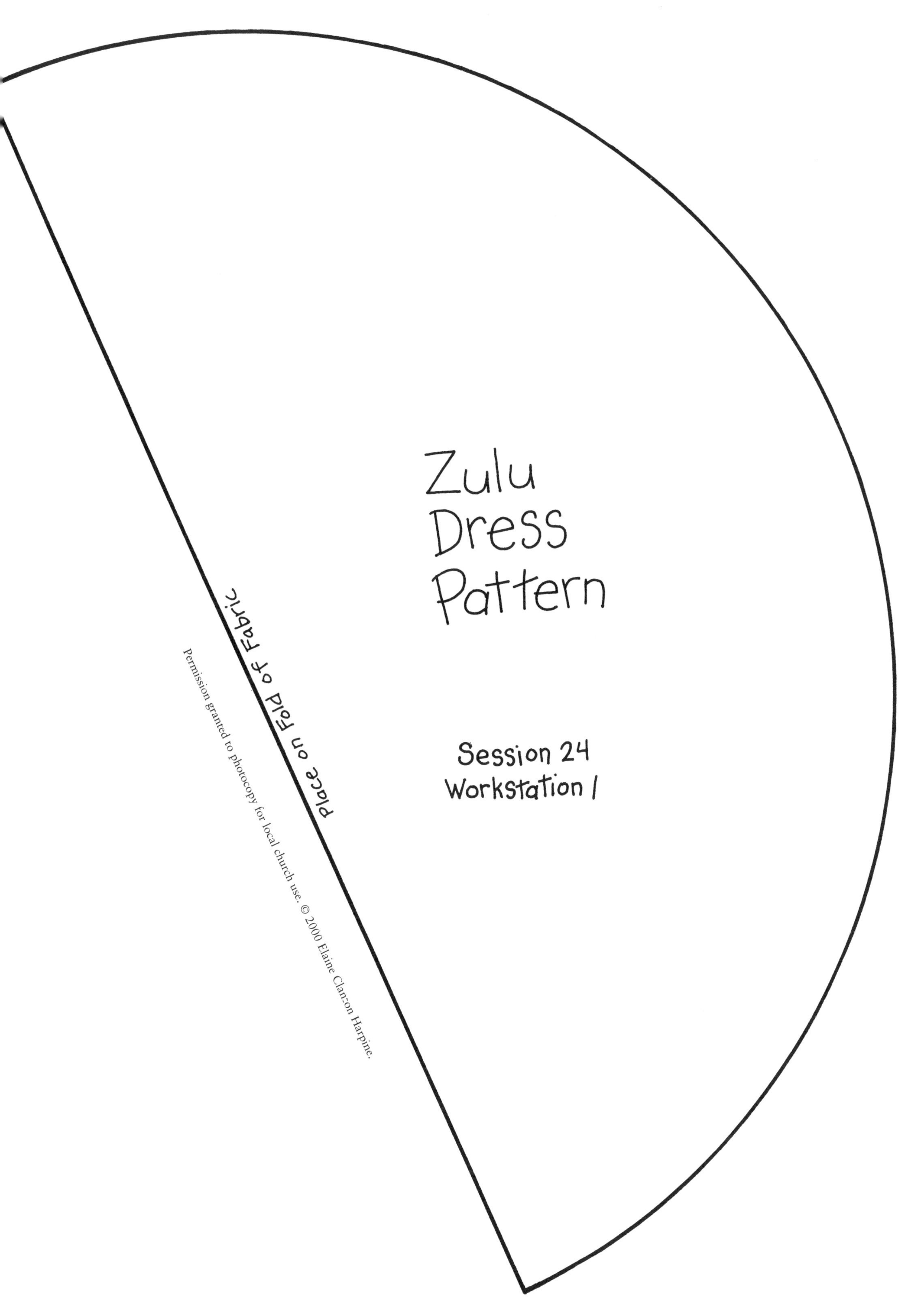

Zulu
Dress
Pattern

Session 24
Workstation 1

Place on Fold of Fabric

Permission granted to photocopy for local church use. © 2000 Elaine Clanton Harpine.

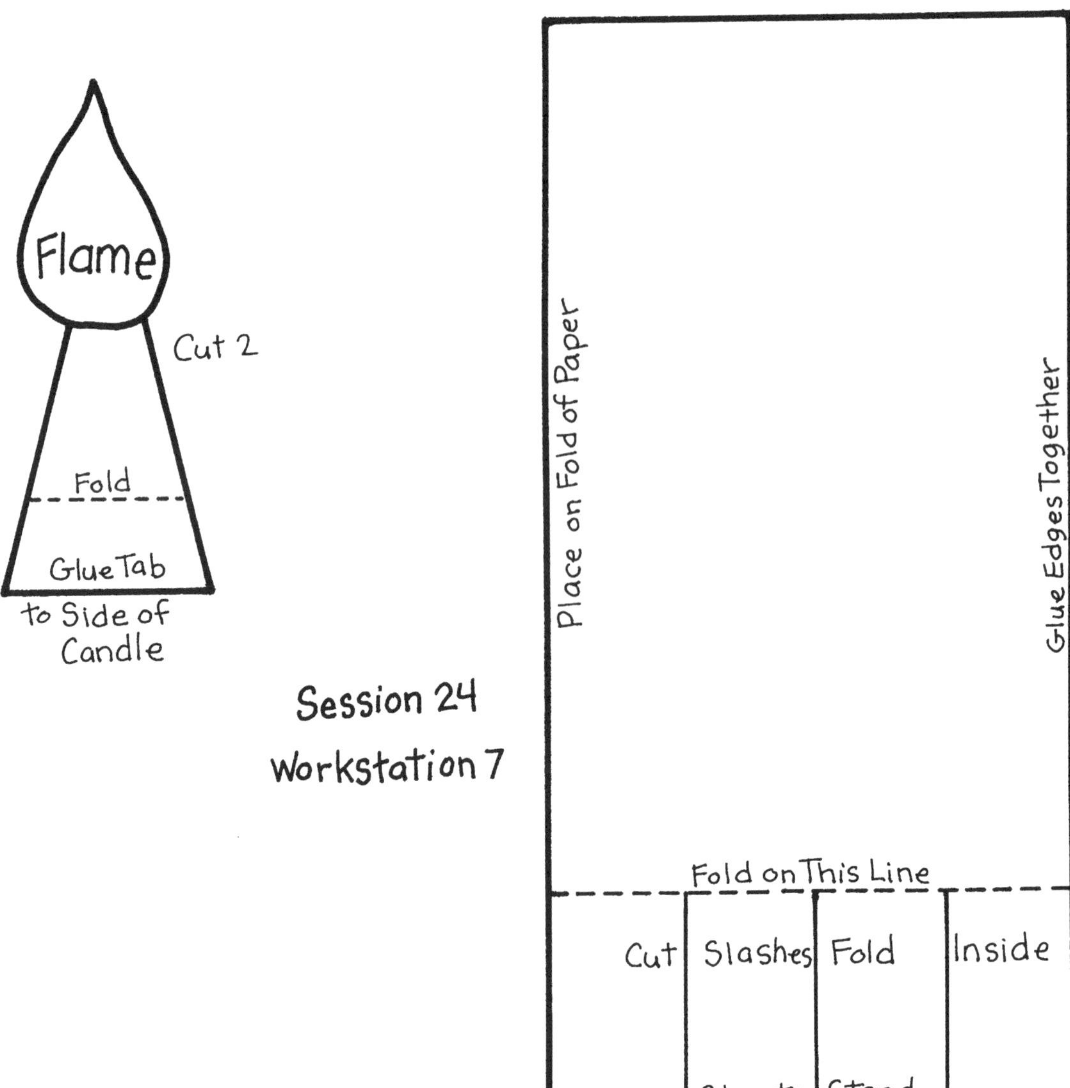

Flame
Cut 2
Fold
Glue Tab
to Side of
Candle
Session 24
Workstation 7
Place on Fold of Paper
Glue Edges Together
Fold on This Line
Cut
Slashes
Fold
Inside
Glue to
Stand

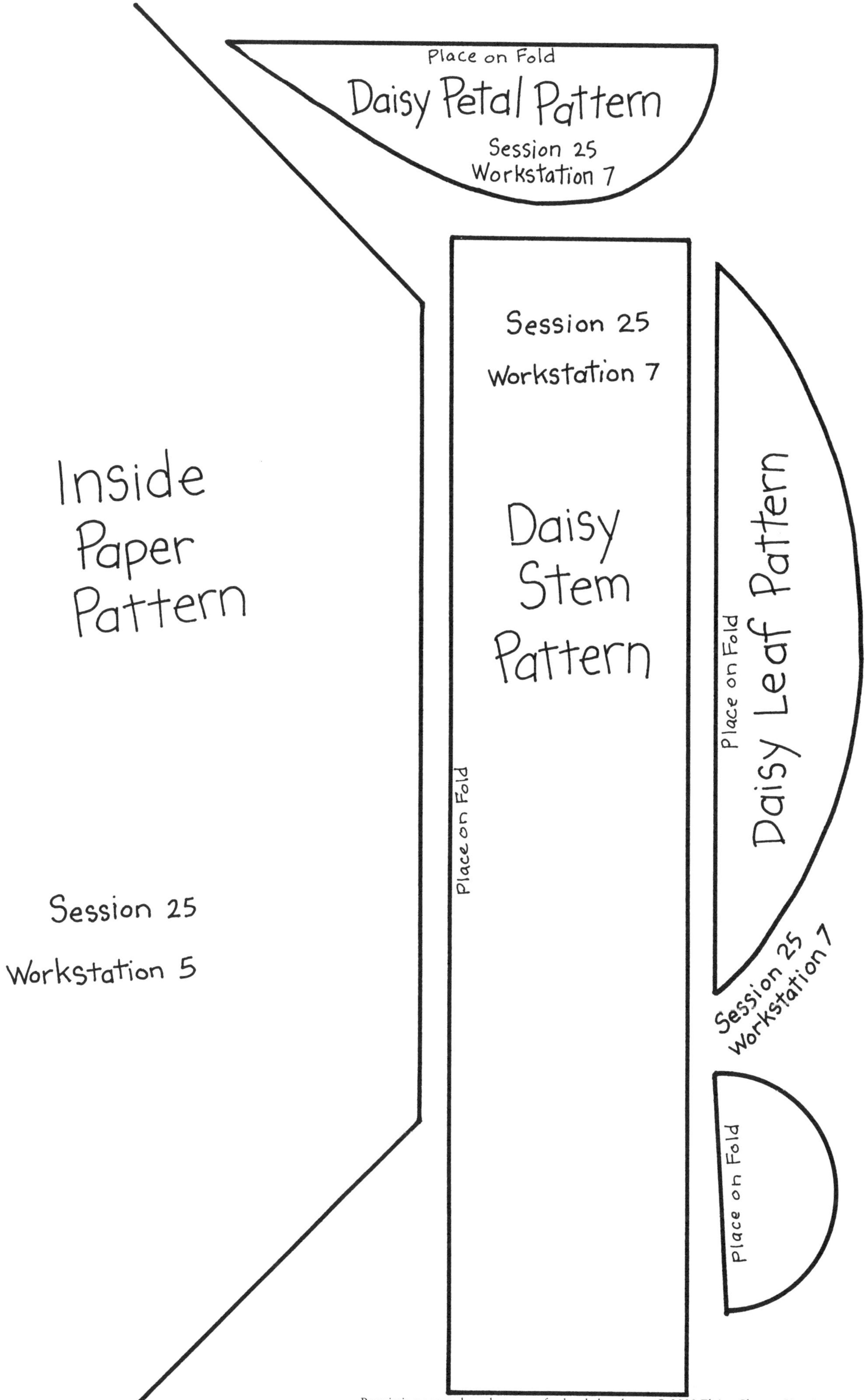

Place on Fold

Daisy Petal Pattern

Session 25
Workstation 7

Session 25

Workstation 7

Inside
Paper
Pattern

Daisy
Stem
Pattern

Place on Fold

Daisy Leaf Pattern

Place on Fold

Session 25
Workstation 7

Session 25

Workstation 5

Place on Fold

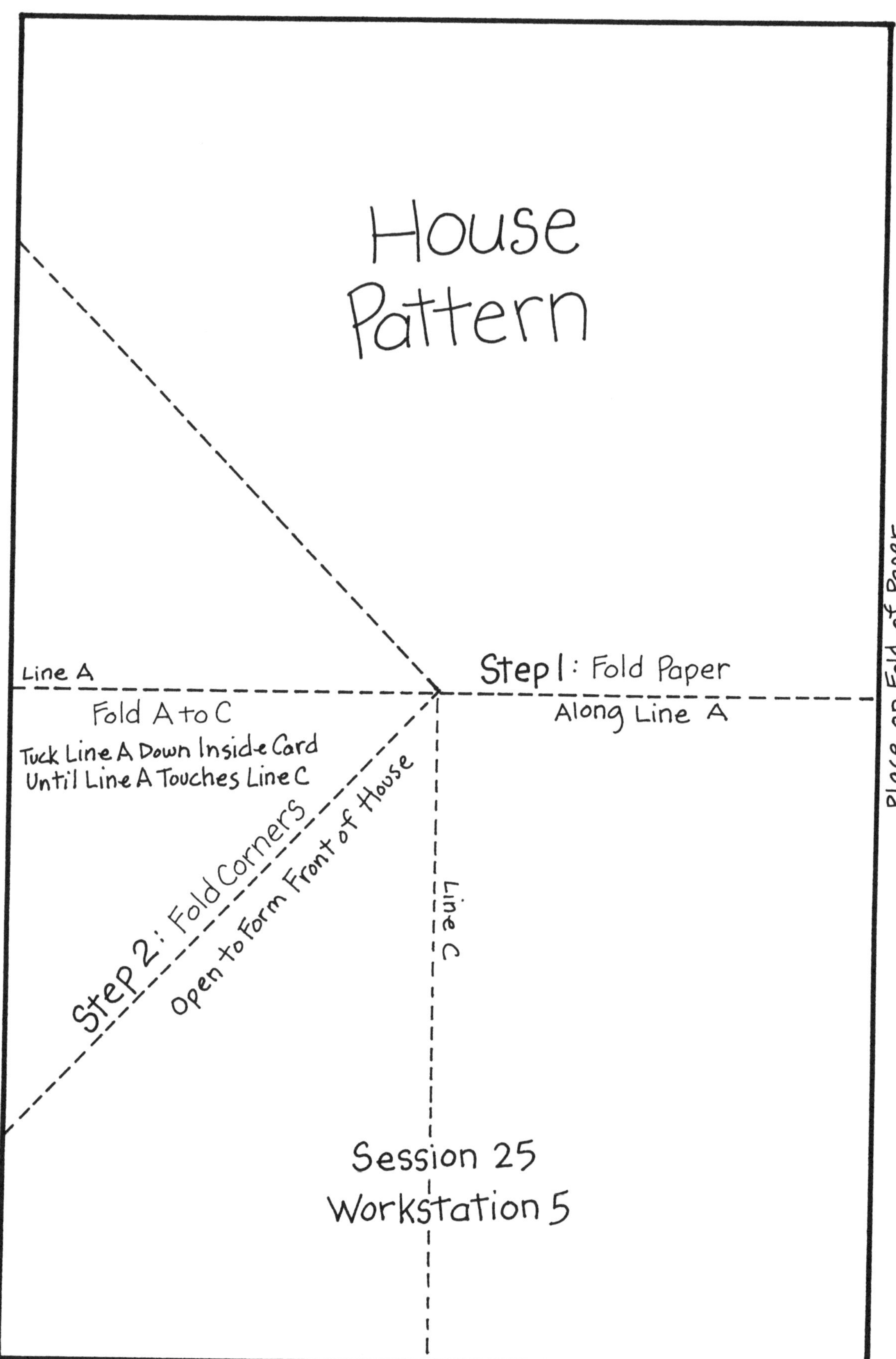

House
Pattern
Step 1: Fold Paper
Along Line A
Place on Fold of Paper
Line A
Fold A to C
Tuck Line A Down Inside Card
Until Line A Touches Line C
Step 2: Fold Corners
Open to Form Front of House
Line C
Session 25
Workstation 5

Fold of Paper
Fold Up
Pop-Up
Heart
for
Inside of
House
Session 25
Workstations 4 and 6

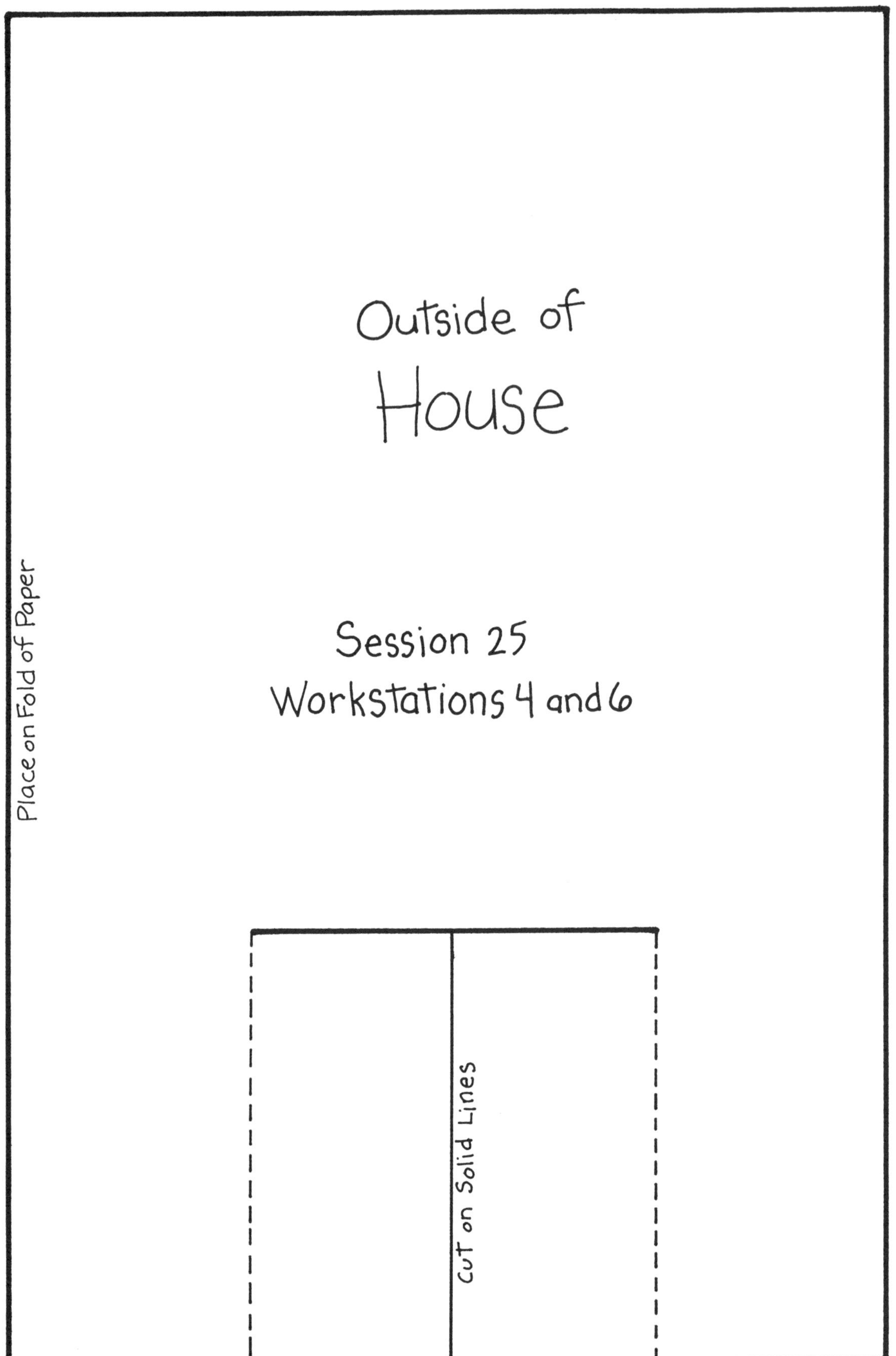

Outside of
House

Place on Fold of Paper

Session 25
Workstations 4 and 6

Cut on Solid Lines

Cut 1

Roof Pattern

Place on Fold

Session 25
Workstations 4 and 6

Place on Fold

Daffodil Petal Pattern

Session 25

Place on Fold

Daffodil Leaf Pattern

Session 25

Daffodil Stem Pattern

Session 25
Workstations 2 and 3

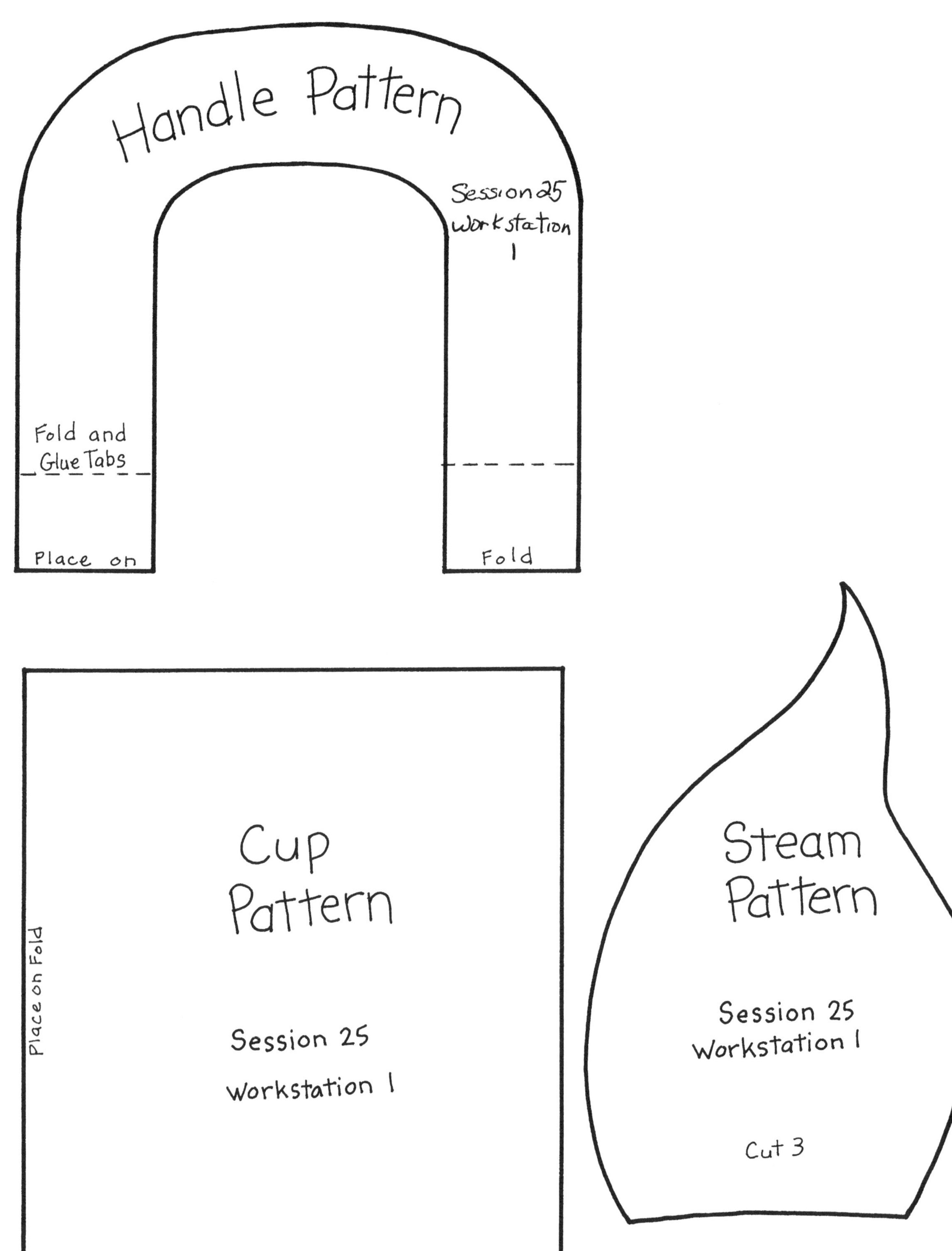

Handle Pattern
Session 25
Workstation 1
Fold and Glue Tabs
Place on
Fold
Cup Pattern
Session 25
Workstation 1
Place on Fold
Steam Pattern
Session 25
Workstation 1
Cut 3

Wheel
Pattern

Session 26
Workstation 5

place on Fold

Shrub
Pattern

Tree
Pattern

Session 26
Workstation
4

Place on Fold

Father's
Day
Card

Session 26

Workstation 2

Fold on Line to Cut Slit for Car and Wheel

Permission granted to photocopy for local church use. © 2000 Elaine Clanton Harpine.

Place on Fold of Paper

Center
Fold Line

Cut   Slit

Place on Fold

Pull Handle for Car

Session 26

Workstation 6

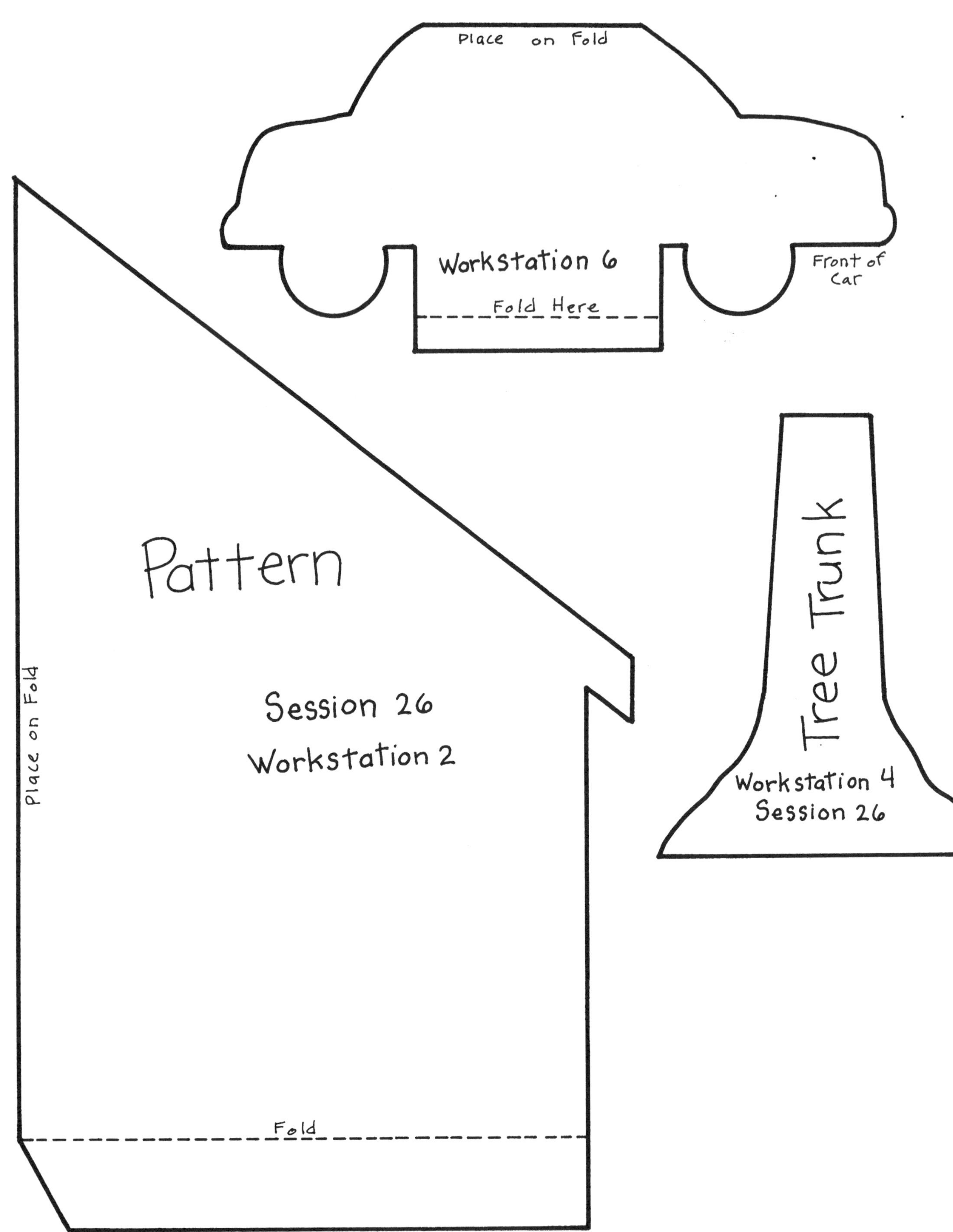

Place on Fold
Workstation 6
Fold Here
Front of Car
Pattern
Session 26
Workstation 2
Place on Fold
Fold
Tree Trunk
Workstation 4
Session 26